Waging Heavy Peace

Waging Heavy Peace

A Hippie Dream

NEIL YOUNG

BLUE RIDER PRESS

a member of Penguin Group (USA) Inc.

New York

blue
rider
press

Published by the Penguin Group
Penguin Group (USA) Inc., 375 Hudson Street, New York, New York 10014, USA •
Penguin Group (Canada), 90 Eglinton Avenue East, Suite 700, Toronto, Ontario M4P 2Y3,
Canada (a division of Pearson Penguin Canada Inc.) • Penguin Books Ltd, 80 Strand, London WC2R 0RL,
England • Penguin Ireland, 25 St Stephen's Green, Dublin 2, Ireland (a division of Penguin Books Ltd) •
Penguin Group (Australia), 250 Camberwell Road, Camberwell, Victoria 3124, Australia (a division of
Pearson Australia Group Pty Ltd) • Penguin Books India Pvt Ltd, 11 Community Centre, Panchsheel Park,
New Delhi–110 017, India • Penguin Group (NZ), 67 Apollo Drive, Rosedale, North Shore 0632,
New Zealand (a division of Pearson New Zealand Ltd) • Penguin Books (South Africa) (Pty) Ltd,
24 Sturdee Avenue, Rosebank, Johannesburg 2196, South Africa

Penguin Books Ltd, Registered Offices: 80 Strand, London WC2R 0RL, England

Library of Congress Cataloging-in-Publication Data

Young, Neil, date.
Waging heavy peace : a hippie dream / Neil Young.
p.   cm.
ISBN 978-0-399-15946-6
1. Young, Neil.   2. Rock musicians—Canada—Biography.   I. Title.
ML420.Y75A3   2012   2012026138
782.42166092—dc23
[B]

Printed in the United States of America
1   3   5   7   9   10   8   6   4   2

Book design by Claire Naylon Vaccaro

While the author has made every effort to provide accurate telephone numbers, Internet addresses, and other contact information
at the time of publication, neither the publisher nor the author assumes any responsibility for errors, or for changes that occur
after publication. Further, the publisher does not have any control over and does not assume any responsibility for author or
third-party websites or their content.

*Penguin is committed to publishing works of quality and integrity.
In that spirit, we are proud to offer this book to our readers;
however, the story, the experiences, and the words are the author's alone.*

Frontispiece. Driving the Jensen at the ranch, 1988.

For Ben Young, my Hero, my Warrior.

And his mother, brother, and sister.

Preface

When I was young, I never dreamed of this. I dreamed of colors and falling, among other things.

## Chapter One

BROKEN ARROW RANCH, SPRING 2011

The Young Family—

Father Neil, Mother Pegi,

Children Amber and Ben

I pulled back the plastic sticky tape from the cardboard box. Wrapping paper was on the ground around my feet. Ben watched from his chair, and Amber and Pegi sat around me. I carefully lifted the heavy weight out of the box. It was further wrapped in packing paper and then a final layer of some foamy quarter-inch-thick protective material. Then it was revealed: a locomotive switcher with handmade Lionel markings. Curiously, it was not a real Lionel. It must have been some kind of prototype. There was a white typewritten sheet in the box from Lenny Carparelli, one of the endless stream of Italian-Americans connected in one way or another to the history of Lionel, a company I still have a small share of. I read the sheet. The model was from General Models Corporation. It was a beautiful switcher, and it was indeed the prototype that Lionel had used to create its own model. As the letter pointed out, this happened back in the days before corporate lawsuits and trade secrets invaded every little area of creativity and design.

Pegi always gives me Lionel collectibles for holidays, and I now have a very extensive collection of rarities, all proudly displayed behind glass in a room with a giant train layout. It is not a normal train layout: The scenery is made up of redwood stumps for mountains and moss for grassy fields. The railroad has fallen on hard times. A drought has ensued. Track work, once accomplished by hardworking teams of Chinese laborers, has been left dormant. Now expensive, highly detailed Lionel steam engines from China traverse the tracks. My railroad is historic in its own way as the site of many electronic development programs where the Lionel command control and sound systems were conceived and built from scratch; then the prototypes were tested and the software was written, tested, rewritten, and retested. Heady stuff, this electronics development. It all started with Ben Young.

Ben was born a quadriplegic, and I was just getting back into trains at the time, reintroducing myself to a pastime I had enjoyed as a child. Sharing the building of the layout together was one of our happiest times. He was still in his little bassinet when the Chinese laborers originally laid the track, thousands of them toiling endless hours through the nights and days. He watched as we worked. Then, after months, it eventually came time to run the trains, and later I devised a switch system run by a big red button that he could work with his hand. It took a lot of effort, but it was very rewarding for him to see the cause and effect in action. Ben was empowered by this.

That was thirty-three years ago, though, and now I have the Windex out and I am cleaning the glass doors on the display shelves where my prized Lionel possessions are kept safe and sound for all to see. Not that anybody ever comes here. You could count the visitors on your hand. Which is unfortunate, considering the amount of care that has gone into the display. The display and layout create a Zen experience. They allow me to sift through the chaos, the songs, the people, and the feelings from my upbringing that still haunt me today. Not in a bad way, but not in an entirely good way, either. Months go by with boxes piled everywhere and trains derailed with dust gathering on them. Then, miraculously, I reappear and clean and organize, working with every little detail for hours on end, making it all run perfectly again. This seems to coincide with other creative processes.

I remember one day David Crosby and Graham Nash were visiting me at the train barn during the recording of *American Dream*, a lot of which we did on my ranch at Plywood Digital, a barn that was converted to a recording studio. We had a truck parked outside full of recording equipment and were working on several new songs. We were all pretty excited about playing together again. Crosby had recently gotten straight, was recovering from his addiction to freebase, had just completed jail time he got for something having to do with a loaded weapon in Texas, and was still prone to taking naps between takes. His system was pretty much in shock, and he was doing the best he could because he loves the band and the music so much. There is no one I know who loves making music more than David Crosby. Graham Nash has been his best friend for years, through thick and thin, and they sing together in a way that shows the depth of their long relationship.

They met in the Hollies and the Byrds, two seminal bands in the history of rock and roll, and then came together with Stephen Stills to form Crosby, Stills & Nash around 1970. CSN's first record is a work of art. It defined a sound that has been imitated for years by other groups, some of which have enjoyed greater commercial success, but there can be no mistaking the groundbreaking nature of that first CSN album. Stephen played most of the music then, overdubbing all the parts during the night with Dallas Taylor, the drummer, and Graham. There was so much Stephen had wanted to do with Buffalo Springfield in the years just before—like producing, writing, and arranging harmonies, as well as playing more guitar—and CSN was his first opportunity to be really creative after the Springfield ended, and he went for it big-time. But more about that later . . .

Anyway, I saw David looking at one of my train rooms full of rolling stock and stealing a glance at Graham that said, *This guy is cuckoo. He's gone nuts. Look at this obsession.* I shrugged it off. I need it. For me it is a road back.

Anyway, now I'm polishing the glass on one of the display shelves that houses my collection. With the glass all cleaned and sparkling, I stand in the room alone and admire the beautiful Lionel models, all perfectly lined up in an order that only I understand.

I leave that building and walk about 150 feet over to Feelgood's Garage. Feelgood's is full of my amps, old Fenders mostly, but also some Magnatones, Marshalls, and the odd Gibson. I remember my first Fender amp: I got it as a gift from my mom. She always supported my music. It was a piggyback model that was on top of the speaker cabinet. Two ten-inch speakers delivered the whopping sound of the smallest piggyback amp Fender ever made. But to me it was HUGE. Before that I had an Ampeg Echo Twin. I used to dream about amps and stage setups in school, drawing diagrams and planning stage layouts. I didn't do real well in those classes.

Feelgood's has my cars, too. I have a thing for transportation. Cars, boats, trains. Traveling. I like moving. Once when I was walking along a street in LA at age twenty-two or twenty-three, I saw a place called Al Axelrod's. It was a car repair place. There was a red convertible's rear end poking out of the garage. I recognized it as a '53 or '54 Buick. When I was young, one of my dad's friends, the writer Robertson Davies, lived near us in Peterborough, Ontario. We used to go to his house every Christmas and play charades at a party. He had a bunch of daughters. Very exciting. Anyway, he also had a '54 Buick. It was brand-new and made a large impression on me, with its beautifully designed grille, taillights, and an overall shape that featured a kind of bump or ripple in the lines at about the midpoint, accentuated by a chrome strip that mirrored it. This ripple emanated from the rear wheel's circular well and was unique to Buicks.

So I went inside Al Axelrod's and saw my first Buick Skylark. It really blew my mind. Only about 1,690 of that model were ever made! It was custom chopped at the factory about the same time as GM introduced the Eldorado and the Corvette. I looked for a Skylark for years after that, and finally John McKeig found one in a body shop in Pleasanton, California. John was a Vietnam vet who was taking care of my cars. He was an excellent body and paint man. I had him do a job for me, and then I hired him to come and work for me taking care of the thirty-five cars I had acquired by then. All of them were wild designs. Mostly from the fifties; a lot of Cadillacs. I was not overly interested in their mechanical condition when I bought them, just wanted those unique shapes. (That turned out to have been a big mistake, because most of them didn't run well and took a lot of time and money to restore. It would have been better and less expensive to just get original cars in excellent condition.) Anyway, after years and years of collecting, I sold a lot of them and just kept the good ones. Most of them were right there in Feelgood's. The best in my collection is a 1953 Buick Skylark, the one that John found, body number one. The first one ever made. That is the Big Kahuna.

So here I am, writing at Feelgood's, looking at my cars and a conference table with a whiteboard. Tomorrow is a big meeting with Alex, a representative who works for Len Blavatnik, the new owner of WMG, my record company. The reason for the meeting is my new start-up company, PureTone. At least that's what we're calling it this week. It's very early, and we are still changing names. The company aims to rescue my art form, music, from the degradation in quality that I think is at the heart of the decline of music sales and ultimately music itself in popular culture. With the advent of the new online music retailers, such as iTunes, has come terrible quality. An MP3 has about five percent of the data that can be found in a PureTone master file, or even a vinyl record. I have an idea to build a portable player and online distribution model to present a quality alternative to MP3s with the convenience today's consumers demand. I want to bring the soul of the music industry and the technology of Silicon Valley together to create this new model using artists as the drivers. My goal is to restore an art form and protect the original art while serving the music lover.

Tomorrow is the big presentation day, and I am going over my approach, which has been guided by PureTone CEO candidate Mark Goldstein, a start-up specialist introduced to me by friends of mine from the Silicon Valley community. These friends of mine are brilliant and very successful. Unlike me, they have mastered the art of monetizing their ideas. I have big ideas and very little money to show for them. I'm not complaining, though. It's not the money that matters; it's doing things right and efficiently that is my goal. I just want to succeed at this so badly.

I dislike what has happened to the quality of the sound of music; there is little depth or feeling left, and people can't get what they need from listening to music anymore, so it is dying. That is my theory. Recording is my first love in the creative field (along with songwriting and music making), so this really cuts to the quick. I want to do something about it. So it is important that I get my thoughts together, impress this gentleman, and get some financial backing for this project, which will surely need it.

My Skylark is right here with me.

## Chapter Two

California, 2011

N ot that it matters much, but recently I stopped smoking and drinking.

I am now the straightest I have ever been since I was eighteen. The big question for me at this point is whether I will be able to write songs this way. I haven't yet, and that is a big part of my life. Of course I am now sixty-five, so my writing may not be as easy-flowing as it once was, but on the other hand, I *am* writing this book. I'll check in with you on that later. We'll see how it goes.

My doctor said it would be good for me to stop smoking weed because he sees a sign of something developing in my brain, and I am listening to him. My dad was a great writer and he lost his cognizance to dementia at about age seventy-five, so I am wary of that. When I stopped smoking weed, I threw in drinking, too, because I had never stopped both simultaneously and I thought it might be nice to get to know myself again. When my daughter stopped

With Crazy Horse—left to right, Ralph Molina, Billy Talbot, Frank "Poncho" Sampedro—on Malibu Beach, 1975.

drinking a few years ago, I was very impressed by the example she set for our family. I love life with my wife, Pegi, and the kids, and want to live as much of it as I can, but not as a burden to anyone.

Although I have not written any songs in a while, a few songs that mean a lot to me and may have shaped my songwriting are listed here: "Crazy Mama" by JJ Cale is a record I love. The song is true, simple, and direct, and the delivery is very natural. JJ's guitar playing is a huge influence on me. His touch is unspeakable. I am stunned by it. "Like a Rolling Stone" by Bob Dylan is as fresh as the first day I heard it—I can still remember that afternoon in Toronto. It changed my life. The poetry, attitude, and ambience of that piece are part of my makeup. I absorbed it. "Be My Baby" by the Ronettes has a sound I always will love. It is in my soul. Ronnie sings it so great. The groove, the beautifully resonant background vocals, the track: It is all one thing. Phil Spector is a genius. Jack Nitzsche is a genius. "Evergreen" by Roy Orbison is one of the most beautiful sentiments ever recorded. I can still hear Roy's voice and feel my girlfriend's love. "Four Strong Winds" by Ian & Sylvia speaks to me always. It occupies part of my heart. There is a feeling in it. I love the prairies, Canada, my life as a Canadian. Of course I love songwriting, so I know someday I will write again.

I also have been thinking about Crazy Horse. To me, that band is a vehicle to cosmic areas that I am unable to traverse with others. Some people have asked me why I play with them. They say, "Why do you play with Crazy Horse? They can't play." The answer is blowin' in the wind. I can go places with them. Pegi just recorded "I Don't Want to Talk About It," written by Danny Whitten, the original Crazy Horse guitar player and singer who's all over *Early Daze,* an album of songs from the beginning of Crazy Horse that I have been working on compiling recently. Danny was every bit the artist that I am, but he died of a heroin OD in the early seventies. Every time I hear Pegi sing that song, it makes me tremendously sad. She sings it so beautifully, phrasing it to break my heart. She does it justice. You can see I have some unfinished business there, reckoning with Danny.

I have been working on *Crazy Horse: The Early Daze* for a few months, collecting unreleased tracks that tell a story of the band that no others can tell. Crazy Horse, formed at the beginning of 1969 with myself, Danny Whitten, Ralph Molina, and Billy Talbot, is still together today, in 2011. I love working on this *Early Daze* record. It makes me feel good. I told Ralphie, Crazy Horse's drummer, about this and how cool it was. He remembered that there were a lot of things that never saw the light of day. Now they will. He was very excited. I just have to finish it. At least get it on the road to being done. I will have to be hands-on for that.

Danny's playing is all over those early tracks. I miss him still. He would have grown to be great, and we would have really made history with him. I have some regrets there, but *this* record will set some of it straight. After Danny's passing, I was devastated, but I was also booked on the road doing the Time Fades Away tour in 1973 with Jack Nitzsche, Kenny Buttrey, Tim Drummond, and Ben Keith. The tour went on. Danny was supposed to play in that band. Only Tim and I are left now.

Back to the Horse. In 1974, after Danny's death, Poncho Sampedro was introduced to me by Billy Talbot, our bass player, and we became Crazy Horse again with Poncho on guitar. It was a different band, great in a new way. To his credit, Poncho would not try to play anyone else's parts. He was Poncho. That was a really good attitude, and it enabled us to stay true to ourselves, pick up the pieces, and move on. So we did, with *Zuma, American Stars 'n Bars*, and *Rust Never Sleeps*. We are a great live band, and playing with Crazy Horse is transcendent for me. If I only had a few new songs . . . I need new to get there.

Redoing old songs doesn't work very well. New blood. That's what the Horse needs. So I have a plan: Crazy Horse at the White House. Get together on my ranch in the big White House, a sprawling ranch-style bungalow made of redwood, painted white, located in the redwoods on the Corte Madera Creek. It has been the center of music-related activity on the ranch since I purchased that part of the property in 1972. (This is not to be confused with the little White House, a small home for working folks on the old ranch back in the day that is now used to house visitors who may be working on musical projects.) The plan: Set up in there and record, leave the equipment at the ready for a year or so until we have a great record. Just keep playing and let the *muse* back into the fold. Gently now. No searching. No working. No trying. Just let the *spirit* come back in and don't be greedy. Be ready. That should put my straightness to the test.

I want to use our old tube recording console known as the Green Board (I think it is the best soundboard ever) and record 8-track on two-inch magnetic tape for the fattest analog sound possible. The Green Board is full of history. The Beach Boys' *Pet Sounds* and "Heroes and Villains," Cream's *Disraeli Gears*, the Monterey Pop Festival, and Wilson Pickett were all recorded through the Green Board. We will run Pro Tools digital alongside just to have the modern tools for fixing our mistakes, but I want that old tube sound. I love the tubes, with their chemical and gas reactions creating the sound. I think this will be fun and will work, and I am going to get that started today. I'll keep you posted.

I want to release this Crazy Horse recording as my first Pure-Tone release. That would really be cool. You know, the way people experience music today is so different from how it used to be. It's not the same part of the culture that it was. I think a lot of that has to do with the quality of the sound, so I am addressing that with PureTone. The music is not the problem. It's the sound.

Years ago, we always would listen to acetates (reference vinyls that can only be played a few times) and hear what we had done in the studio. That is how we listened. The feeling would be there immediately, and off we would go into the spirit world, listening, feeling, and absorbing the waves of sound. That was an amazing time. It is gone now, but we could get it back with a quality sound that is visceral.

Today music is presented as an entertainment medium, like a game, without the full audio quality. It's like a cool pastime or a toy, not like a message to the soul. So things have changed.

So I am making music again. That is the plan. Go for the music again. So here I go. It's always been good to me. I just want to feel it. I need to feel it in my body, sing lyrics that make me want to play my heart out in long instrumental passages that only the Horse can carry me on. I remember once in the studio we were recording and I caught Ralph's eye. He was in pure ecstasy just for a moment; we made visual contact, and I have never lost that feeling. It is like we felt the force of the Horse all at once! Now Ralph always says, "Don't look at me while I'm playing." I know why. He wants to not think about how he looks. He wants to play. So we ride together, but we also ride alone. Crazy Horse is an animal unto itself. Anyone who has witnessed a full-on barrage from the Horse knows that of which I speak.

When I think about music today, I am struck by the history of it all, how important that has become to the audience. Knowledge of the roots of rock and R&B is coveted. Tracks of that music will live forever. Those times were magic, and I know that they will never be lived again. I know that if I can bring them all back in their pristine glory with PureTone, it will be a revelation for music lovers today, to actually hear these songs the way they were with the original resonance, creating the feeling that moved a generation's hearts in the beginning. This is getting closer with every passing day . . .

I'm going back to the train barn to see if I can fix the derailment that ended my last visit. It should be easy. After that, I will let a little time pass and see what happens in there. Maybe take my computer with me and keep on writing this. That is the way I wrote the script for *Greendale*, by not stopping for anything. I just carried a pad with me and would write whenever something came to mind. At first I didn't know I was writing a story, just thought it was a bunch of songs that featured the same characters. Anyway, I'm going to pack this thing up and go over there.

It's summer now and the insects are all out. On the way to the train barn I notice that the swans who live in the lake in front of our house have no way to quickly make it back into the water if they are out walking and sense a bobcat, mountain lion, coyote, or other threat. We have lost a few birds lately, and this is something that needs to be taken care of.

Back at the railroad, the derailment was between two cross-over track switches. That is where two mainlines now coincide. There used to be two mainlines at this location. Originally, Chinese laborers, working for the railroad, had built some beautifully intricate trestle bridges over a feeder track that passed under the original twin mainlines. When an earthquake shattered the ancient structure in the early eighties, the railroad, having fallen on hard times, was unable to finance the reconstruction. To get things moving again and recover lost revenue as quickly as possible, the mainlines were quickly consolidated into a temporary bridge that carried a new single mainline over the underlying feeder track that was still in use. This resulted in a congested location that was not originally planned for and has consequently become the site of more than one derailment and ensuing safety inspections.

It was not an easy task to fix the derailment, and took over five minutes. The two switches had to be placed into manual mode for the reassembly of the train after the derailed cars were re-railed. Once again, my expertise at re-railing by touch instead of vision— the result of many years' experience—saved a lot of time and got the railroad up and running before an official inspection was necessary. Having dodged that bullet, I sit down to continue my writing.

## Chapter Three

I have to tell you what happened at the meeting yesterday at Feelgood's.

The gentleman representing the new owner of WMG came by, and I took him and my partner Craig Kallman, CEO of Atlantic Records, for a ride in my 1978 Cadillac Eldorado to listen to PureTone. It was very important that the gentleman, Alex, understand what we were doing and advise his boss it would be a good idea to finance this endeavor, so I gave it my best. He got the difference in sound quality immediately, and I was very happy. So was Craig. This is important stuff. The making of musical history, repossessing our sound, and bringing it back to the masses. After all, improving the quality of life is the ultimate goal of technology.

With that in mind, I was demonstrating the Revealer, a feature that allows the listener to compare PureTone with lesser formats like CDs and MP3s. Suddenly, Craig was tapping my shoulder rather frantically. Looking up, I noticed I was on a collision course with another vehicle! I stopped just in time to avoid a head-on crash. It was my road and I was not expecting a visitor, but the lady driving the other car was the wife of the catering chef I had hired for this meeting, and she was bringing down some BBQ sauce. With that episode in the past, I regrouped and moved on with the demo.

Mark, our PureTone CEO candidate, had told me that as part of the demo I should show the video I had made of musicians riding in the PureTone Eldorado, listening and testifying to how they loved the sound of PureTone. Tom Petty, Mike D of the Beastie Boys, Flea of the Red Hot Chili Peppers, and Kid Rock were all in the video, along with Mumford & Sons and My Morning Jacket. They were all espousing the merits of PureTone, truly enthusiastic about the prospect of listeners actually hearing the same quality that the artists heard in the studio when the masters were recorded. Mark had told me to show Alex the video on the iPad— the same iPad I was using as the user interface to control the PureTone player. That would be the Silicon Valley way. And, after all, we are a Silicon Valley company, bringing artists' music and record companies together with the Cloud to save the sound of music. I deftly extracted the iPad from its holder, brought up the video, and played it back *from the middle*! Realizing my mistake, I took it back from Alex and got the main page up, returning the video to the top and starting again—only to realize that I had turned the sound off, mistaking the sound control for the control for the position of the video. Mr. Silicon Valley! Was I cool or what?

This demonstration was going nowhere, but I finally got it back on track. Thank God the video is very cool and makes a great point. Alex said he liked it a lot, and the whole idea seemed to be a hit. It will be the first of many episodes we plan on rolling out on Facebook just before the launch of PureTone, one video per day for over a month. What a demo! We still don't know what Alex is going to tell his boss: invest or pass? This is a heck of a business, this start-up thing. Not for the faint of heart.

It's the next day. I'm back at Feelgood's waiting for a three-o'clock meeting with our new partner, WMG, to get a grip on our PureTone plan going forward. The Skylark is looking good. I just got new license plates for it. They are old California plates I bought on eBay. Other cars in Feelgood's right now include a '47 Buick Roadmaster Estate Wagon woodie I brought to the ranch in 1970, a '54 Corvette I bought back in '74 (in which I first learned that Carrie, Zeke Young's mom, was pregnant), a '57 Eldorado Biarritz convertible that Pegi and I bought at the San Mateo County Fair Antique and Collector's Revival back in the day, and a '57 Jensen 541 I bought in Fort Lauderdale in 1975 while I was refitting the *WN Ragland*, my 1913 Baltic Trader, with my old buddy Roger Katz. Every car tells a story. They are all packed with good memories. My latest purchase, a 1963 Avanti, is in the shop getting ready to take up a residency in Feelgood's. Someday I hope to write a history of every car I have ever owned. Cars all have stories to tell.

I used to think that buying a car or a guitar was like buying someone's memories, feelings, and history. I would always get a song out of it. I will do anything to get a new song . . . An old car can take you new places. An old guitar, well, that's a whole other story.

The Green Board is sitting twenty feet away here in Feelgood's, looking like a museum piece. I want to bring it back to life—and myself with it. Sitting around here waiting for this meeting with all these things and stories attached to them, that's the way my life is. I'm a material guy it turns out, looking to unload in a way that helps everything get lighter.

Waiting is not my strength in most matters. I may be a very impatient person when I am focused on something I would like to see happen. I think things are moving along, but I can't play them like a guitar. That is obvious. Being a musician enables a person to bend the notes and express things that are inside you, no matter what. That is probably why I am so happy when I am playing music or making a record. I am very excited about using the Green Board to record this next album. I love the sound, and though I don't have even one song or idea at this point, I am looking forward to expressing something through music, anything. It is this process of getting away from music and doing other things that lets me stay really into music. I need relief from music so that I can appreciate it when I have the chance to partake. Just thinking about playing makes me feel more at home.

My friend Paul feels the same way. He loves music but has to get away from it to stay vital with it. It is certainly a balancing act. Paul and I are friends because we both knew and loved Linda, who I met first during Buffalo Springfield days. Linda was a wonderful girl and lady. Today we are in touch periodically and talk about music or whatever. I like Paul a lot. He played at the Bridge School Benefit for us a few years ago and was really great. He reminds me a little of a modern-day Charlie Chaplin, the way he moves and the attention he pays to his art.

Next week there will be a big meeting about Lincvolt, another project of mine that I have been working on for four years now, repowering a huge car to make it more energy efficient. Why? Because if I can do this with a big car, people will imagine what can be done with a small car. And people in this country are big. They have an urge to travel long distances—the roads in North America are long and beautiful. The scenery is God. Using a big car for an electric project resonates with the wandering spirit of America and brings attention to the cause, makes people talk about it—even if they think it's a dumb idea and go out of their way to say why it is, I am succeeding because people are talking about how they would do it better. How do we lose our dependence on fossil fuels? By not using them and doing it in dramatic ways that attract attention.

That is one reason the generator in Lincvolt runs on ethanol. Oh my God! *Ethanol?* I have heard so many bad things about this fuel. It uses food stock and takes away from the supply of food. No! There is a lot of misinformation about ethanol. Ethanol does not replace the food we are using. The amount of corn we are using for food has been the same for years. It is flatlining. We are using ethanol from corn, but it is not taking away from our food. It isn't taking away from our feed for animals, either. Ethanol suppliers like POET in South Dakota actually produce food for animals from the waste of ethanol production. I have gone another route with ethanol. Lincvolt uses cellulosic ethanol from biomass—and we have a lot of biomass on this continent. We could use it for something constructive.

Even Henry Ford was intrigued by the possibilities. The other day, when I was doing some research, I came upon a paper by Bill Kovarik, a Ph.D. who works at Radford University, called "Henry Ford, Charles Kettering, and the 'Fuel of the Future.'" Here's my version, partly derived from Kovarik's defining work. It's called "Lincvolt and the Ford Legacy."

Back in the early 1900s, Henry Ford was thinking about the future and was receptive to building electric cars. As time passed, news reports had Ford's EV coming in 1915, then 1916. Details varied: It would cost somewhere between $500 and $750 (between $10,000 and $15,712 today) and would go some-where between fifty and a hundred miles on a charge. Thomas Edison, Henry Ford's business partner and friend, divulged no details in an interview with Automobile Topics *in May 1914. "Mr. Henry Ford is making plans for the tools, special machinery, factory buildings, and equipment for the production of this new electric," Edison said. "There is so much special work to be done that no date can be fixed now as to when the new electric can be put on the market. But Mr. Ford is working steadily on the details, and he knows his business so it will not be long."* —Bill Kovarik

We will never know how Henry Ford's vision of the future would have turned out if his dreams of biofuel-powered cars

had come true in the early twentieth century. What would it have been like if we had not powered our cars with gasoline? A classic Lincoln Continental convertible originally produced by Ford Motors in 1959 may just give us a glimpse. Repowered as a series hybrid with a 200KW prime mover and a Ford Hybrid 2.5L Atkinson engine, Lincvolt may be like Henry Ford's dream car. Lincvolt's Ford 2.5L is fueled by E 100 ethanol or E 85 ethanol from biomass. An A 123 battery pack stores the power for silent running around forty miles. The Lincvolt Continental Electro-Cruiser, built with American components, will be on the road in late 2012, making many aspects of Henry Ford's dream a reality.

The innovation will not end there. Building on the tradition of user-friendly technology, Lincvolt will feature the world's best-sounding audio system, PureTone. Taking full advantage of Cloud-based libraries of recordings by your favorite artists, Lincvolt will simply sound like no other car on earth. Lincvolt passengers will enjoy PureTone SQS (Studio-Quality Sound), making Lincvolt audio sound superior in quality and digital resolution to any music ever heard in a car.

Am I a dreamer or what? I write blog articles like this all the time, hoping I can make it happen one way or another. Now I have AVL, a prototype builder of electric cars for many automakers, building the electric drive train and controls, Paul Perrone of Perrone Robotics making it autonomous to help it gather even more attention, and Roy Brizio of Roy Brizio Street Rods building the final shape around this behemoth concept. A 1959 Lincoln Continental convertible is one of the largest cars ever built, measuring 19.5 feet overall and weighing about six thousand pounds with my modifications. It is smooth as glass and whisper quiet, runs about forty miles on a charge—about an average daily commute—and has unlimited mileage without stopping to recharge because of its ethanol-fueled generator system, the result of years of experimenting and failing with different approaches.

I did that experimenting, and it wasn't always fun. It sucked watching a tape of my electric car in a warehouse burning to the ground at three A.M. (more on that later). It hasn't been easy to do, but we just keep trying and knowing eventually a solution will rear its head. Many talented people have had to come together to show this could be done, and it is being built right now and on schedule for completion in 2012. Sometime I'll tell you a few other parts of that story, like the many times I had to go to Wichita, where the car was being repowered, and wait for something to happen that never really did happen. Or the two weeks my good friend Larry Johnson and I spent waiting around in Wichita, after taking a train from San Jose, having been assured by Johnathan Goodwin, the master mechanic hired to perform the repower, that Lincvolt was ready to roll out of Wichita as soon as we arrived. Yes, sometime I'll tell you . . .

It can be frustrating and it may stress relationships with family to the limit, and there is no guarantee of success or recognition of success. I don't know why I have to try these things and become so engrossed and obsessed with them. For sure music is a huge release from these types of projects.

## Chapter Four

Ontario

My bedroom in Omemee was the home of my first train layout. It was an L-shaped layout my dad made for me, and I had a Marx train. The couplers were flat and fit together in a way that made them stay together, but if you tilted them one way the cars would come apart and disconnect. I still remember that layout well, so it made quite an impression on me. It was right across from my bed in the corner where I remember emptying my Christmas stocking at dawn to see what Santa had brought me and finding a great barnyard set with tiny horses, cows, and fences.

It was where I remember being when the doctor, Dr. Bill, came one day with his black bag and told my mom and dad something important out in the hallway. I was about five years old. My mommy was crying, and my daddy said, "Sure, Doc, right away. We'll go today." Then, after breakfast, I was taken to the car. It was hard for

At almost five, fishing on a bridge over the Pigeon River, Omemee, Ontario, August 1950.

me to walk for some reason. I slept on the floor in the back of the car. My older brother, Bob, was there with me in the backseat, and Mommy and Daddy were in the front with Dr. Bill.

The next things I remember are this big metal table and the biggest needle I had ever seen. It turns out I was getting a lumbar puncture. That hurt like hell and scared me to death. I really think that was my first big trauma. Then there was a hospital bed and a nurse who always sang "Beautiful Brown Eyes" to me. Then I was trying to walk across the floor to my mommy from my daddy in a little room. My mommy had her hands open and said, "Come on, Neil!" So I went over to her in stiff little steps and everyone was happy. The whole thing took about a week, and then I was on my way home. My brother Bob remembers it this way:

> *In November of 1951, Neil was six. It was prior to that, I believe in the spring, that he contracted polio. Salk vaccine had not been invented. It was a very serious situation. It was obvious that his life was on the line. I could feel it from both my mother and father, but I knew it anyhow. He was taken to Sick Children's Hospital in Toronto in our car, a 1950 or '51 Monarch, with my father and Dr. Bill Earle, and Neil and me in the backseat. I think it was raining and dark. Neil was lying on a board on the floor. A lumbar puncture was done at the hospital and confirmed he had polio. The treatment was lengthy but it worked and he survived. When he came home he had to learn to walk again. I remember him trying to get from one part of the living room to another by hanging on to furniture to keep his balance. He was unsure of what had happened with his battle with polio.*

"I didn't die, did I?" he said. It was a serious question. There were two children across the street, one of whom may have contracted polio also. I believe their family name was Goddard. I spent a lot of time as a child in Omemee being quarantined because of diseases that caught Neil. There was polio and diphtheria, measles, and others. His health has always been an issue. Later, there was epilepsy. We both had to deal with that. I do not know why Neil has had to contend with all these things. Later in his life, vertebrae in his lower back had to be removed as a result of polio. He wore a brace for a long time and even toured in that condition, including his famous concert recording at Massey Hall in 1971, which so many people hold close.

Walking was hard for a while, and my back hurt. We had a quarantine sign on our house that said POLIOMYELITIS on it and warned people about not entering or something to that effect. No one wanted to be near me for a while. The neighborhood kids stayed away, and when they ran away up the street, I couldn't catch them. I remember not being very good at sports, and my back hurt when I was skating and leaning over, so my position as a goalie was in jeopardy on the rink. I couldn't skate that well, and the puck scared the hell out of me. I was not meant to play hockey—but my brother Bob was. He was great! He was so fast it was scary, and we went to his games for years, cheering him on. Then he gave up hockey and became a golfer full-time. Of course, it was summer when I got sick. I am just putting that together now.

We lived in a small Ontario town—OMEMEE, POPULATION 750, a sign at the outskirts of town said. That is where I remember

*With my brother, Bob, and our mom, Rassy Young,
at Summit Golf & Country Club, Richmond Hill,
Ontario, circa 1958.*

growing up the most. We had a house on the main street, which was Highway 7, and my dad's typewriter was upstairs in the attic. No one could go up there. Of course, I went up there to see why not. Daddy was always able to stop typing and talk to me. He called me Windy.

"What's on your mind, Windy?" he would ask.

Then I would tell him about the turtles in my sandbox or something along those lines. He was a writer, and that's what he did up there. That's all I knew at that point. He went up there every day and sat down and wrote on his typewriter. It was a big old Underwood with ribbon, a truly amazing machine that my dad loved. My mother used to edit for him, cleaning up his spelling and grammar, I suppose.

Now, here I am with my computer, sixty years later, finally following in my dad's footsteps. I am well prepared. It turns out he taught me everything I need to know, and it's just now that I have gotten around to using my training. He said, "Just write every day, and you'll be surprised what comes out."

He was a good dad. We spent a lot of good time together. For a while after my parents broke up, my mom was always bad-mouthing him, but I always knew he loved me. He stayed in Omemee when my mom and I moved to Winnipeg—I wish I had seen him more in my formative years. (What the hell is a formative year compared to a normal year? That is a ridiculous phrase. *Formative years*. I am striking that from my repertoire.) I really loved him, and he loved me. Once, years later, when I needed his sage advice, I told him about a big problem I was having, and he just kept staring forward in his chair. I realized he couldn't answer me. He was there and not there. That's when I saw it for the first time. Dementia, Alzheimer's, you can call it whatever you want. It's just a name. He was gone. His eyes and hair and face were all turning gray at once. He never answered. Once he told me he couldn't write anymore. He said he couldn't remember what he was writing about. I said, "Try poetry, it's short." He said that wouldn't work. Damn. That was at his farm.

The last time we were at the farm, we went for one of our many walks. We always took long walks in the forest together when I visited him, at the farm or anywhere. Once in Ireland, when he was living there, we went for a long walk on the heath, crossing fences and covering a lot of ground. But on that day when we were back on the farm walking, Daddy got lost. That really was the last walk we went on together. All good things must pass. Why? When he died in 2005, I cried like a baby at his funeral service. Completely lost it. Life.

Chapter Five

D avid Briggs used to say, "Life is a shit sandwich. Eat it or starve." David was my producer. He worked on all of my good records, as he used to say. His records were the ones that invoked the memories of the artistry created by Roy Orbison. He always mentioned Roy to me at critical times, knowing I admired him and his unique voice and songs, his willingness to be different. David was hard to work with for many of us, but we all loved him because he was the best. "Be great or be gone" was another one of his favorite expressions. I could go on and on about each session I had with David, the drugs, the women, the booze, the rock and roll, the fights, the laughs—but not yet. I am sure this will all come out eventually as I meander through my experiences in this walk through life. He was also my best friend, then Larry Johnson, my filmmaking collaborator, was after David passed, and now Elliot Roberts is. Earlier in the scope of things, Elliot was my manager and the necessary strength in my dealings with others. Sometimes he was seen as a villain, sometimes as a savior.

Although unpopular at times with my musician friends, Elliot

With Elliot Roberts at the USA Film Festival, Dallas, 1973.

is consistently there for the art, there for the artist, protecting me from the sharks, while sometimes being accused of being a shark himself. Elliot is the friend I call every day at least five times, no matter what. We live through every deal together, every project. I am harder and harder for him to deal with as I get older and more certain of my opinions on business matters, but he still protects me from others and tries in vain to protect me from myself. I will do anything to get started on something. I will use my own money when I shouldn't just because I hate waiting. That may be why I have spent so much money and built so many things. I just like to do it myself. I hate waiting for approval, because I have my own Approve-o-Meter. It works like a charm.

I put in the money to do it myself and do whatever I need to do to get the money, promise that I will deliver a record and get advances, anything I can do to get the cash to make something happen the way I envision it. So I get into a lot of trouble, though I also get a lot of things done. I did it with Shakey Pictures' *Human Highway*, *Greendale*, the Lincvolt movie in progress, the PureTone videos in progress, *Journey Through the Past* (my first film), the Lincvolt construction and development, the Lionel TrainMaster Command Control development, the Lionel RailSounds development, the Lionel LEGACY Control System development, and probably some others I have forgotten. None of these things would have happened if I hadn't done them myself. No one believes in my ideas until I actually do them. I am never able to get backing for anything I want to do other than records because I am the only one with money who believes in them—and I don't do them to make money. I am entrepreneurial. I do them because I can see it before it happens. That is the good, the bad, and the ugly, all rolled up into one big ball.

Mostly now, though, Elliot is able to save me from myself. As I said, he is a true friend, and also one of the funniest people on the planet. We have at least one disagreement a day. Whatever deal he gets, I ask him for more. And mostly he gets more. I have learned that taking less is not that good. It's not the money; it's the respect. And the money.

We have to have control. We fight for it tooth and nail. My father-in-law, T. A. Morton, Pegi's dad, lived by the fifty-one percent rule. You need that much for control. I have tried to be true to that, but some ideas are just too big for me to carry by myself. I hate the fact that the PureTone idea is probably going to get out of my absolute control one day. I hate waiting for other people to okay what I want to do. Ideas are the driver. There is nothing worse than having a great idea and losing it because you can't control the process. Working with me must be hell under those circumstances. I don't feel bad about it, though. I know I work well with people who want to get things done.

I dislike firing people. Since my first high school garage band, I have had to make those decisions and have those conversations. Although I always was the leader, there were times when I have been a wimp and had others do my dirty work, but I have learned that is not the way. No one can do that and feel good. Honesty is the only thing that works. It hurts to be honest, but the muse has no conscience. If you do it for the music, you do it for the music, and everything else is secondary. Although that has been hard for me to learn, it is the best and really the only way to live through a life dedicated to the muse.

Sometimes I am in a groove and everything is going great with the band—and then I wake up one morning and its over. I can't say why, but it is definitely time for change. This change is not arbitrary or capricious. It is spawned from an underlying sense of what is needed to keep the creative process alive and thriving. Sometimes a smooth process heralds the approach of atrophy or death. So the change must be made, disruptive as it may be. Then the hard stuff starts. People have families, need money, have obligations, need security. Or everyone thought it was cool, and it was, but now it isn't. The muse says, "If it isn't totally great, then don't do it. Change."

"Be great or be gone." Thanks, David Briggs.

"Quality whether you want it or not." Thanks, Larry Johnson.

"How can I help you?" Thanks, Elliot.

These are my guys. Whether they are still breathing or not, they are in me, in my music, in everything I do. But there is a lot of damage. A lot of times, spontaneous change is seen as irresponsible, uncaring, and self-serving.

So what do I do now that I'm sixty-five? Retire? Nope. I can't stop moving long enough to do that. I am going to go to Hawaii tomorrow and will keep writing this. I love it there and I kind of decompress. Pegi is going to Hawaii, too, in a few days, but I can't wait that long to get over there. She has just made a great record and wants to finish up all the business around it before she joins me. But it won't be long and we'll be together again. I love that. She is my life partner. My confidante. I can tell her anything. After all these years together, I am still getting to know her. I would be an island without my ocean if we were not together in our hearts. I am the luckiest man on the planet to be able to go to Hawaii and rest for a while and wait for her to join me. Not that I really know how to rest like others do. Creative work and writing are relaxing to me.

Seeing my friends Marc and Greg and Lynne and Vicki over there will be fun, too. Greg and Vicki have the Napa Valley Wine Train, among many other things. Marc and Lynne have Salesforce .com, and Lynne has the Homes for the Holidays program. Pegi has the Bridge School and her career as a singer/songwriter. We all have our jobs. We are lucky as hell. Pegi and I have shared some really good times with these friends.

I wrote the song "Leia" for Marc and Lynne's little girl. Her name is Leia. (See how creative I am?) We were just hanging in the house one night, the six of us and Leia, and I went over and started playing the piano so she would come over and play it, too. She is musical. She came right over and started some jazzy stuff while I was playing a simple percussion part. Next thing I knew, I was writing the song in my head. Lynne loved the chorus or bridge . . . I don't know what it's called. It goes:

Old people watchin' with their eyes aglow
Mother gently smiling as she watches the show
Leia, Leia, Leia

She is a little sweetheart.

Love is everywhere. Marc says, "There is a river of love." I'm holdin' on to that thought.

The Bridge School, started in 1986 by Pegi and two of her friends, Jim Forderer and Marilyn Buzolich, is dear to my heart. It is a school that teaches communication through technology to children who have severe speech and language challenges. Quite often these students have cerebral palsy like my son Ben.

Recently I was sitting at a Bridge School board retreat in San Mateo, California, and we were all talking about the future of the school. Later in the day the board broke for the evening, and I asked Bryan Bell, a board member, and Brian Morton, Pegi's brother who is also on our board, if they would like to go to a local toy store, Talbot's Toyland, with me.

I like to wind down at the toy store after Bridge meetings. It's kind of a habit. I used to always go with Larry Johnson back in the day. He was a board member, too. He was our technology guy. Larry really gave a lot to the Bridge School. It is immeasurable what he did. He took kids to hockey games, using my set of season tickets for the San Jose Sharks while I was on the road, and he would take Ben Young with him all the time, too.

Anyway, Bryan Bell followed me over to Talbot's to kill an hour before we had a Bridge School board dinner at a nearby restaurant. When we got there, I asked him to jump in my '78 Eldorado in the parking lot and listen to PureTone.

Afterward, we went into Talbot's Toyland, where a new Hudson steam locomotive was waiting for me. This was the first Chinese-built model of the venerable classic 5344 NYC Hudson first made by Lionel in the 1930s. This engine represented the pinnacle of Lionel's expertise at that time and was the flagship product for the first hundred years of the company. Now the trains are manufactured in China, and Lionel and I had packed in every feature known to man, and had almost introduced the next revolutionary feature unknown to man, but not quite. (It wasn't ready, so we left it out of this model.) I was pretty jacked about getting it and taking it back to the train layout after the Bridge retreat was over the next afternoon.

At Talbot's, I met Keith from the train department. He broke out the Hudson from its brown made-in-China box with the familiar orange Lionel box inside, then we put a piece of track on the counter and hooked up the Lionel LEGACY Command Control System to the track. The remote was on the counter, and Bryan commented on how cool it looked. I got a good feeling from that. A lot of love went into its design. It is a pretty cool-looking retro modern remote, kind of old, with levers and sliders as well as a rotary throttle, but it has a soft key grid. We put the Hudson out on the track where I tested it with the remote to make sure everything was working correctly. I got it going, and we listened to the incredible LEGACY RailSounds system, the smoke puffing perfectly synched with the chuffs while the wheels were turning, the bell swinging back and forth while it rang, the steam coming out of the whistle every time I blew it with varying intensity from the sprung slider on the remote.

Bryan was intrigued. It was the first time he had ever seen the Lionel LEGACY system in action, and this was a top-of-the-line steam locomotive with every available feature. I eagerly, as always, demonstrated the loading effect technique by applying the train brake and listening to the heaviness of the chuffs increasing against that added load. Those little engines have so much technology in them . . .

I am very proud of the work I did with Lionel. I was instrumental in creating a series that celebrated Lionel's history with a bunch of made-in-the-USA classics that we reissued with the new sound and command control systems I had developed and tested in California along with the first generation Lionel TrainMaster Command Control. I had paid for that development myself, and it was helping to save the company. These were the last Lionels built in the USA. All we had to sell was collectibility, and we did it really well in that instance. It was all we could do, and it kept us alive during an assault of brand-new Chinese-manufactured models from our competition.

Lionel made the move to China years ago to keep competitive with another American train maker who was kicking our ass with Chinese detail and low manufacturing costs. I became an owner of the company when that happened, because as the company was being sold, I was able to parlay my investment in technology development into ownership participation. It was sad. But we hung on with the Postwar Celebration Series and "celebrated" our way through our transition to Chinese manufacturing by making products in the USA. Although the competition eventually caught on, copied our sound, and developed a proprietary control system, we made it over to China just in time to avoid bankruptcy. So here we are today, still manufacturing in China. Another great American brand, no longer being made by Americans. What a story. It was either go to China or go out of business. That NYC Hudson engine was kicking ass in that little toy store.

The next thing model trains need to do is abandon modeling the sounds by user input and become real. The effort involved in pulling a load needs to be measured, and algorithms that used to be based on user input need to be newly based on the locomotive's effort measured to pull the load or perform the task. Then there is little to do but drive the train down the track, allowing it to measure its own efforts and trigger sound and smoke effects and speed changes to reflect the laboring that is being measured. That is the next step, the future of modeling, or at least part of the future. Everything is there now in the Lionel system to make this happen on a basic level, except a good measurement of the effort being put out by the locomotive model to pull its load. Not just some gross measurement like measuring the electric motor effort, but an electromechanical high-resolution capturing of each nuance of the laboring. That will be nirvana, and I will be celebrating my ass off when that happens! And it almost happened on that 5344 Hudson at Talbot's. Almost, but not quite.

From Talbot's we took off to the dinner with the Bridge board and walked down to the restaurant together. When we got there, the ladies from the board (Vicki Casella, Executive Director of the school, and Sarah Blackstone, an expert in the field of Augmentative and Alternative communication) were already having a little wine and winding down. I would have had a beer or something, but as I said, I quit drinking, and I really don't miss it that much. I had a cranberry and soda mix, which is what I like these days. Steve Atkinson, another board member, showed up and said he had just missed us at the toy store and people were all talking about the fact that I had just been there. (That is always surprising for me to hear and think about. I guess a grown man who happened to be famous geeking out with a train in a toy store with two other guys is somewhat interesting and could be seen as news.)

The next day we returned to the retreat and finished at about noon. We had to come up with a few concepts on how to ensure the Bridge School's future. I have been able to help with concert fund-raisers, but Pegi is the force behind the Bridge School. The catalyst. It was her idea. One day when Ben Young was young and we were looking for school placement, after a particularly depressing look at a local California classroom for the disabled, Pegi was near tears. She just blurted out, "Why don't we just call your friends and put on a concert to raise money and start a school? We could get Bruce Springsteen!" I just looked at her, dumbfounded by this audacious idea.

Because of his grace, Bruce did it and made our first concert a sellout. We started the school on those funds. Bruce Springsteen is the real thing. He was at the first big peak of his career, and his appearance was amazing on all levels. We also had super performances from Nils Lofgren, Tom Petty, Don Henley & Friends, Robin Williams, and an unannounced CSN. The Bridge School was born. And it all came from Pegi. Elliot and Marsha Vlasic have been booking the Bridge School benefits since the first one, choosing the artists to be invited and making sure they are all taken care of.

Bruce is still my friend. We don't talk much. We don't have to. He is great and in his own league. I am not him and he is not me. But we are on similar paths, writing and singing our kind of songs around the world, along with Bob and a few other singer/songwriters. It is a silent fraternity of sorts, occupying this space in people's souls with our music. Last year, I lost my right-hand man, the pedal steel guitarist Ben Keith. This year Bruce lost his right-hand man, the saxophonist Clarence Clemons. It's time for another talk; friends can help each other just by being there. Now both of us will look to our right and see a giant hole, a memory, the past and the future. I won't play with another steel player trying to re-create Ben's parts, and I know Bruce won't play with another sax man trying to play Clarence's. Those parts are not going to happen again. They already did. That takes away a lot out of our repertoires.

Bob Dylan doesn't have anyone like that, I don't think, although maybe it was once Mike Bloomfield—now there was a great guitar player. Bob is painting now, and Elliot—who once was Bob's manager, too—says he is a master. I'm not surprised. I'm sure Bob has the master's touch, whether he is painting from a photograph or a memory of something he has seen. He chooses his images. He has been doing that for a long time. His songs have known no bounds in their influence, and the folk process transfers well to painting. He may just be getting started. Like music, the world of art has its own rules to break.

## Chapter Six

Mort

A t age eighteen, I purchased Mortimer Hearseburg, or Mort, a 1948 Buick hearse that was for sale from a local mortuary. I had seen an advertisement in the paper for the hearse and went to a place where several hearses were parked. I thought a hearse would be the ideal band vehicle, something that could finally replace my mother Rassy's car. We always spent a lot of time loading and unloading her small Ensign, an English car made by Standard Motors. It wasn't big enough for our band's gear, but we made it fit. I must mention here that Rassy was the biggest supporter of my musical endeavors and believed in me from the very beginning, offering her encouragement always. (By the way, her real name was Edna, but her daddy nicknamed her Rassy.) While we lived in Winnipeg, she had supplied her little car for all the Squires' gigs up to that time, allowed us to practice in the living room of our little flat, even lent me money to buy my instruments

With Pam Smith, at Falcon Lake, Manitoba, August 1964.

and amps when my dad wouldn't because of my terrible school grades. Once she took me over to a relative's house with my amp and guitar and had me play "Malagueña" for them because she thought I was so great. I didn't even know the song, but I loved to improvise on the chord changes, which I thought were genius.

She got really pissed when my dad did not help me buy my instruments. When my dad's book *Neil and Me* came out in 1984, she was incredulous beyond description! She would quote from the book and then say, "Oh, for God's sake, what a load of shit!" noting that he didn't have any relationship with me compared to her and had done nothing to support my musical life.

She never forgave him for leaving us. I did.

Anyway, when I arrived at the place where the hearse was supposed to be, behind a wire fence, there was a gated area where two identical hearses were parked. The only real difference between the two was that one had a blue interior and the other had a burgundy interior. The interiors I am referring to are the inside velvet trim in the back of the hearses. The exteriors were wild! They were at least eight inches taller in the hood than a normal Roadmaster, and they were very long. The wheelbase was 156 inches. The name *Flxible* was on the side of the front fender. Two 1948 Buick Roadmasters that had been custom-built as hearses! I loved them.

In the back there were really nice curtains and a headliner of plush velvet with pull-down shades, and there was a sliding divider window between the front and the back. There were rollers on the floor for moving the caskets easily in and out of the back through a gigantic rear door. What could be better than that? Perfect for rolling amps and PA in and out, sleeping and storing equipment, I thought to myself. The price was $125 for either one.

They were both in good running condition. (That was the thing about hearses; they were always in good shape because of what they were used for.) I made a choice. The blue interior was the best, so I took that one. Rassy paid the bill. Thank you, Mom! I couldn't believe my good fortune. I was high as a kite! At the first gig with Mort, I felt like the Squires had a new identity. The hearse was an amazing attention-getter, and that is what being in a band needs. When you get to a gig, you got to be cool. We were the coolest thing in town with Mort. No one else had anything like that. Nothing they had could touch it.

Of course, Pam Smith's dad was not so sure about it when I pulled up in front of their house in the residential area where they lived. The neighbors all thought that someone had died. Pam was my steady girlfriend, my first real love. We went together for about a year, maybe less, as I remember it, a long time for someone that age. I saw a recent picture of her a while back, and she still is beautiful today. She was wearing a flannel shirt in that photo that looked like the same kind I love to wear. Even after I left Winnipeg, my thoughts kept coming back to Pam, and occasionally I would send her long rambling letters, which she did not answer, probably not knowing what to say. Long and short of it is, she was my first real love, my first companion of that kind, someone I could talk to, and as with old friends there is always going to be a warm feeling there. Sending good thoughts to you, Pam.

Today I have a hearse identical to Mort, given to me by Taylor

Phelps's partner, who said Taylor wanted me to have it when he died. I drove Taylor to his funeral in it. That car is in *Year of the Horse*, a cool film about Crazy Horse that Jim Jarmusch did. That film is very special to me because it has my dad in it. I loved my dad, and during that time, I started to see that he was not himself. Once I left him on one floor of the hotel in Dublin where we were filming with Jim, and he got lost. That was unsettling. Despite what my mom said, I know he was a cool guy. He was always doing what he thought was right for me.

One beautiful morning in 1963 or '64, Mort was parked in front of our triplex at 1123 Grosvenor Avenue in Winnipeg. We packed up Mort with everything we needed, and then we headed southeast to Fort William, Ontario. It was our first big road trip, and our first nightclub gig was booked at the Flamingo Club. I was eighteen. I felt on top of the world. (Mort had a straight-eight and a three-speed manual transmission. Mort was a good runner, and to save gas I used to go into neutral on downgrades, not knowing that this practice was putting unnecessary strain on the drive train, which I would pay for later. Even in those days, I was very energy efficient! Of course, Mort was a giant vehicle like Lincvolt, so nothing has really changed.)

We made it to Fort William with no problems, and three wide-eyed kids were finally in the big time. When we got to the Flamingo Club—a brightly decorated, multilevel supper club with a dance floor and long bar known locally as the Flame—we were ready to play, doing three to five sets a night for the $325 weekly salary plus meals at night. The first night we were nervous, but we did fine.

We played six days a week. The money was great! It was the most money I had ever made at that point, and I was on top of the world. We lived at the YMCA for a small payment, so after food expenses we made a little bit of profit. There were three of us splitting it evenly. Bill Edmondson on drums and vocals, me on guitar, and Ken Koblun on bass. Ken, my school classmate and an original Squire from the very beginning, had been keeping a diary since our first gig.

The Flamingo eventually put us up at the Victoria Hotel, and I was writing a lot of songs for the gig there. We were going Jimmy Reed–style big-time because I loved Jimmy and knew that kind of music would be perfect for the club. I wrote a couple of R&B songs in that vein right away, "Find Another Shoulder" and "Hello Lonely Woman," at the hotel. I wrote a lot more then, too. One older song that was the same type of beat was resurrected. It was called "Ain't It the Truth." These tunes were all R&B-based and we did a good job on them. We did "Hi-Heel Sneakers" and "Walkin' the Dog" and countless others of that type as well. A lot of local musicians came to hear us there, and local DJ Ray Dee also came to the club to check us out. Ray later recorded us at the CJLX studios and booked us in the area. He was a great help to the Squires in Fort William, offering his leadership and advice.

We made friends with many of the local musicians, and they hung out with us. Danny Hortichuk of the Bonnevilles was just one of them, and I remember him as being a really good guy. Being from out of town was working for us big-time like I had hoped it would. There is nothing like having no preconceptions to live up to or down. Today my past is a huge thing. Everybody has an expectation of what I should do. There comes a time when these things start to get in one's way. Expectations can block the light. They can shadow the future, making it more difficult to be free-flowing and creative. I need to find that freedom again today if I want to fly.

Meanwhile, back at the Flamingo Club, we were doing "Farmer John" every night and tearing the place up with it. Writing songs at night and in the morning, playing multiple sets every evening at the club, I was living the life I loved and every day was a new opportunity. We were very successful there and got asked back with a raise to $350 per week. I woke up every morning with a clean slate. No expectations weighing over me, and no history binding me to the past.

At night, I had something else on my mind. I was looking at the used-car ads in the paper. Back in Winnipeg, I had spent some time sitting in a 1959 Cadillac convertible that belonged to my school friends Brian and Barry Blick's dad. He owned a TV station in Pembina, North Dakota, and used to drive back and forth between there and Winnipeg in this big Caddy. It was red with a red leather interior. The car made a big impression on me, so I used to sit in the YMCA in Fort William figuring out how long I would have to work gigs like the Flamingo Club until I had enough money to buy a car like that. I checked all the ads in the paper for similar cars and compared prices. I actually have one today, but it's all in pieces because the fellow who was going to rebuild it never did get around to putting it back together, for a variety of reasons. I may still get it done, though. It would be worth it just to get closure. Today that car is worth a fortune and it would cost more than it's worth to put it back together. It would fit right in as part of Feelgood's.

This car used to run fine. It's too bad I had it dismantled to rebuild. You live and learn. David Briggs had named it Nanu the Lovesick Moose. It had an interesting feature where the windshield washer had so much pressure that it would overshoot the windshield altogether.

Here's a memory: Once we pulled up at a gas station in Nanu with the top down and there was a car full of really fine babes right beside us, filling up with gas and looking like a million bucks. They were gorgeous and looked like real fun-loving girls. Knowing exactly what would happen, Briggs said a big "Hi" to the girls and then hit the windshield washer button. Water squirted out of the jets right over the whole interior without touching it and landed on the trunk lid eight feet behind us. He had made his point: It was an impressive and grand display of male virility. David just sat there like nothing was happening. I was laughing so hard I couldn't stop. We had some really great times, David and I! That was only one of them! I am laughing my ass off right now just thinking of the fun we had! How lighthearted. That was when Nanu was in her prime. I have to get that car running again. What a wonderful thing that would be! That would make me tremendously happy.

One other time we were in Malibu driving down the Pacific Coast Highway in Nanu. We had a gram of coke with us, and Art Linson, who was David's friend and Nils Lofgren's manager and friend, was in the backseat. David and I were sitting in Nanu's bucket seats up front. We were cruising Malibu and feeling real good about life. A Malibu sheriff pulled up beside us and turned his lights on. He was pulling us over! When we stopped, he got out of his car and walked up to ours.

I rolled down my window and asked, "What's the problem? Is it against the law to drive a '59 Cadillac convertible in Malibu?"

He was taken aback by my question.

"This car was made for this town!" I said.

He shook his head, smiled at me, and said, "Just take it easy. Have a good evening."

We drove away. After holding our breaths for a minute, it dawned on us.

"I've never seen anything like that," said Briggs. "You just blew my fucking mind." Linson just stayed put in the backseat, shaking his head.

Sometimes timing is everything. There was ZERO thought process involved in that. I had absolutely no idea what I was saying or doing. It just came out. It was a spur-of-the-moment event. We drove away laughing, counting the minutes till we did another blast. Those were some big times, a long way from the Flamingo Club.

## Chapter Seven

Why This Book Exists

Remember the goose that laid the golden egg? This book is all about that. This book will keep me off the stage (except for a few benefits—Farm Aid and the Bridge School) for over a year. I need to go away and replenish. This book is one thing that I am doing to stay off the stage. It all started when I broke my toe at the pool.

Back at the ranch, Pegi and I were having a great time with Amber and Ben up at the pool. The pool is up a hill behind the house. Anyway, we were up there and having a great time on July 3 celebrating Father's Day, because Amber had been in Montana at an art retreat and Pegi had been down in LA working on her new record on the real date. So now we were together and celebrating Father's Day and all was cool. That's when I stubbed my toe on a rock and broke it. My little toe!

So I have to slow down. That's why I am writing this book *now*.

Or maybe it's because I'm not smoking weed anymore. I am a lot more focused now. That's odd. On one hand, I am wondering whether I can write songs straight, and on the other hand, I am saying that because I am straight I am probably writing this book. Someone should take note of that for his or her own research on the subject of sobriety, but not me.

I am feeling very fashionable, even trendy, for having stopped smoking and drinking. I should be in *People* magazine or on *Entertainment Tonight*. I am missing a lot of exposure. (Actually, I cannot imagine anything further from my mind than doing that type of thing, thank God.)

I am no fun to watch TV with. I am constantly heckling and criticizing and making fun of it. I suppose I will be on TV *hawking* this book, though.

Jonathan Demme recently made another movie about one of my performances. This is the last one of a trilogy. It's really about life. It's a docu-music-entary, what was once clumsily called a rock-umentary. Promoting it, I could be on *Colbert*! Now that guy is really funny. Or Jon Stewart! Thank God for humor! Those guys are brilliant. I am always getting scared that I will be in the middle of some long-winded story and forget what I'm talking about and my secret that I am slowly losing my mind will be out. It is a real fear. Everyone will know! But that is not new. That is not a recent development. I have always been like that. That is what makes detecting the onset of early stages of dementia in me so difficult. Maybe there won't ever be any. Maybe it's all in my mind.

## Chapter Eight

My first band that worked a lot was called the Squires. We formed in the early sixties in Winnipeg, Manitoba, and were made up of Jack Harper on drums, Allan Bates on guitar, Ken Koblun on bass, and me. The band went through a lot of changes over the first years, but that was the starting lineup. We played high school dances, church dances, community clubs, and the odd outside gig on the back of a flatbed truck. Once we even played a wrestling match.

Those were the kinds of gigs we did in the beginning. We made very little money, sometimes as little as five dollars for the whole band. This was our beginning. We didn't know where we were going, but we were going. There were good and bad gigs, but they all added up. Eventually, the Squires started getting booked out of town, and we would travel fifty miles to make a gig. We had my mother's little Ensign packed so full that I could never see out the back when I was driving to the gigs. It's a wonder we weren't pulled over. We never were.

Ken's amp was homemade and it was a big wooden box that

provided a huge bottom sound for the bass. Eventually we had to cut it down because it was too big for the car. Ken drove that speaker with a Heathkit amp he purchased as a kit and built. We had the shoddiest equipment in the beginning. My guitar, a Gibson Les Paul Junior, was hard to keep in tune. I didn't know that the intonation could be adjusted, so it went on like that until I got my next guitar, a Gretsch Chet Atkins "Horseshoe," just like Randy Bachman's from the Silvertones and the one I played later in Buffalo Springfield. My first amp was an Ampeg Echo Twin, until I graduated to a Fender Tremolux, which was a really big deal for me: The Tremolux was the smallest of the piggybacks, but it was my first big amp.

There was also a band in town called the Galaxies. They had three huge Fenders, two Showmans, and a Band-Master. They were the coolest band as far as equipment went. Then there was the Silvertones; they had a Fender Concert amp and they got big. Randy Bachman played guitar in the Silvertones. They were the best musicians in town, and Ken Koblun from the Squires and I used to watch them all the time whenever we could. They played everywhere and got all the big gigs. They were simply the best.

Randy's playing was the inspiration for a lot of my sound. He had an echo sound he derived from using a tape recorder to get a slapback effect from a tape loop. That is achieved by recording the note and automatically playing it back a split second later. The split second later comes from a length of tape between the two magnetic heads: one records, one plays back. The delay is created by the distance between the two recording heads that is heard when the tape travels from one head to another.

Randy was very advanced, and his echo sounded just like Hank B. Marvin's of the Shadows whenever the Silvertones did one of their Shadows instrumentals. I would go to their gigs with Ken and we would just stand there transfixed. The Silvertones did not have a weak link. Their singer, Allan Kobel, was really great. Bob Ashley on piano was unreal. He could really rock and play anything from Floyd Cramer to Professor Longhair. Jimmy Kale, the bass player, was totally unreal, and he helped us a lot. We got Ken's first bass through Jimmy—he connected us to order it through Cam's Hardware, a local shop that sold some musical instruments. Cam's had a connection to Silvertone, the musical instrument and amplifier company, in the States, and Silvertone made a cool bass. Later, Jimmy would lend us his concert amp for recording and big gigs. He was a real good friend. Thanks, Jimmy!

Eventually, Jack Harper, an original member, was replaced by Ken Smyth as drummer. Allan Bates knew Ken from high school. That configuration of the Squires recorded "The Sultan" and "Aurora."

Allan eventually wanted to further his education and was replaced by Doug Campbell (who later quit because his mother didn't want him to take a chance on music). Doug was a genius and played lead guitar. I say he was a genius because he actually worked on his guitar, shaving the frets down and adjusting the intonation. He was able to create a "fuzz tone" by doing something inside his amp. He knew no boundaries. He was really impressive. Too bad he couldn't go with us when we took off, but that's the way it goes. He left a hole and I had to fill it myself, but I had learned a lot from Doug.

The Squires played my own songs and rock arrangements

of folk classics like "Oh, Susanna," "Tom Dooley," and "Clementine." We got that idea from the Thorns, another band that came through on the circuit. We learned their arrangement of "Oh, Susanna," and I developed a theme doing other old folk songs along that way, with new melodies and arrangements that rocked. Tim Rose, leader of the Thorns, was one of those credited with writing "Hey Joe," later made a big hit by Jimi Hendrix. The Thorns were really great. I don't know what happened to them. They should have been huge. But we know life has her ways. Nothing is obvious, and you never know what is going to happen. The Thorns and Danny and the Memories were great bands that could have been huge, but just disappeared. Who knows what is next or why it isn't?

The Squires eventually became the number-three or -four band in Winnipeg, and we got really good. We had the most original material of all the bands. I was writing a lot, because I always was thinking about music. First it was instrumentals, and then songs with words that I had to start singing. That set us apart. I knew that and I took advantage of it. Original music was the key to moving up. Doing covers was good for gigs, but I wanted other bands to be doing my songs. A few years later, the Guess Who (formerly Allan and the Silvertones) actually recorded one of my songs, "Flying on the Ground," fulfilling that dream. I was very happy about that. They did a great version.

Original songs were not found that often in the bands that competed with us in Winnipeg. I never had to try to write. I learned to be ready to write when an idea came into my head, whether it was in school or wherever. I learned to drop everything else and pay attention to the song I was hearing. The more I did that, the more songs I heard.

We also had a constantly changing lineup. We had Al Johnston on drums, then Bill Edmondson, who moved in across the street from me when he arrived from Montreal with his mom and grandma. He was a genuine rocker with all of the attitude required. I was a big believer in attitude; I think that set the Squires apart as well. Bill Edmondson played on "I'll Love You Forever" and "I Wonder," eventually recorded at CJLX in Fort William and produced by Ray Dee, the number-one Fort William disc jockey who adopted us when he heard us at that first Flamingo Club engagement. Bill ended up marrying the secretary from CKRC, where we had our first sessions in Winnipeg, and ultimately stopped playing with us because she missed him so much when we were out of town. There were many reasons why guys dropped out of the Squires, but I never did really get them. I was in for the long haul.

Then, just before we left Winnipeg for the last time, we got Bob Clark. Bob was game and traveled with us to Fort William. He was really cool, and we rehearsed in a room above his brother's store where he gave drum lessons. He and his older brother were mostly into jazz, and there was a big jazz scene in Winnipeg, but Bob was into playing rock and roll and liked where the Squires were going. Bob Clark was a fine musician. He was really into it. With Bob on drums, we really had the version of the Squires that could move out of town and be successful. Bob sang, and Ken was getting better at singing, too. I thought we were ready to go. As I mentioned, we packed up Mort and headed to Fort William.

A list of some of my early shows with the Squires,
from Ken Koblun's diary, 1963.

			463				accio 158
round 10/16 + All + act	St. Peter's Mission		N. 22	45	11.25	-	12 séparat
40	St. Agnatuis P.Y.O.		N. 29	50	10	-	
	St. Marie C.Y.O (HOFNER)		D. 6	45	2.25	=	
			D. 13	125	23.75	=	more 124 play others
v	Dauphin		D. 20	60	12.00	-	
v	Charleswood Coll.		1964 J. 3	50	10	-	
v	St. Agnatus C.Y.O		J. 24	0	-	-	
45	Kelvin Hi		J. 25	0	-	-	
	4th Dimention		J. 31	60	11.30	-	Jazz man
v	Miles MacDonell Coll.		F. 1	57	11.75	-	
v	Glenwood C.C		F. 5	-	-	-	
	4-D		F. 7	25	7.50	1	
50	Paterson's Roadhouse		F. 8	5	-	-	
	4-D		F. 9	50	10	-	
v	St. Pauls of the Apossil		F. 14	50	10	-	
v	Our Lady of Victory		F. 21	60	10	-	
v	Portage le Prairie		F. 22	46	4	-	
55	Maleens United Church		F. 29	-	-	-	
	4-D		M. 7	25	5	-	
	Paterson's Roadhouse		M. 14	24.25	7.5	-	
	Glenwood C.C		M. 26	0	-	-	
	Paterson's		M. 28	50	9	1	
v 60	Paterson's		A. 2	70	1		
	Inland Broadcasting		A. 2	Recording			
	C.15.R.C		A. 3	40	10	-	
	Crescentwood		A. 4	60	12.50	-	
v	Norberry C.C		A. 5	50	10	-	
65	St. Paul's of the Apossil (bill is paid 55)		A. 11	55	5	-	
Practice Chire 47 →	Paterson's (		M. 8	25	6.50	-	
	Winiakwa C.C (Annapeg twin)		M. 15	A.35	387		
	Grandell C.C		J. 9	0	-	-	
	Nortee Dame Aud.		J. 12	40	6.25	-	
70	Maple Leaf C.C.		J. 15	-	-	-	
	Towers-T+C		J. 19	-	-	-	
	Weston-C.C		J. 5	20	5	-	
	Profeen		J. 24	30	7.50	-	
no mail	Cellar		J. 31	36	9	-	
80 Cellar			4.6	0	-	-	Bass man
last Practis	Towers T+C						

In Fort William, Ontario, a working-class port town at the head of the Great Lakes where the Squires first played the Flamingo Club and hit the big time, we stayed and settled in. We played the Flamingo a few more times and sent our tapes out to record companies. Nothing happened. One of them is a song about Pam, who I have mentioned before, a beautiful, soulful girl I met at Falcon Lake who was my first love, in a fantasy setting by the ocean, which of course I had never seen at the time. I called it "I'll Love You Forever." We used sound effects of waves. I thought it was really cool. Another song I had written, "I Wonder," was recorded at CJLX, too. Those tapes live in my archives now.

I was writing more, and the Squires played the Hootenanny at the Fourth Dimension Club, a local coffeehouse in town that had entertainment all week long; the Hoot was on Sunday or Monday nights. There were 4D clubs in Fort William, Winnipeg, and Regina, and they became known as the circuit. One of the acts that came in was called Two Guys from Boston—they were Joe Hutchinson and Eddie Mottau. They were really good. They sang together and had a 45 rpm record that they played for us called "Come on Betty Home." I loved that song. I was so impressed that they had a record.

One day they received some black ganja in the mail and they were ecstatic. I had no idea what it was, and still really don't know whether it was hash or weed, but it was something and they were happy as hell. I hadn't smoked either weed or hash at that time, and I didn't then.

Around then, the Beatles had "Ticket to Ride" out, and it was on the jukebox at the Fourth Dimension as well. "Come on Betty Home" and "Ticket to Ride" got a lot of play. Many bands and performers played the 4D circuit. Mostly they were from the States (as we call the United States up in Canada). I saw Lisa Kindred, Sonny Terry and Brownie McGhee, and Don McLean before he had his hits "American Pie" and "Vincent," plus a lot of other performers. Don was traveling in a Dodge van, and he had changed the letters *DODGE* to read *DOG*. These were the early days that left such a mark on me. I was always fascinated and impressed by these groups and artists. I was so envious of them for being from the States and on the road.

The next band to come in and play on the circuit was called the Company. There was a guy singing in that band who was really great. He played guitar and sang, and it sounded like he was a soul singer. You had to look at him to be sure he was white. His phrasing was amazing. I really noticed him. He walked up and introduced himself to me. His name was Steve Stills. We got along real well immediately. We struck up an instant friendship after he heard us playing at that Hootenanny. It was amazing to me that after hearing us play he was so impressed.

A great friendship rose up between Steve Stills and me that goes on to this day. Stephen is a genius. Like any genius, he is sometimes misunderstood, and I misunderstood him many times when we were young. Later on I came to recognize him and understand him better. When I left CSNY to do my own thing, I missed him. Although Crosby and Nash loved him and his music, I always felt they never completely got the point with him, and he became a little reclusive in his creativity because of that, in my opinion. No one really knows him like I do, though. He is my brother. We went through so much and learned from each other along the way, discovering our music and life at the same time. It was all so new to us, and we discovered it together, like brothers, and I don't think we are finished with that yet. The way we play off of each other, the joy of that, is something seldom found. I never felt that David and Graham had that same sense about him; of course, we were older friends and both lead guitar players who could play together in a way that made it hard for us to tell who was playing what. David and Graham did not have that with Stephen in the same way. I think I respect Stephen's talent and genius in a way that they don't. They see something else, and now they have spent a lot more time with him than I have. When I spend time with him today, I still see that original genius. I want the Buffalo Springfield to play yet again, with a drummer who can drive the band in a way that we have never really had, and that goes way back to Stephen's original problems with Dewey Martin, our first drummer. There is still more to do there and no reason not to do it.

Before the Company left Fort William, Stephen gave me an address on Thompson Street in New York's Greenwich Village, where I could find him if I ever went there. Then the Company left to go to Winnipeg, and the Squires stayed at a motel called Dinty's Motor Inn. We were able to live there for nothing in exchange for playing Saturday and Sunday afternoons at the Fourth Dimension Club. Gordie Crompton, "Dinty," owned the motel and the Fourth Dimension. After we finished at the Fourth Dimension we got some other gigs around town, but times were rough and we had little money. For a while, we lived on Spam and Ritz crackers we bought in a little liquor store across the street from the motel.

Eventually we got kicked out of Dinty's Motor Inn and moved to the YMCA. Then we started playing at a place called the Pancake House on Sunday afternoons. That was okay, but it didn't make us enough money to live.

We played a lot in Fort William until I left after a long period of doing that and moved on to Toronto. That was a very sudden move. Late one night I was hanging with a bunch of guys from local bands, some guys from the Bonnevilles and Terry Erickson, a bass player who also played good guitar. We were thinking of him becoming a Squire and had even taken some pictures together. I decided to drive Terry to Sault Ste. Marie in Mort. We jumped in the hearse and left. Just like that. Ken was back at the YMCA, so he missed the trip and was left behind. Bob Clark and the Bonnevilles came along with us. We took Terry's motorbike with us in the back of Mort.

We were about halfway there, near a town called Blind River, when we broke down. Mort's transmission was toast. We got towed to Bill's Garage, a harrowing experience with the hearse being towed backward, the rear tires in the air and me steering in reverse. After holding on for dear life at a high speed and terrified, we finally got to Bill's Garage in Blind River, Ontario. Bill said he could find us a part to fix the hearse and get us going. Several days later, we were still there and running out of money; we were living on roasted potatoes from the market. We hung out in an old junkyard/dump near the edge of town.

A graveyard was just across the gravel road from that dump.

We were a funky lot. The Bonnevilles hitched back to Fort William for a gig they had that weekend. Bob went with them. Realizing that Mort was gone, I thought being in Fort William without the hearse would be nowhere. It was a feeling. The hearse was part of the whole thing. The picture. The image. There is an intangible to a group and a persona. You can't lose that. If you do, you have to start again. I felt that Mort was a large part of my identity, so I took off with Terry to North Bay to see his dad and try to get some cash. I don't remember what happened to Terry's gig in Sault Ste. Marie, but I do remember that when we got to North Bay, we saw a lounge band, the Mandala, with a great guitarist named Domenic Troiano and George Olliver, a fantastic vocalist. Wow! Those guys were really cool; very slick and professional R&B. I eventually went back to North Bay later on to do a folk club as a solo, working out of Toronto, just before I met Bruce Palmer and Rick James and joined the Mynah Birds.

But anyway, back in North Bay, Terry's father, who was a policeman, had no cash for us. We were offered Kellogg's Corn Flakes and Scotch in the morning, though, followed by a Coke. That was how Terry started his day, with Coca-Cola. His dad was enjoying the Corn Flakes. There was no milk. That was something new to me, Coke in the morning, and I tried it for a while.

Eventually we headed south to Toronto to get some help from my dad. We were treated well, but it was a little stiff and uncomfortable around there and we didn't stay too long. I felt like we were in the way. My father had remarried, and I met my little sister, Astrid, and her mother (by the same name) there for the first time. Little Astrid was very young then, three or four years old, taking oboe lessons. I started exploring the Yorkville music scene, the Canadian equivalent of New York's Greenwich Village. I called Ken and Bob, and after some apologizing for blowing off our last gig in Fort William, I convinced them to come out and give Toronto a try.

That was really the end of the Squires, though. Ken, Bob, and I tried to put together something in Toronto, but it was not that easy to get a gig there. We rehearsed in the lobby of an old theater that my dad was able to arrange for us. He was supporting us, and that made me feel like he was behind us. I think when he saw me up close in Toronto he realized how serious I was.

There was not a lot of room for us to break in in Yorkville. It was nothing like Fort William, and times were tough. There were many bands, and the competition for gigs was great. A manager I had met, Marty Onrot, brought people by to listen to us, but no one really bit. We had Jim Ackroyd in the band for a while, and he was really good. He had played with the Galaxies, the number-two group back in Winnipeg, and we filled out a lot with Jim playing guitar. We did a song called "Casting Me Away," and it sounded great. But no one hired us. There was zero success, and we got no jobs. Bob eventually left the band and went back to Winnipeg. Ken and I tried a few different players, got a new drummer named Geordie McDonald, and did maybe one gig at a ski resort in Vermont. It was an audition gig, and they didn't take us.

We didn't succeed in taking Toronto by storm. It was a tough time. We were small fish in a big pond, had no reputation, and really there was nothing special about us in the big city. We were out of our league. We tried, auditioned, practiced, but nothing panned out. Ken and I were living in a rooming house on Huron Street near Yorkville Village, eating macaroni with wieners and beans that we cooked up in the communal kitchen in the house. There were maybe six or seven other rooms with tenants. It was bleak. I met a girl named Sandy Glick, and that was the high point. I had a friend. I skirted around drugs and parties. I escaped.

Perhaps Jack Harper and Ken Koblun are the Squires I remember the most, Jack because he is still in contact with updates on Winnipeg and is still in the Squires in spirit, and Ken because he was so much of a friend and always gave everything he had. Ken was really the heart of the Squires. He lived it with me and went through all the same changes I did.

The breakup with Ken and the Squires was one of the hardest things I can remember. I probably handled it very poorly and that's why it is hard for me to remember. Ken did well for a while, actually better than I did, playing with the Dirty Shames and a few others in the Toronto area. I tried playing some solo gigs and did one in North Bay and another in the city, and a guest shot at the New Gate of Cleve on Avenue Road when the headliner was sick.

I went down to New York for an audition at Elektra Records that Marty had set up, went to Greenwich Village, and met Richie Furay, who had been in a group with Stephen Stills before the Company and was living for a short time at the address Steve had given me on Thompson Street. Richie said Steve had gone to LA to start a band! I taught Richie "Nowadays Clancy Can't Even Sing," and then I did that demo session at Elektra Records that went badly. They had me set up in a tape storage room. I had my electric Gretsch to play and I ended up not using my amp because

I had a bad guitar cord. (I had dragged my amp all the way to New York; I still remember lugging it through Port Authority Bus Terminal. I asked someone for a hand with it, and he replied, "You're in the Big Apple now, kid—carry it yourself!") Anyway, I ended up doing the demo without it. I sucked. I flunked the audition. They didn't take me.

I told Richie to say hello to Stephen if he heard from him and headed back to Toronto. Richie then heard from Steve and went to LA to join in a band with him. Back in Toronto, eventually I sold my Gretsch and got an acoustic twelve-string. The Gretsch had a white case that had been signed by everyone I had met to that time, including Stephen, and I am sorry I sold it. I was out of money and I didn't know what else I could do. I wanted to give the acoustic solo thing a try in the Village (Yorkville). That Gretsch guitar and signed case is probably around somewhere. I sold it at a music store on Yonge Street, and of all the things that are out there of mine, that is the one I wish I still had. That was my first Gretsch, just like Randy Bachman's, but it was gone and I took my acoustic twelve-string to a few gigs and got some bad reviews. My first review dismissed my songs as full of clichés. They probably were! What's wrong with clichés? I thought I was pretty good, myself. I had an arrangement of "Oh Lonesome Me" that I really liked, and people laughed at it, thinking it was a parody or something. I used it on *After the Gold Rush*, and that worked.

Once I went down to Detroit to the Chessmate Club and tried to get a job, but that didn't happen. I did write a song on a napkin in the White Castle across the street called "The Old Laughing Lady." I stayed at Joni Mitchell's house with her and her husband,

Chuck, in Detroit while I was there. Eventually they left, and after one night sleeping in some girl's basement, to the amazement of her parents, I left one morning in a snowstorm and returned to Toronto. It was cold and I didn't have any warm clothes. That was a long trip.

It was rough in Toronto, and then I joined the Mynah Birds. I didn't know it at the time, but Ken actually took off down to LA and played with Stephen and Richie for a week while I was in the Mynah Birds. He didn't like it and came back to play with the group he was with, 3's a Crowd. He was doing a lot better than me at that point.

In Toronto I became acquainted with Bruce Palmer, who I think I met with some folkies at David Rea's flat in the Village. That is where I smoked my first weed. I got high and loved it instantly. The music sounded like God. We were all playing. David was an excellent acoustic guitarist who played with various folk acts like Ian & Sylvia and the Allen-Ward Trio as an accompanist. Bruce was just there hanging, and we became friends quickly.

He asked me to come and check out the Mynah Birds, who had just lost their lead guitarist. I joined the band and played my acoustic twelve-string with a pickup. It was pretty different. I really liked playing rock and roll again, and the Mynah Birds decided I was in. Eventually, the backer of the band, John Craig Eaton, bought more equipment for us, and that included a Rickenbacker electric for me to play. I missed my Gretsch, but we did a lot of gigs.

Ricky James Matthews, as he was called then, was our lead singer, and he was known as the Black Mick Jagger. He sang his ass off. Living with Rick in a basement apartment on Isabella, near Yorkville Village, I became introduced to other drugs. I was trying amphetamines and smoking a little hash. Looking back, I could have gone a lot deeper. Luckily I didn't get too far in the stronger drugs.

The band definitely rocked, and eventually we started doing some tunes Rick and I wrote together like "It's My Time." Mostly we did Stones covers in the beginning. I was so jacked on pills that once I jumped off a stage and pulled out my cord! That was a high school gig somewhere in Toronto. But we got good and landed a recording contract with Motown.

It was early 1966, and we headed down to Detroit and stayed in a big hotel, the Pontchartrain. While we were there I saw the Newbeats, the group that had a big hit, "Bread and Butter," going up the escalator. They all had dyed blond hair and matching powder-blue suits. I was very impressed. A real recording group, right in front of my eyes! I thought the sessions went great at Motown's Hitsville U.S.A., 2648 West Grand Boulevard. Smokey Robinson dropped in and was helping us, and some of the Four Tops would come in and back up our vocals, standing behind us as we sang. They made us sound cool. Everything was going great! It was just a big family feeling around Motown.

It was a very cool time and place. We even went to choreography school to learn how to move, and I'm sure we flunked, but they treated us well. They fitted us for clothes. We were on our way to the big time! And then Rick, who was a U.S. citizen, got busted for evading the draft for the Vietnam War. He was gone, just like that. It was over. Zip.

Then, two days later, Morley Shelman, who was our manager, OD'd on some heroin he had bought with our advance money. The cash was all gone, and so was our manager. We went back to Toronto and the band broke up. It was time to make a big move. That night I met with Bruce Palmer at a seedy little club on Avenue Road called the Cellar.

## Chapter Nine

Playing with Fire

I made a film once, *Human Highway*, in which I burned four wooden Indians in a bonfire. It was a great scene in the movie, and it had a lasting effect on my life. One of the wooden Indians, the chief, had lived for a long time in the trees outside my beach house in Malibu, where Pegi and I were married in 1978. Sometime after the filming of that part of *Human Highway*, I went on the road in my bus and toured America. It was a 1973 Eagle bus we had fitted with wooden wings on the side and car tops, a Studebaker and a Hudson, on the top. The interior was all custom woodwork. It was a wild machine used prominently in the movie. I called her Pocahontas. Whenever I was asked about the bus, I would say, "Give a hippie too much money and anything can happen."

Now I'm going to relate to you three stories; I think you'll notice a pattern . . .

First story: In 1974, CSNY did a tour of North America and

Driving Pocahontas, 1978.

actually made it to England to finish up at Wembley Stadium for a final show with Joni Mitchell, The Band, and Jesse Colin Young. Most of these big stadium shows were just no good. The technology was not there for the sound. It was all about the egos of everyone. The group was more into showboating than the music. It was a huge disappointment. Listening back to the tapes of Wembley, it is pretty obvious that we were either too high or just no good. I am saying too high. I know we were *really* good when we were at our best. I heard it and I felt it, but not on that tape.

When the big CSNY tour started in the United States, I leased a brand-new GMC mobile home and took it on the road. David Cline (aka Ranger Dave), Jim Mazzeo (aka Sandy Castle), and I were on board, along with my older son, Zeke Young. It was a journey to remember. The GMC was a poorly designed unit with double back wheels and front wheel drive, and every thousand miles or so the front tires would need to be replaced. We did not have that unit for very long. We ended up abandoning it and flying to somewhere near Cleveland, where we purchased a 1954 Cadillac limo for a few hundred bucks and tried to make that work. It did work well for a while, until it had problems, too. We had it fixed, and then Taylor Phelps came out to drive it home to California, where I had it restored.

Eventually we purchased a 1960s Flxible bus that worked pretty nicely for the rest of the tour. We named it Sam. At the same time, we purchased a 1973 Eagle bus that I saw on the road and planned on converting to a motor home. Mazzeo, an artist I knew, and I had been talking about ideas for that bus for months. When the project finally got under way, Mazzeo introduced me to a master woodworker/artist/designer, Roger Somers, who took on the job in Sausalito, right on the San Francisco Bay. Roger was the sort of character only Mazzeo could have found. He built, with the help of a mechanic named Bart Ehman, a motor home that was completely over-the-top. Work was done over the period of a year and a half in a boatyard.

No one who saw it in real life would ever forget it. This was simply the most outrageous bus in history. So over-the-top in every way that it should have ended up in the Smithsonian as a testimony to what might have happened if Ken Kesey was a millionaire and a sex addict.

Roger Somers named the bus Emily Flowers. Its interior features were all slanted toward being phallic or sexual in some way or other. All of the details reflected a highly tuned awareness of sexual pleasures in subtle and not-so-subtle ways. I was not aware of this aspect of what he was doing. It never occurred to me that the bus was being made for someone other than myself! Considering how shy I was sexually, I was very uncomfortable in the bus until I started to change a lot of these details and mellow it out. It took years to get it to that point. It was a lesson of sorts.

I liked the exterior of the bus, except for one decorative part that sort of resembled Medusa of Greek mythology to me. You may remember her as the woman with snakes for hair. I changed that design several times until it finally became a cow skull on a redwood bark background. Eventually, after years of refinement and simplification, the bus became a very comfortable place for me to be (although it was still outrageous, like a giant woodie with its wooden wings and car tops on top). We renamed it Pocahontas and toured around the country for years and years in it.

First Zeke Young, then Ben Young, took the position of shotgun and grooved away the miles with me, both of those boys having the time of their lives! I loved traveling on that bus with my boys, and they loved being on the road with me. Drivers came and went. David Cline, Jim Russell, Paul Williamson, Dave McCleod, and finally Joe McKenna, who was with us the longest time of all. Bigger motors, better brakes, new air conditioners, better generators; we kept upgrading, tour after tour, show after show. Just the memories of life on that bus could make a whole book. It had a shower where you could climb out the top through a skylight hatch and dry off on the roof or just hang out in the sun on a beautiful teak deck. Its kitchen was fully equipped so we could cook whatever we needed on the go. The beds were super comfortable, with one of them below the floor in a luggage bay. You entered that one through a hatch in the floor. Zeke loved sleeping there and looking out the round portholes that were on either end. The big bus was insulated with lead and was so quiet it was eerie. Pocahontas was so heavy she was nicknamed the "lead sled."

One day I was at the train barn and the phone rang. It was Joe McKenna. He was crying. "Oh God, Neil! I lost the bus. It burned to the ground. I just couldn't put it out. I'm so sorry, man! It's gone." He was on his way to the Pittsburgh area to have the bus worked on as part of its regular maintenance. He was calling from the side of the road on the Pennsylvania Turnpike, where that great bus met its demise. I would probably still be riding in it today had that not happened. The 12-volt system had caught on fire somehow, and it was unstoppable. I consoled Joe. "Don't worry, man. It's only a thing." It had been a good run. There was nothing more you could say, unless I write another book just about that bus.

We brought Pocahontas's remains back to the ranch and buried her in a eucalyptus grove, up on a ridge. We began building another bus right away and were able to use some of the interior pieces from Pocahontas that we salvaged. The whimsical wooden wings were gone, though. Two Buick Fastback car tops from 1947 replaced the original Studebaker and Hudson in topping off the new bus, a 1993 Eagle, which is bigger and has a lot of aluminum siding. While it doesn't run as smoothly as Pocahontas, it is equipped with a special lift and bedroom for Ben Young, our spiritual guide. There is a slight vibration in it that I always attribute to something I can't explain. It's not a good vibration, but it's not a particularly bad one, either.

Second story: At the end of our 1978 tour, when we returned in Pocahontas to Los Angeles to play the Forum, we noticed a lot of smoke in the sky. You could see it for miles. Wildfires were burning, and the fires were traveling fast. It was on TV. I made it to the Forum and performed my show with Crazy Horse. Afterward, the mood was upbeat until we got backstage. Something was off. It turns out our Malibu house burned to the ground during that performance. Nothing was left but the fireplace and a plaster mask of my face some girl had done after a wild night of partying at the Crazy Horse Saloon in Malibu.

And a third story: One weekend not long ago, Pegi and I were on our own little retreat in Desert Hot Springs, visiting one of our favorite places, Two Bunch Palms. It is a spa with a great hot springs that really is relaxing. We always try to stay in the Al Capone Suite. That is where the notorious gangster stayed when he was there a long time ago with one of his starlet sweethearts. Pictures of her are all around the place. There is a cracked mirror in the room with what appears to be a gunshot in it. The place has great vibes. Anyway, we were at the spa and this was one of the times we were unable to book the Capone Suite. Early in the morning, the phone rang. I picked it up. Ben Johnson, Larry's son, was on the other end of the line. "Oh my God! It's gone, Neil! The car has burnt to the ground. It's gone! Lincvolt is gone!"

We got on the Internet and watched it burning on the morning news. They didn't mention the car specifically, but I could see the taillights reflecting through the fire. They just reported that a warehouse in Belmont full of things owned by rock star Neil Young was burning and there were a lot of tapes and archival materials in the fire. We jumped on a plane and headed home to view the site firsthand.

A day or so later, I watched Lincvolt burn on a closed-circuit Internet camera that recorded the car 24/7. It was devastating. Three and a half years of work gone because one of the team had left it plugged in and forgot to go back and unplug it. It was not ready to be left plugged in to charge alone yet. It was still in development. That part of the system was untested. Operator error. I started to rebuild the car immediately (having a new regard for insurance that I had not had previously). The filming of the rebuild continues. This time it went forward with new people on the team. They are the best that the world has to offer.

With regard to the three fires, draw your own conclusions. Here are mine: I am betting three is the charm and we're done, what goes around comes around. I am gratified that the Great Spirit has chosen to make material examples. I am always in awe of Her power.

Chapter Ten

I suffered a temporary delusion. I thought I was the chosen one. Somehow I thought I could accomplish what no one else had been able to do. I wrote that phrase, *chosen one*, somewhere, and Pegi told me that was a wrong way to think about myself. She sure was right. It was ego-based. I was thinking it was all about me. Wrong. I thought I was the one who could solve the world's energy problems, just by persevering and following my dream.

I have sometimes become so infatuated by a goal that I can visualize myself doing unbelievable things. I learned about men who had powered cars on water, and met some very interesting garage mechanics and backroom scientists who shared both the dream and a lack of knowledge of physics. I thought these folks were brilliant, and backed them all the way. That was not to be. Maybe they are brilliant, but they weren't in their work with me.

I have made a lot of mistakes, and that was a big one—something is not so just because you believe in it and wish it to be so. What if it had worked? The planet would have been safer without the oil wars, cleaner without the pollution, but that was not to be. At least not yet. But I have faith in the human spirit and innovation, creativity and determination. Someone or some group will eventually figure it out.

The Lincvolt project has been my longest-running to date, and it is still a work in progress. In the beginning, Larry Johnson and I set out to make a movie about a couple of regular guys, with no experience, trying to repower the American Dream. We just kept moving, changing teams, and continuing. Then, with the sudden passing in 2010 of Larry, my co-conspirator, partner, and friend, coupled with the spectacular fire that almost completely destroyed the car, it seemed like all was lost.

Thankfully, Lincvolt was not destroyed. We rebuilt it. We added rear quarter panels and the deck from Miss Pegi, a 1958 Lincoln Continental that Pegi gave to me for my birthday to use for parts. Can you see why I love her so? That is part of life. Now it's part of the movie Larry's son Ben and I are finishing together. But Larry is bigger than that. His spirit will live forever in the films he has made and the people he has touched, in his children who now work alongside me with the same endless energy, optimism, can-do attitude, and brilliant minds. Our Lincvolt film will be finished, and our car will travel this country with Larry's spirit in it alongside me. That was the dream, and it will be the life.

Lincvolt will be clean, powerful, and sexy. This has to happen. It is going to. After four years looking at alternative fuels, I have learned a lot. Lincvolt's generation system will be powered by biomass when the car hits the road again. That is where the car's electric energy will originate. Look at all the waste we have in this country. We are number one. Biomass is everywhere. According to U.S. Department of Energy studies conducted by Argonne

National Laboratory of the University of Chicago, one of the benefits of cellulosic ethanol is that it reduces greenhouse gas emissions by eighty-five percent over reformulated gasoline. We need to change the way we get around. That is obvious. Checked the weather lately?

I am going down to São Paulo, Brazil, to speak at the SWU Festival. It is an environmental festival. SWU stands for "Starts with You." I hope I do a good job. Yes, it is scarier to do this than to play in front of thousands of people. I am cashing in some of my fame now to try to make a difference with it. What else is it good for? I have never really considered myself to be an activist. I just want to have a voice. You can call me whatever you want. Rock star? I have never really spoken in public before except once. It was at the SEMA (Specialty Equipment Market Association) show in Las Vegas, when we showed Lincvolt one week before the fire nearly destroyed it.

So as I said, I am going down there to São Paulo to speak and motivate young people to think about what they can do in their day-to-day lives to make a difference in the health of the planet. I guess that is one thing I can do now that is useful. I hope so. I want to do a good job, and I hope my part of the program is solid and constructive. It's a new ball game for me. I need to prepare. I can't just go down there and run off my mouth for half an hour. I can't just talk about the car. I need to go deeper. Into the conscience, the inner spaces where people can be empowered to do what they only have dreamed of doing before. Young people are prime candidates. They are wide open. Note to self: Prepare.

## Chapter Eleven

L ast night I saw a movie about Conan O'Brien on cable. It was a documentary about his tour of America during the time between when he ended his network show and the start of his TBS show. This was a road movie, and it made me uncomfortable. I saw Conan, a friend of mine (I played on his last NBC show), on the road falling into every pothole it had. His people were doing their best, but they did not know what they were doing. The shows were not the problem. He was just not handled correctly. Nobody knew how to preserve and protect him on the road. The road is not easy under the best of circumstances.

There are a lot of things that can go wrong on the road. If you get sick, you still play, but people think you are losing your edge. If you have half a house, people don't feel that they are part of something. If you don't have a great crew, your shit doesn't sound right. If you don't have the best equipment, your show may not sound as great as the last one or the next one. If you have a reputation, it is on the line. If you forget what you are doing, it shows up on YouTube. If you remember what you are doing, it shows up on YouTube. If you do something new that isn't ready, or something old that you screw up, it is on YouTube. If snot comes out of your nose while you are playing the harmonica and slithers down the harmonica rack onto your T-shirt, it is on YouTube. If you say something stupid . . .

It is a lonely job out there performing. I have to do it because I always have. I probably always will. I love the music part. I like it when the sound is right and the audience is into it and the music is relevant. If one of those elements is missing, you are screwed. You are killing yourself slowly. You need all three elements. At this age, I think relevancy is the big challenge. With Crazy Horse, I need to perform new songs on the next tour for me to feel anything other than ancient history up close. So that is why we will record at the White House before we book anything. We need to be sure the new songs and music are ready and are meaningful to us. They are our ticket, our vehicle to the future, and without the new songs we are just reliving the past.

We need a real reason to believe in what we are doing. I hope it's there. It always has been, and we are all still breathing. There is a lot of love, a lot of baggage, and a lot to give. I think we will make it and it will be great. I will be so thankful if we have another shot at being great. There is nothing to prove, other than the fact that we still care enough to not just run through our hits and misses. We just want to give ourselves the opportunity to show our audience who we are. It is a very special thing we have, the way we play off of one another, the real deal. But it all comes from the songs, the images in our minds and hearts, the lyrics and the way they resonate. That is the fuel for the band. That is what will make the music relevant.

Poncho is my neighbor in Hawaii. When I get there, we will talk it over and I'll see if he is in. Ralphie is in already. If Poncho is in, I will talk to Billy next. Ralphie, Poncho, and Billy. Drums, guitar, and bass. I am looking forward to the whole trip. Recording, writing, playing, doing it straight. That will be new and different.

## Chapter Twelve

And Now, a Word from PureTone . . .

I t would be a historical moment for recorded sound if all of the recording companies would bring their labels together and agree on a concept for the good of music. Create the new gold standard. In trying to present PureTone to the leaders of all of the music groups—WMG, Universal, EMI, and Sony—I need to present an image. Here is an illustration I made to show what it is like to listen to different types of digital sound—if you are Jacques Cousteau!

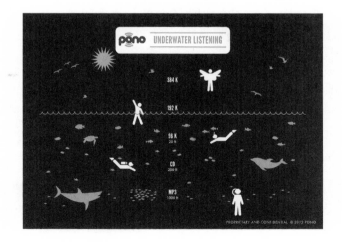

I believe this accurately represents the experience! It is important to understand that we cannot descend much further in quality or we will hit rock bottom. Cloud music streaming will get very close to stirring up whatever sediment may be down there. Right now, we all live in a yellow submarine.

Music is now like a game. Turntable.fm, Spotify, and all the rest are the new radio. If someone likes a song or album they hear on the new radio, they would have a new option to purchase this music for listening. In my dream, the listening option would be PureTone—the new gold standard.

PureTone resolutions are 192 kHz and 384 kHz. Although 192 is here today, 384 is on the horizon, and both could be presented by PureTone in the future. PureTone is the best it can be in the digital realm, signed by the artist and certified to be studio master–quality recording.

Of all of the projects I have undertaken, this one most closely affects my music. Technology is supposed to make life better for everyone. That is its aim. This goes a long way toward doing that. There is a feature in the PureTone user interface called the Revealer. It enables you the listener to take a PureTone recording and instantly degrade it to CD or MP3 quality so you can show your friends why you listen to PureTone. This is a way to share the knowledge without the need for long philosophical and abstract discussions over what can be heard and felt and what the human ear cannot comprehend. There is no need for that discussion with the Revealer. It is true that I like this sound of music better than Apple's iTunes, but I think iTunes and the other MP3 dealers and the new streaming services that provide musical discovery play an important part in getting music out to listeners. The listeners can decide whether they would like the PureTone version of any particular recording. PureTone players play MP3s from iTunes, too, but they will sound better than the other players because of the digital-to-analog conversion at the heart of PureTone technology. It has to be better to play back the high resolution of PureTone masters, and so that helps MP3s sound a lot better, too. Pure-Tone players will be portable, everywhere players, usable at home, in the car, or in your pocket with earphones. Additionally, Pure-Tone home players could be bigger and better, with more memory and audiophile features galore for the extreme listener, but basic PureTone is for the masses, for music lovers. "Quality whether you want it or not," as Larry Johnson used to say.

Chapter Thirteen

In 1970, when I was twenty-four years old, I visited Northern California, and CSNY's road manager Leo Makota told me about a piece of property that was available. I wanted to see it right away. I was ready for a change from Los Angeles where I was living and had seen this beautiful area of land from the airplane on my trips to the Bay Area. Looking out the window, I saw rolling hills above the ocean with the grass a wheat color, looking like velvet on the hillsides. In the canyons, redwoods had stood for centuries.

There used to be an airline called PSA that had stewardesses who dressed in short, short skirts and white go-go boots. That was a great airline. You could fly between LA and San Francisco for $9.95. Flights left every half hour. I flew up one day from LA, got directions from Leo, and went down to see the property in the Santa Cruz Mountains. I knew I liked the place even before I got to it. It was on a long road through the forest, actually at the end of the forest, where it opened up into pastureland and a breathtak-

With the Stray Gators in the barn at Broken Arrow Ranch, 1971. Left to right, Tim Drummond, Jack Nitzsche, me, Kenny Buttrey, Ben Keith.

ing view of the Pacific coast. I knew I couldn't get on the property, because there was no realtor involved yet. I loved the place, though I only got as far as the outside gate.

Later I found out that wasn't even the right place! The place Leo had pitched me was even farther down the road! The realtor and I made arrangements, and I went down there and saw the whole thing. A ranch foreman named Louis Avila was living on the property. He lived there with his wife, Clara. Louis gave me a ride around the ranch, all 140 acres' worth, in an old blue army jeep I still have today. The property had two lakes, two houses, and a beautiful old barn. It was owned by a couple of lawyers, Long and Lewis, and was called the Lazy Double L.

"How does a young fella like yourself have the money to buy a place like this?" Louis asked.

"Just lucky, I guess," I replied.

Later, while I was living there in my first months, I wrote the song "Old Man" about Louis. My dad thought it was written for him, and I never told him it wasn't, because songs are for whoever receives them. It was a beautiful place to live. I was absolutely in love with it. I decided to call it Broken Arrow Ranch.

Driving up north to the ranch from Southern California to move in to the house was a great trip. I had a '51 Willys Jeepster that I had purchased in Santa Ana, California. It had a top speed of only fifty-five miles per hour. Loaded with all of my worldly possessions, mostly gold records and musical instruments, I took off north from LA. I had been living in the Chateau Marmont hotel for a while because I had broken up with my first wife,

Susan, and it felt good to get on the road to start again in a new place. Johnny Barbata, CSNY drummer (and former member of the Turtles), wanted to live up north, too, and was going to look for a place, so he was riding with me. As we left LA, there was a fire burning on both sides of Highway 101. Through the smoke and flames we went heading to the future!

Behind me was Bruce's white 1958 Caddy limo. It took about eleven hours to reach the ranch. Late that night, on September 23, 1970, we reached the ranch. It smelled unreal, all the plants and the redwood forest; there was just something about that smell I loved. Home. It was the smell of home. I had finally made it.

As soon as I got there with my friends Johnny, Bruce, and Guillermo, who were going to live in the area too, we started tearing the house apart. It was just a little ranch house built on a lake in the fifties out of plywood siding, and it had some pretty cheesy interior features as well. We took down the cheap plasterboard paneling with phony wood grain that was on the old cabin walls. After a few days, we replaced it with beautiful redwood planks I picked out myself at the lumberyard. I went through stacks and stacks of twelve-inch-wide planks of rough-sawn A-grade redwood, choosing the ones with the most beautiful sap and grain. Maybe I took one out of every twelve. I loaded them carefully into the back of my '51 Willys pickup truck. When we got the redwood to the ranch and inside the house, we cut the planks carefully to length, choosing the exact grain detail we wanted to see on the wall, and then put them up. I chose every piece and placed each one carefully, taking my time to examine the grain, then deciding where to put it. These planks had a lot of sap in them and a unique grain. They were not the best grade for structure, but they were my favorite and I was using them only for a wall covering. Pegi and I still enjoy them in the living room today.

Since we also tore out the low ceiling and exposed the fir roofing and beams, I thought it would be a good idea to stain them with some teak espresso stain. I had learned about this stain because it was used in my first house in Topanga Canyon. That house also had redwood A-grade inside. Anyway, after a little application of the teak espresso stain, I decided it wasn't working. It was way too dark. I stopped right there. It is still there in one small corner of the living room. It makes me feel good to look at it because it reminds me of how innocent I was. I feel good just thinking about it. That was a really good time for me. I love new beginnings.

The house stayed basically like that for about eight years, until 1978, when Pegi and I were married. We expanded and built on a whole new wing that was designed to house the whole future family. It was four times the size of the original house, but even with all that room, who could have foreseen the arrival of Ben Young, our spastic, quadriplegic, nonverbal spiritual leader, with all of his special support equipment and his team of caregivers? So onward we went, designing a space for Ben and his crew . . .

If there is one thing I love almost as much as making music, it is building things. Houses, boats, cars, buildings of all kinds, control systems, sound playback systems, and model railroads have all been built and rebuilt either by me or people I have commissioned during my time on the planet. Why do the processes of people, artists, designers, and engineers involved in building or developing things fascinate me? I suppose it's because I am not sure if an idea will work when a project begins. This creativity is fascinating. I love to watch and try to guide what is happening, expanding the goals and reach of a project as it unfolds. Some people think that is the wrong way to do things, but I think it is the true way to discover. Each tangent offers new possibilities for exploration and discovery. A job is never truly finished. It just reaches a stage where it can be left on its own for a while.

Next to the ranch there was a place called Star Hill Academy. It was my neighbor Jimmy Wickett's place, and it was sort of a commune. (California communes, places where hippies lived together on the land, were popular in those times.) I heard about it, and one day I went over to see it. That's where I met Mazzeo. He was calling himself Sandy Castle at the time. A lot of people were living there in makeshift dwellings. One of the most interesting was Ken Whiting's tree house. Mazzeo took me over there. It was accessed by going out on a funky gondola type of thing, which was hanging from a steel cable between the tree and a building left behind by the loggers who had used Star Hill as their headquarters while they were harvesting the native redwood growth from the forest. Ken's tree was way down in a canyon, and the building was up on the rim of that canyon. So the cable extended straight out to Ken's house, about a hundred feet up in the big redwood tree. It was a straight shot. The canyon was full of big redwood trees, and Ken's house was in one of the biggest.

I was convinced to ride out on the cable car, which was actually just a sheet of metal hanging from some clothesline pulleys that ran along the cable out to the tree. I jumped on a little hesitantly to ride out. The sheet of metal plating hung from the cable, and away I went. I got almost all the way out there when the car stopped moving and started traveling backward toward the middle of the sagging cable. I hung out there in midair! Then Ken started pulling me in toward the tree with a safety rope that was part of the design. There were no railings on the metal sheet. They hadn't been added yet. Just wire connectors to the four corners. These connectors were joined at the top to a big clothesline wheel that was turning over the cable as the "car" moved along.

I began to notice some of the weaknesses in the overall design. It was important to stay in the middle of the metal plate and maintain good balance. People were cheering. Ken was pulling me in, and the car tilted more and more as I reached the tree. I realized when I arrived at the tree that I was the first person other than Ken who had used the cable car. It took a while for me to get up the nerve for the return trip. Getting in and out of the device was a difficult move from the tree. There was a beautiful girl up there with Ken who had climbed up the tree to get to the house. She was impressive. Her name could have been Sun Green, and she was part of the inspiration for Sun Green, the heroine of a film/album I did, *Greendale*, years later. Or maybe that is all in my mind, where my imagination has taken charge. That kind of thing can easily happen.

When I was buying my house in Topanga, Billy Talbot was already living nearby. He was in a place up Fernwood Pacific that he had rented from the music historian Michael Ochs, brother to the great songwriter Phil Ochs. That house was a small place farther up another side of the ridge from mine. It was smaller than what the previous renters needed, so they had moved out and Billy and his family—his wife, Susan, and baby son, Chris—moved in.

They had Chris's crib set up in a little room, and there was a really creepy painting on the wall above it. The painting was so creepy that Billy covered it with wood paneling. The previous renters had created it and left it there. It was only later that Billy realized the previous renters were Charlie Manson and a small group of girls.

Around the same time, just a bit later, I was visiting with Dennis Wilson, who I had met with Buffalo Springfield when we toured the South with the Beach Boys, doing three shows a day in different cities, leapfrogging across Florida. Dennis and I had become pretty good friends. I wanted to show him some songs I had written. At the time, Dennis had a nice place on Sunset Boulevard near Pacific Palisades—it had been Will Rogers's old compound, a single-story mansion with a huge pool and a great main room, a very gracious design I remember as being really impressive, with a huge front room featuring a magnificent old fireplace. I really appreciate the old Spanish architecture in the Los Angeles area because it is art and reflects the culture and the times of old Hollywood. Those must have been great days to live in.

Anyway, I went to visit Dennis there and found him living with three or four girls who were kind of distant. There was a detached quality about them all. They were not like the other girls I had met in Hollywood or Topanga, or anywhere else for that matter. He had picked them up hitchhiking. They had a pretty intense vibe and did not strike me as attractive. After a while, a guy showed up, picked up my guitar, and started playing a lot of songs on it. His name was Charlie. He was a friend of the girls and now of Dennis. His songs were off-the-cuff things he made up as he went along, and they were never the same twice in a row. Kind of like Dylan, but different because it was hard to glimpse a true message in them, but the songs were fascinating. He was quite good.

I asked him if he had a recording contract. He told me he didn't yet, but he wanted to make records. I told Mo Ostin at Reprise about him and recommended that Reprise check him out. Terry Melcher was a producer at that time who made some very influential hit records. Apparently Melcher had already been checking out Charlie and decided not to go for it.

Shortly afterward, the Sharon Tate–LaBianca murders happened, and Charlie Manson's name was suddenly known around the world. We couldn't believe we had played with him. Those grisly murders took place in Terry Melcher's recently vacated house. Sharon Tate was the new tenant who had just moved in.

## Chapter Fourteen

A Few Thoughts . . .

I have been told that MIT evolved from a train layout. If that were true, I could understand. Of course, that is not true— I believed it until I Googled it and learned the history—but it still made sense to me. Almost all technology can be found to have some roots in the science of railroading and real railroad operations. During development of what is now Lionel's system for control of action and sound on a model railroad, I became obsessed. There are so many ways to model the actions and sounds of a machine like a locomotive, it is endless—and the complexity involved is like a drug. For instance, every action has a sound and every sound has variables. Every sound variable needs an algorithm based on an action, and every action needs a variable control mechanism and a sensor to monitor its position or at least predict its position, possibly based on the positions of other related moving parts of the machine's systems. To me, this is a stimulant. I am fascinated by it, by all of the possibilities. Every sound needs to be recorded in such a way that it is variable by an algorithm based on the mechanical action or by the controller. You can see how I get hung up.

The end result is music.

I always leave these projects and go on to make music. A completely different part of my brain is used for music, and it feels like I am massaging my soul when I make music. The senses and the feelings evoked by the lyrics and melodies and execution of the instruments in cooperation and sympathetic reaction with other musicians is very similar, yet totally different from the act of building and creating. It's cosmic, dude. (Is this *Wayne's World* or what?)

L ife is exciting.
Jonathan Demme's new picture is the third concert film we have done together.

Jonathan shot a show I did up in Massey Hall (Toronto) and is really happy with it. It was the last show of my solo Le Noise tour. We also filmed in a '56 Ford Crown Victoria on the way to the theater from Omemee, my hometown, for about three hours, and he has intercut that with the concert. I'm giving a tour, from the driver's seat, of my old haunting grounds.

I love Demme. You know, he's made films like *Philadelphia*, *The Silence of the Lambs*, and *Stop Making Sense*. His energy is infectious. He is so positive, knowledgeable, and up about all aspects of a project; it makes him a complete pleasure to work with. He has now made a trilogy of performance films with me—and I am very honored. The guy is a G-man (G is for genius)! Anyway, Elliot and I

*With Jonathan Demme at the WNYC studio in New York
to talk about* Neil Young Journeys, *2012.*

both know the most exciting time for any project is when it's done, when people are experiencing it for the first time, and it hasn't been released yet. It doesn't get better than that. Elliot will call me after he sees a screening and deadpan what a disaster it is and how we have to sue Jonathan. That is a great review. (We have our ways.)

Here in Hawaii, in the real world (ha!), Poncho Sampedro just graduated from a gardening course that taught him all about Korean microbiological gardening, where there are no chemical sprays and the earth takes care of itself. He is very high on that. We talked about it for a long time, and I can't wait to walk over to his house and see what he is up to. Even during Crazy Horse's most active years, Poncho worked on *The Tonight Show with Jay Leno* to keep his independence, live his own life, and have a constant income without relying on the group. He worked with Kevin Eubanks, the orchestra leader and a great guitarist, taking care of Kevin's equipment and helping him with his projects. He worked there right up until the Leno–Conan controversy and departed at that time to come with his cat, Kitty, to Hawaii, where he has a great place just up the road from Pegi and me. Kitty, who has been with Poncho a long time, has adapted well after a couple of months. Poncho is a unique person to know and make music with, and he has a big heart. Like everyone in Crazy Horse, his playing is very sympathetic to what he is hearing and feeling.

I love these long-term relationships. Poncho and I talked about doing a Crazy Horse thing again, and he is in. I am very happy about that. Next I will call Billy Talbot, our bass player, and we will talk as well. Billy is up in Zeona, South Dakota, with his wife, Karin, a lovely lady we have all known for a long time. They first hooked up during the *Greendale* sessions at Plywood Digital in 2002. Plywood Digital was right across the barnyard from an old Victorian house that Karin was living in, where she had raised her children with her husband, Larry Markegard, who had passed away a few years before. Larry was the foreman of my ranch for a good twenty-five years and was there long before I purchased that land. He and Karin came to California from the Midwest, settled down, and raised a family. It was a hard time for us all when Larry died in 1996, because everyone loved him so much. He was a really cool character and a very good man. Now it's Karin and Billy Talbot. Bless both their hearts for finding each other at this point in their lives. Billy had been pretty much a wild man most of the time up to then, and Karin was always such a sweetheart. I think that it is beautiful, although at first I couldn't believe it because Billy never seemed to settle. Billy finally did with Karin. Love.

Chapter Fifteen

Cars and Guitars

H ank is my 1949 Cadillac convertible, baby blue with a tan top and blue leather seats. She is a beautiful car, named after Hank Williams, the great country music icon singer/songwriter. I first met Hank (the car) through an ad in the paper. I was down in Hollywood with Ben Keith and Rusty Kershaw, recording *On the Beach* in March of 1974. We were recording at Sunset Sound on Sunset. That place is still there today, and as a matter of fact that is where Pegi just made her new album, *Bracing for Impact*. It is also where we made "Expecting to Fly" with Jack Nitzsche and Bruce Botnick, the great engineer who did the Doors' albums with Paul Rothchild. Stephen Stills and I did "Rock & Roll Woman" and many other Buffalo Springfield tracks there. I recorded "I Believe in You" and "Oh Lonesome Me" with Crazy Horse there, too. It is a great place with lots of history for many of us. Today, it looks pretty similar in some ways, although it has

Old Black and my amps, 2012.

grown to include the building next door, incorporated a little courtyard with a basketball hoop, and has a parking lot behind the studio. Stephen and I used to park our Cadillac right where the basketball hoop is while we were making *Buffalo Springfield Again*, but the rooms where music was/is played remain pretty much exactly the same. These old studios are so wonderful—imagine a building constructed so that music would sound good in it.

Anyway, I was there in 1974 with Ben and Rusty, and we were recording *On the Beach*. I picked up the paper and saw this ad. I was always in the habit of rewarding myself for doing a project and completing it. I would buy a car or something to celebrate and have a material memory of that time. (As I said before, I am a material guy.)

In December 1974, I took Pegi for our first date. I picked her up at her little cabin in the redwoods in Hank. Zeke Young, who was then about two, went along for the ride. She was living in a very small town called Loma Mar, about fifteen miles from the ranch. I had Zeke with me and thought we would all have a nice day together. We went on a cruise down the Pacific Coast Highway toward Santa Cruz. The beautiful blue Cadillac convertible in its element on an oceanside drive, we were just talking, taking in the sights, getting to know each other. Pegi, twenty-two years old, was a beautiful girl. I loved the way she smiled so brightly, and her blue eyes really caught my attention. I already knew there was something different about her and that I was feeling things that I hadn't felt before. We stopped in a little town called Davenport, but there was nothing going on there, just looking around. When we got back in the car, Zeke tried to bite her. I think he was anxious for all my attention, since he did not see me every day. I should have known that.

Zeke had a rough start in life, with his mom, Carrie Snodgress, and me breaking up right when he was just getting going. Zeke was born in 1972 with cerebral palsy and had to wear a brace on his foot. Like any other kid who was a bit different from others, Zeke Young was picked on by his peers, but he is a resilient and loving person, with a heart as big as life itself, and he has become a man I am so proud to call son. He is hardworking at his daily job, one he found at the Home Depot, where he started part-time and has stuck with it to become a full-time senior employee.

Zeke had gone to an audio recording school and learned all the technical theory behind recording. He used to work with me on my tours, recording my shows on a Pro Tools system. One day he came to me and said, "Daddy, I think I should get another job, because I need to be independent and you will not be doing this forever. I don't want to be relying on you for a job." I think any father would be really proud to hear those words from his son, and I was very impressed with Zeke.

Although he possesses a lot of varied talents, he has made a commitment to work every day for the security it brings. He is well respected at his job, and specializes in handling complaints, one of the hardest things to do. He does it with a smile. Everyone loves Zeke. His sense of humor is legendary. You don't get away with anything when he is around . . .

But back to Hank. When *Harvest Moon* came out in 1992, MTV was in full swing and the video age was upon us. We made a video for the song "Harvest Moon," and Hank is featured in the video. Larry and Karin are in it, too. (Larry is the guy in the video with the big white beard.) It is beautiful to watch them together.

Speaking of cars, during 1983, I was touring with a band called the Shocking Pinks. We had a lot of cars with us. The Pinks were a throwback to the days of old rock and roll. Every night we had a different Cadillac to leave the stadium in, and it was part of the show. At the last note of the last song, we would make a mad dash to the car with the cameras following us, then we would jump in the car and drive away while the crowd watched on a twenty-foot-high model of a portable TV that was onstage. We had this announcer, Dan Clear, who would be chasing us out of the venue, trying to get one last-minute interview. It was a lot of fun! The video is ridiculous! That was about when my record company sued me for making music "uncharacteristic of Neil Young." Point is, there were a lot of cars.

Old Black is my guitar. This is the guitar I have played on almost every Crazy Horse recording I have ever made. Black is a 1952 Gibson Les Paul model that I got in a trade with Jimmy Messina back in the days of Buffalo Springfield. Originally, Old Black must not have been black, but was most likely gold. Someone had refinished it and changed the color a long time ago. That was obvious to me when I first got Black in 1968, because by that time Black had aged tremendously—was well-worn, you might say. Someone, probably the same person who made Old Black black, had special chrome-plated metal pickup covers and pick guard made. All the original gold tops had cream-colored plastic pickups (at least they seemed plastic to me—maybe they were not, but they were definitely not steel). Black's pickups were shrouded with chrome steel covers. They were beautiful.

That is the way the guitar was when I recorded *Everybody Knows This Is Nowhere* with Crazy Horse. That was our first record, and I played Black on every track that called for an electric guitar. I had added a Bigsby tremolo arm, or wang bar as it was called, to the guitar at some point very early on. (Matter of fact, I think it came that way in the trade. I'm pretty sure the same work—the black paint, the chrome-plated metal pickup covers and pick guard, the Bigsby—were all done by the same person. Special bone inlay was also added, but most of that had fallen out by the time I got it from Jimmy.) Then I used it on "Southern Man" and "When You Dance" from *After the Gold Rush*.

Sometime after that I decided to get the pickup next to the bridge fixed so that it wouldn't hum. It hummed like hell when there was a transformer or weird wiring or lighting in a building, and you had to orient the guitar a certain way in space or the hum was as loud as the notes. I took it to a guitar shop down on Western Avenue in LA and dropped off the pickup to get it wound again; there was a procedure that supposedly fixed the problem. I'm glad I only gave them the pickup, because when I returned later to retrieve it, the store was gone. Not a trace. They left with my pickup! Shit! That sucked. What a bunch of assholes!

I was shocked. My guitar was damaged beyond anything I could have imagined. Later I replaced the stolen pickup with an old Gretsch pickup.

I was never really happy with that Gretsch pickup. It just didn't sing like it used to. I knew I had to change. Larry Cragg, a master guitar tech and old friend who traveled on the road with me taking care of my instruments from the mid-seventies until 2010, is a very conscientious character, taking wonderful care of my guitars and amps. He played countless parts in my stage shows as well, from "Grandpa" in *Greendale* to "Farmer John" in *Ragged Glory*. He always gives it everything he has, no matter what he does. One night in the early to middle seventies, Crazy Horse was playing a coliseum somewhere and Larry ran up to me very excited. He exclaimed, "I have found the perfect replacement for Old Black's pickup. It's a Firebird, and it screams." He was so excited. Larry was really into his work and was always trying to make things better. It really did scream, like a banshee, and I played it for years. It's still on Old Black today. Larry takes care of much of our equipment now from his shop at home, and spends a lot of time playing steel in bands around the area. He is happy to be a playing musician, and he plays with Pegi when she goes out on the road, too. It's great to know he is still there to help if we get in any real trouble with our equipment. Thanks, Larry!

"Like a Hurricane" is probably the best example of Old Black's tone, although if you listen too closely, it is all but ruined by all the mistakes and misfires in my playing. That was a memorable recording, though, for the feeling that comes out of our instrumental passages.

I always record every note played, whether it is a run-through or not, and the recording of "Like a Hurricane" is a great illustration of why I do that. When you do that, you catch everything. Most often the first time something is played is the defining moment. That is what I like to capture in my recordings. It is a strict rule that my engineers are there to record *everything*. The master recording I used for the final version of the track was the run-through when I was showing the Horse how the song went. That is why it just cuts on at the beginning. There was no beginning. There was no end. It is one of those performances you can never repeat; the cherry, the original expression of the song, the essence. We just kept wailing on those changes until we couldn't move anymore.

One night in late November 1975, I wrote the "Like a Hurricane" lyrics on a piece of newspaper in the back of Taylor Phelps's 1950 DeSoto Suburban, a huge car that we used to all go to bars in. Taylor was a great friend who lived on the mountain, and everybody loved him. He and Jim Russell were my buds back then. Jim was a cowboy who drove big machinery and was a really nice guy. In the mid-seventies, Jim and I hung out a lot and went to bars looking to get lucky. We had both recently broken up with our kids' moms, and Zeke and Jenny, our two kids, would be in the truck in the parking lot when we went into the bars for "Daddy's Boogie." There was an Alaskan Camper on the back of my new 1975 Dodge Power Wagon, Stretch Armstrong, and Zeke and Jenny used to hang in it while we were doing our thing.

As was our habit between bars, we had stopped at Skeggs Point Scenic Lookout on Skyline Boulevard up on the mountain to do a few lines of coke; I wrote "Hurricane" right there in the back of that giant old car. Then when I got home, I played the chords on this old Univox Stringman mounted in an old ornate pump-organ body set up in the living room. It was painted antique white, and I had gotten it from Dean Stockwell, the great actor and another friend of mine in Topanga. None of the original guts were left inside the thing, but it looked great and sounded like God with this psychedelic Univox Stringman inside it I had hooked up so that it was hammering and overdriving a Fender Deluxe. I played that damn thing through the night. I finished the melody in five minutes, but I was so jacked I couldn't stop playing.

A few months later at the Village in LA, I put on all the vocals as overdubs. I just had to hear that song finished. Crazy Horse had never sung it or even heard the words. It was just a rundown of the track, and it became the master recording of "Like a Hurricane."

Taylor didn't go bar cruising with Jim and me, though. It turned out he was gay. He was such a cool guy. I knew he had something else going on. Later, he started One Pass Video in San Francisco and became very successful. Then, when he suddenly retired and dropped out, I said, "Hey, man, why are you dropping out now? You are going to be a huge fucking success. You are a natural. You could produce movies."

He just looked at me and said, "I can't do it anymore. I have more important things to do now."

About a year or so later, maybe a little more, Taylor died of AIDS. At the time, AIDS was still a relatively new thing with a stigma attached to it. People were just starting to understand what it was. Son of a bitch. That was sad. I really miss him. He was one cool and funny and smart guy. What a drag. He was one in a million. Unique as hell. Taylor had the gift of gab. When CB radios were popular, he talked like he was on a CB all the time. "Breaker

breaker, come back?" He outfitted all of his vehicles with them. He was always trying new things. Once he took on the character of a paramedic and drove around the mountain in his Yukon, full of emergency medical stuff, talking on his CB. Then he bought a semitrailer tractor truck and drove that everywhere. He was a very likable and a one-of-a-kind character. Life again.

## Chapter Sixteen

As You Can Tell

I am getting aware of the fact that I keep writing and thinking about people who have died. I love living. I do not want to die for a long time because I am not ready. I suppose if I thought I was going to die, I could get ready given a period of time, but I am not sure about that. Some folks think that is not a good thing to think about. I envy the control they must have over their thinking processes.

As you can tell, if you are still with me, I don't have much control over that. I have only rewritten about one paragraph so far. There is no such thing as spell-check for life, though. There is a big wind blowing today, and I'm part of it. I want to make a difference, and above all, I want to be a good person from here on out. I can't change the past. Don't look back. Thanks, Bob. I needed that. "How many roads must a man walk down before you call him a man?"

Chapter Seventeen

How many seas must a white dove sail before she sleeps in the sand?"

My first time hearing Bob Dylan was back in Winnipeg around 1963. I was trying to figure out how to get to the USA and had met some friends who had told me about a possible job working on the railroad. Following up on that, I visited one of them. They were all sitting around listening to a record I had never heard. Some guy was singing, playing harmonica and acoustic guitar. We were all listening now. Hanging on to the words he sang. There was something about that, the way it sounded. I thought it was folk music, but not like the folk music of the Kingston Trio. I started to hear more and more of Bob. One day he came over the speakers of my radio singing "How does it feel?" over and over. The lyrics pounded their way into my psyche, this new poetry rolling off his tongue.

He spoke for a lot of us without knowing it. I felt connected to him in a moment. That was in Toronto, '64 or '65. Bob left his mark.

Buffalo Springfield, Malibu, June 1966. Left to right, Stephen Stills, Richie Furay, Bruce Palmer, Dewey Martin, me.

I had to avoid listening to him for a long time in the late sixties and early seventies because I thought I would assimilate so much that I would suddenly be copying him. It was a conscious thing to avoid being too influenced. I am like a sponge in that when I like something, I become so influenced by it that I almost start to *be* it.

Eventually I was able to pick up the harmonica without thinking I was copying Bob, just influenced by him. Dylan's words are part of the landscape, like country names on a map. I have heard people try to sound like him, and it turns me off. People have tried to sound like me to the point that my dad thought "A Horse with No Name" was mine! (Hey, wait a minute! Was that me? Okay. Fine. I am back now. That was close!)

I am currently tired of my musical self. I have reached a point where I have OD'd. When this happens, it is temporary, but my capacity to enjoy music disappears totally. Everything I think of musically is a joke and I reject it completely. That is part of the process. It has happened a few times before. The last time was near the end of 2009; I finished that tour and had to stop. Too much of a good thing. Even other people's music turns me off when I am like this. It all sounds the same.

I did, however, hear a group called Givers on TV a few nights back, and they blew my mind. It was completely original! WOW! It sounded like they were in a complete other zone from the rest of music. "Land of a Thousand Dances" did the same thing to me when I heard Danny and the Memories do their version on YouTube. So I am not dead. Just sleeping. Hibernating, like music lovers who can't feel what they used to when they heard music because of the low sound quality. They are hibernating bears. They will come out of their caves only when the sound of music shines like the sun again.

Anyway, when I first heard Bob, back in '63, I was just getting used to being independent, looking for a reason to stay in Winnipeg and finding a reason to leave. It was very hard to get out of there. I went down to the railroad station and could not get a job. I thought workin' on the railroad would be a good way to get out of town and go to the USA. Then I found out I needed a work visa. I didn't think I could get a visa, because I didn't know what I was going down to the USA to do. What was I going to say, "I'm going to write songs and play my guitar"? No. There was an American who could already do that job; we were just talking about him. You have to be unique to get a visa. Do something no one else can do. I was stumped.

So I made up my mind that someday I was going to sneak in. It took a long time for that to happen. A few year later, in 1966, I was in Toronto, in the middle of the night, sitting in a funky after-hours dive called the Cellar. I was with Bruce Palmer, bass player for the group I was in at the time, called the Mynah Birds. The group had just broken up. Bruce and I were just sitting there, probably pretty stoned, and I asked Bruce if he wanted to go down to LA. I targeted LA because that was where all the music was happening. Bruce and I knew that. He said yes, so we sold all the band's equipment (even though it had been purchased for the Mynah Birds by the group's backer, John Craig Eaton) to buy a '53 Pontiac hearse. We loaded it up with three girls and another guy, all from Yorkville Village in Toronto. We immediately headed for Sault Ste. Marie, the most nondescript border crossing we could find.

With six lids of grass and a few musical instruments, we crossed the border. As we headed into the States, we were laughing our way into the promised land. The U.S. immigration guard asked us where we were going. We said, "Vancouver, but the roads are so much better down here, we are dipping south to use them." With a compliment like that, six wide-eyed kids made it through!

We headed straight south. The roads *were* better. We were surprised at how good they were. They were made of gray concrete with yellow lines down the middle, and made a slight *ba-bump* sound as we rolled along. These roads all were smooth and looked brand-new. Most of the highways in Canada were black asphalt with white lines, and they had bumps and places where they had been repaired. It was a very different sensation, riding on these roads.

Having heard about Route 66, we headed for it south of Chicago. We broke out a lid, rolled a couple of joints, and smoked them. Then we just drove. Next thing I knew we were down in Texas and got pulled over by a state trooper. Oh shit. He asked us for our draft cards. We told him we did not have draft cards because we were Canadian and we were just on our way to Vancouver but the roads were so good, etc. He took down our Ontario plate number, went back to his trooper patrol car, and we sat and waited. Miraculously, he told us to keep going and obey the signs. We were off on our way again.

The girls were driving me nuts. It's hard to say why. I don't remember. I was just very stressed. One of them drove occasionally, and I didn't like the way she treated the car. I thought for sure it would break down because of how she drove. We had to start putting oil in it. We knew only a little about caring for a car. I was exhausted from driving, not eating much, and really not feeling well. We got to Albuquerque and stopped there, took up residence at a crash pad some hippies we met turned us on to, and hung out and rested for a few days.

Looking back, maybe I had my first epileptic seizure there. I know we went to a hospital emergency room, but I don't recall much about what happened to me there. Afterward, I slept on a mattress on the floor of the house for a really long time, probably a couple of days. When I started coming around, Bruce and I decided two of the girls were stressing us out too much. Things were not harmonic. So we hatched a plan. Bruce and I, along with the one of the three girls we liked who was really nice and kind of lost, would get into the hearse in the middle of the night and leave the others at a folk club in town where they had been hanging out. We felt a lot better after we left them behind.

Traveling through some tremendously hot and dry country, the next thing I remember is coming down a really steep hill near San Bernardino. And then we got to LA. It was April 1, 1966.

There was a freeway exit called Juanita Street, and Bruce and I, thinking that was particularly funny, were saying "Juanita" with big Mexican accents over and over and laughing our asses off. *"Juaneeeeeta, Juaneeeeta!"* We were really giddy with happiness at having finally made it to LA. Then, of course, we had to find Hollywood and 77 Sunset Strip! I had a picture in my mind of the TV show where Kookie used to park the cars. I was looking for that building. We drove through Hollywood looking, but the numbers were way too high. So we turned around and headed west on Sunset toward 77. Finally we got to the ocean—but no 77!

There we were at the Pacific Ocean! A trio of Canadian kids in an old hearse with Ontario plates, in a parking lot off the Pacific Coast Highway, looking at the sea. It was a little cold and foggy, but finally we were there. The sandy beach was right between where we were parked and the waves. We got out and walked across the sand to the shore, full of wonder. And I mean FULL of wonder! We forgot all about 77 Sunset Strip! Eventually we headed back up to Hollywood on Sunset Boulevard, reversing our tracks. When we got to Hollywood again, I saw the building! I saw 77 Sunset Strip, just like the TV show. But it was not really 77. It was some other number. That was one of my first lessons about Hollywood. The numbers are not always what you think they are.

A long time before, back in Winnipeg at the Fourth Dimension Club, I had met a singer named Danny Cox. He gave me his phone number to call him should we ever make it to LA. I called him. He was there. We went to his house off of Laurel Canyon and visited. We couldn't crash there. It was just a small place in the hills, but he fed us and let us take showers, and that felt real good. (Thanks, Danny.) So we slept in the hearse on a side street parallel to Laurel Canyon Boulevard. I remember that every time I pass by, and I have passed by a lot in the last forty-five years or so. We lived there for almost a week. We used the bathrooms at gas stations and restaurants. It was cool. We weren't scared. We were fascinated by the whole scene in Hollywood.

We spent our days looking for Steve Stills, who I knew was down there. Richie told me that Stephen was down in LA trying to put together a band. That was all I needed to know. I remembered Stephen from Fort William, four hundred miles southeast of Winnipeg, at the Fourth Dimension Club, where I had first heard him play in a band called the Company. We had talked about playing more together then.

Bruce and I went to the Trip, a cool club on the Sunset Strip where the Byrds played. We asked around. No one knew Stills. We visited a place called Huff's on Sunset. It was a hippie hangout. I had never seen so many hippies in my life! Where did they get all those cool clothes? Where did all these girls come from? They looked so cool and unreachable. They had tie-dyed dresses and T-shirts, so colorful and beautiful. It made me feel like I was from another planet, but I loved it. We made a living that week by giving hippies a ride between Huff's and Canter's, another cool hangout that was down on Fairfax. We charged about fifty cents a ride. (These hippies mostly were rich.) The girls were really something; I had never seen anything like it. I was completely in awe!

One day, Bruce and I were walking down Sunset toward a hotel, the Colonial West, we visited regularly that we gave people rides to and from, and we found a joint on the sidewalk. Of course, we smoked it right away and got so high, we were completely flying. What the hell kind of pot was that? It smelled really pungent. So we walked along toward this hotel. Some places you can just feel are havens for drug users, heavy drug users. These places have a feeling to them. I sensed the dark seed (which is a phrase I've stolen from Stephen and Kristin Stills's twelve-year-old son, Henry, who used it to describe a Disney movie). There was an opening on the strip that led to a parking lot that was surrounded by about three stories of rooms, so the place was kind of separated from everything else, like a fort. Musicians lived there along with drug dealers, actors, and rich hippies I suppose. It was a scene, and you could feel it instantly. Bruce and I had never experienced anything like this. It was all new to us.

We couldn't find Stills anywhere. Eventually we gave up on LA and decided to head north to San Francisco, where Flower Power was in full bloom, with Jefferson Airplane and Big Brother and the Holding Company. Human Be-Ins were happening in Golden Gate Park. Hippies were everywhere. We were on our way to Mecca! The Great Pilgrimage was about to begin!

We made our way along Sunset and got caught in a traffic jam. It had dawned on us that we may not have enough gas money to get to San Francisco, but we were working on a solution when we heard a voice shout, "Hey, Neil!!! Is that you?"

I looked around out the driver's window of the hearse. It was Stills! We got out and hugged right there on Sunset Boulevard in the middle of traffic. Horns were honking! To us it seemed like everybody was celebrating! Something was happening, but we didn't know what it was. It was fucking Buffalo Springfield, that's what it was.

Stills and Richie Furay were living at Barry Friedman's house on Fountain Avenue. Barry had a background in the circus and the entertainment business. He was a smart guy with a great musical sense. He was managing Stills and Furay, which is how I met him. Stills had convinced Richie to come to LA from New York because he had a group going. When Richie arrived, Stephen explained that the group was now Stephen and Richie!

Richie was a natural vocalist. They had been working on a vocal sound, and they were really great. They sang like birds together. They were doing "Nowadays Clancy Can't Even Sing" (which I had sung for Richie in New York when I was there doing a demo tape in December 1965), and they sang it really great. I sat in and added a little guitar and a high voice here and there. This was going to be good. We needed a drummer, and Barry had contacted the Dillards, a great vocal group with a guy named Dewey Martin on drums—just when they were changing to all acoustic. We tried him out and took him, although Stephen was not a hundred percent sure. Dewey was country and took a little speed, I think. He was moving right along.

But Stephen, who was a genius, had an amazing groove. He possessed his own sense of rhythm that was uncanny, like a clock but with a feel, never rushing or dragging. There was a rub between him and Dewey because Dewey tended to push the beat and rush sometimes. I had never been aware of that type of thing until I met Stephen and started to learn from what he was saying.

We went outside onto Fountain Avenue and saw a big steamroller on the side of the road. BUFFALO SPRINGFIELD, read the sign on the side. What a great name for a band! Buffalo Springfield was born that day. We lived and practiced at Barry's house in West Hollywood. I slept in a little room with the band instruments. Every day we would go to Pioneer Chicken on Santa Monica Boulevard and have a meal. Barry gave us the money. We ate once a day. Stephen always had a cheeseburger with mayonnaise only. Good taste is timeless.

Chapter Eighteen

Stephen and I recently talked about the Springfield and writing books. We talked about the future. About musicians and friends, about loyalty, about the difficult decisions in life around loyalty, loyalty to friends and loyalty to the muse, how sometimes there was conflict, where serving one meant not serving the other. This is a heavy subject, and we, as two old friends, treated it well. It has not been an easy part of life for either of us. I think most musicians would agree with that. Stephen and I have this great honesty about our relationship and get joy from telling each other observations from our past. The past is such a big place.

I have heard it said about me that I have a rep for being difficult to work with. My decisions are made with the music in mind. For instance, I like to play to an audience that is into it. I dislike people sitting in the front rows talking on cell phones. Of course, these people are sitting in the most expensive seats, the ones they get through ticket scalpers and other services that somehow corner the market on the seats. Capitalism collides with music in this area. It was not like that when I started. The people in the front were music freaks, the real music fans, who knew every song, every lyric, every piece of information about the band that they could find. They were stoked to be there in front of the stage, and they were ready to rock. So these cell phones and rich folks who can afford the big bucks for prime seating distract me from what I am doing and make me feel like I am on display in a museum. It is not good for the music, which a lot of times feeds on the energy of the crowd. There is a thing called "festival seating" where the area in front of the stage is without chairs. People can stand there. Only a certain amount of people can get into that area, and it is not more expensive. It is general admittance. First come, first served, as far as proximity to the stage goes. Medium ago, I decided to sell festival-seating tickets at all my indoor shows so people who really wanted to see the band could get up close and watch, moving freely. There is a financial hit involved with that, because those are generally the expensive seats and they are all gone with this type of presentation. I had to really be firm about it. When we got festival seating, the feeling at all of the shows was much better. The band and I really enjoyed that change. Things like that enable me to continue and enjoy playing with a band. Recently I was planning a tour and it was just being announced. Venues were already booked. At the last minute I checked to make sure it was still festival seating. It wasn't. Feeling that I had already established that as the way I liked to play indoor shows, I insisted on it again. All the deals had to be redone at the last minute. It was a very complicated thing to do. I, having already been through this once, was amazed that no one had remembered the way I liked festival seating. If that gives me a rep for being difficult to work with, I earned it.

Because Stephen and I have been friends for such a long time, and we were really young when we met, some of these things run deep. He is really my oldest friend, and confiding in him is easy, once we get started. There is nothing to hide between us. We talked about the love of playing together and being in the groove, and about the fact that we need to have solid support from musicians on our level everywhere on the stage. Festivals are where you need that kind of strength at the core. That is how you elevate the audience and take them with you. We both love doing that.

We talked about playing with Chad Cromwell and Rick Rosas on the Living with War tour around five years ago and how solid that was. It was perhaps the most overtly over-the-top group of songs I had ever written, but we did what we did and I don't feel bad about it. There was no attempt at an artfully crafted message. It was just a straight shot. Stephen was uncomfortable with the political nature, singing songs like "Let's Impeach the President" and "Living with War," which were written as if they were from a raving political maniac. Hey! Maybe it was art. Like someone standing on a soapbox in the park, I didn't waste any time on a melody. The message wasn't worth a carefully crafted one. Production, pretty melodies, and the like would have been a waste of time on that record. It was delivered in a cheap paper bag like something that came with no desire to decorate it. We discussed that. I told him I thought it was a worthy part of our history. It was uncomfortable at times and pushed the limit of what our audience could handle. I was more okay than he was with that. But we talked it through.

Niko Bolas was my co-producer on *Living with War*. I met Niko in 1986. He was the engineer at Record One, a studio in LA's

San Fernando Valley where we made a record called *Landing on Water*. I liked Niko right away. We worked fast and did a lot together over time. *This Note's for You* with the Bluenotes in the late eighties, *Freedom* with "Keep on Rockin' in the Free World" in 1989, and *Living with War, Chrome Dreams II,* and *Fork in the Road* in the 2000s. I always liked Niko and enjoy working with him. He and John Hanlon (*Ragged Glory*) are both guys I can relax with in the studio and be myself with, like I did with Briggs. They know they are not Briggs. No one is like Briggs. But they know who he was and respect him and his memory. He was a legend. They try to keep his feeling going on, and that helps me a lot.

As for *Living with War*, we probably won't be doing any more of those types of records, but we did that one. Buffalo Springfield was not that kind of band anyway, and I think that will be our band for the next big run, whenever and wherever that is.

So I spoke to my old friend Bruce and told him I was feeling it, his loss of Clarence. We talked for quite a while, and there is no need to go into what two old friends had to say to each other at this point, except to say that two old friends spoke to each other about their music, their muses, their partners in crime, their proof, their friendship, their souls, and their lives. Ben Keith was my Clarence Clemons. Clarence was Bruce's Ben Keith. When he died last year, it touched me to the core. I don't want to ever think of anyone else playing his parts or occupying his space. No one could. I can't do those songs again unless it's solo. So I told Bruce, "Waylon once looked at me and said, 'There's very few of us left.'" He liked that. I told him when he looked to his right I would be there. That's enough. I'm not talking about that anymore.

When music is your life, there is a key that gets you to the core. I am so grateful that I still have Crazy Horse, knock on wood. You see, they are my window to the cosmic world where the muse lives and breathes. I can find myself there and go to the special area of my soul where those songs graze like buffalo. The herd is still there, and the plains are endless. Just getting there is the key thing, and Crazy Horse is my way of getting there. That is the place where music lives in my soul. It is not youth, time, or age. I dream of playing those long jams and floating over the herd like a condor. I dream of the changing wind playing on my feathers, my brothers and sisters around me, silently telling their stories and sharing their spirits with the sky. They are my life. How often can a guy make a living doing that? Not that often is my guess, so I accept the extreme nature of my blessings and burdens, my gifts and messages, my children with their uniqueness, my wife with her endless beauty and renewal. Am I too cosmic about this? I think not, my friend. Do not doubt me in my sincerity, for it is that which has brought us to each other now.

## Chapter Nineteen

Hawaii 2011

Writing this book, there seems to be no end to the information flowing through me. There is always more waiting to come out, whereas songs are nowhere to be found at the moment. Since I have never written a book before and my father, who was a writer of books and taught me how to write many years ago, is gone, I am alone but am comforted by the eternal presence of my father and his old Underwood up in the attic. I am both down here and up there. Omemee was my town, and that's where the house was. That's where the attic is. Someday I want us to live on a lake up there in North Ontario for a while. I have been there visiting my brother. This is not the time for us to go there, though. Maybe it will never come, and that's all right, but I want to do it someday, and that is important to me. It is part of my Canadian self. I feel it stronger these days than in days past, yet I know it may not ever be, and I accept that I cannot have every dream come true at once. Life is too short for that.

Anyway, the word count on my computer is a marvel. Think of

counting the actual words one by one and keeping track. My dad would never do that. That's not going to happen with me, either. I am beginning to see that the rest of my life could conceivably be spent as an author, churning out books one after another to the endless interest of, say, fourteen people with Kindles. Seriously, though, this is a great way to live. No wonder my dad did this. There is no live performing, which I love to do as long as I don't *have* to do it, and writing could be just the ticket to a more relaxed life with fewer pressures and more time to enjoy with my family and friends—and paddleboarding!

I suppose that sounds like the end of something, but I look at it as the beginning. I'm even considering starting a second book titled *Cars and Dogs* because there is so much more to say than I could ever say in one book. There is a lot of room there for me to wander, which I am very fond of doing. Maybe it would be disruptive to put out two different books at once, one in hardcover and one in digital, both memoirs, since the book industry is on its heels from the tech revolution. Disruptive is good in technology. No matter how many books I write, I will eventually get to fiction. That is where I am going.

When I injured my toe, I was amazed. It didn't hurt that much after the first shock of stubbing it on a rock. The next day, however, it hurt like hell. I took a picture of it and sent it to my doctor, Dr. Rock Positano, in Manhattan. He sent me back an e-mail. "You broke it." That was his diagnosis.

Pegi thought I should get it checked and X-rayed, but of course I didn't do that because I was busy writing this book. I am not trying to make you feel guilty. I am always busy doing something. I am sure it's broken. It's nine days later and it still hurts. I have a special pair of sandals that Dr. Rock sent to me with a wrap to put on my toe to hold it in place. I haven't used the wrap yet, but the sandals are quite stylish so I wear them, and I will use the wrap very soon, Dr. Rock. (The sandals kind of have the Devo look! Booji Boy would love to wear these babies!)

As I've said, I think the toe has had a lot to do with the book. It was the catalyst to get me started. Art and medicine have come together in a whole new way. Neither one of them is recognizable in the novel configuration we find them in with this project. Now when I walk around every step is a loud *clop*. It is not a stealth thing. I am debating whether to wear them tonight to dinner next door at Greg and Vicki's. We will be having grass-fed beef. I will keep you posted, as you no doubt have noticed.

With sunset coming on I feel particularly good at this moment. The day has developed nicely and I met the Master Gardener at Poncho's. He really seemed to be a Master, walking around and smelling things in the garden, followed by his wife and some other Korean folks who were very nice and very interested in Poncho's plants. Poncho's plants look exceptionally healthy and strong to me, and he is using absolutely no chemicals on anything. He is watering a lot less and spraying some organic microbiological liquid very sparingly.

I did feel I was in the presence of a highly evolved being when the Master was around. He definitely has a wealth of knowledge I don't have. I was very impressed with all of them, him and his friends. One of them was Poncho's teacher, and she did a lot of translating for the Master during the visit. Poncho was very nervous to be around him, and he was very respectful. Poncho really loves gardening, and to have the Master visit his garden and property was a great honor. They covered every area of the property and gardens and made detailed comments on everything Poncho was doing. Poncho has all kinds of blends of "inputs," as they called them, that he has brewed himself on the property just from natural ingredients and a little vodka, beer, and rice. The Master and his friends smelled and tasted all of these bottles and containers of inputs and made comments to Poncho through translation on how he was doing with the blends. When you are in the presence of someone obviously more knowledgeable than you are, who is very gracious, speaks no English, and treats you with a lot of respect, you really feel it.

Toward the end of the visit, Poncho gave the Master one of his famous apple pies, and the Master gave Poncho a pat on the back in thanks and invited him to a special meeting they were having to discuss even more advanced gardening techniques. Later, after they all left, Poncho confided in me that he did not feel qualified to be at the meeting, and I assured him that the Master knew what he was doing. I am sure Poncho is qualified. He is a highly evolved being himself, meaning that he is sensitive to his surroundings and the life around him, whether it is plant, human, or otherwise.

We shared a piece of Poncho's apple pie, and I told Poncho about PureTone. Like all serious musicians, he is depressed by the quality of sound the people's music is delivered in today. That is the impression I have gotten from every musician I have met. Everyone. After he heard PureTone, Ben Bourdon, one of Ben Young's caregivers, asked me if I was making war on Apple. I said, "No. I'm waging heavy peace."

I see online streaming services like Rhapsody, Spotify, and Pandora as the new radio. Apple's iTunes is the new radio, too. The sound is highly compromised, but people can get whatever they want, whenever they want. There is a lot of value to that convenience, but it has created a huge void in quality that begs to be filled. Turntable.fm is a lot of fun and exposes music to the masses in a new way. This is all very good for music. The only thing missing is quality.

Sound is very complex. It is not enough to just be able to recognize a song and hear the melody. There is a significant amount more to music than that. Many young people have never heard what I have heard, and that was not the case when I was young. In the age of technology we have grown used to many things being convenient and easy. We have grown up in the age of convenience and expediency. Videos can be shared and viewed around the world, and so can music, just like any document. The only problem with this is music is not like that. It is a storm on the senses, weather for the soul, deeper than deep, wider than wide. It is more than what you see or hear. It is what you feel. That is missing in today's technology for music, although many things have come along to replace it and distract from its absence.

I will not rest until the impact has been made and PureTone or something like it is available worldwide to those who love music. This is the sound of the twenty-first century, the sound we are capable of delivering. It is music. It has been an art form denied. There is something new now. Music as it should be heard. The promise of digital fulfilled.

But I am a pain in the ass now. I can't go anywhere without the annoying sound of MP3s or some other source of bad sound grating on my nerves and affecting my conversations. Everywhere is an elevator with bad sounds. Like tea bags that were hit with boiling water and scalded into submission, and like coffee that has been bombed by a boiling pot, my mind has been assaulted and has become edgy by this phenomenon of bad sound. This used to be my life, music. So I need to find or create a solution. Let everyone live, including those who crave quality. Mostly so I stop ranting about it.

L iving in Hawaii, with the horizon of the ocean meeting the sky, is soothing. There is a magical healing to the Big Island, and I love this life. How many places are there on earth that really are healing places? There must be countless ones where people each can find their own peace. I hope you find all of yours and I find the rest of mine. In this world it is truly awesome how lucky we are, yet we keep hurting the planet in ways nature could never have come up with, mostly in the name of progress and moneymaking. It is hard to not get angry and discouraged on a quest for the health of the planet. Countless obstacles have been erected to impede that progress. Many souls have felt the pain of defeat. Yet the spirit endures and people try to spread the word. Ways to grow food without damaging the earth, ways to consume without excess waste, ways to use waste for fuel. Ways to serve and preserve the health of the planet are all around us, yet we stumble and repeat our old habitual ways, ignoring that which is speaking to us so clearly, not seeing the signals and signs. Somehow can we break the cycle? Somewhere can we see the light? Will we be served as we have served the earth? Is there fear in that thought? Then why oh why do we sing the same song over and over? The song, the song, the song.

here was a thing in Hollywood in the sixties called Teen Fair. It took place near the corner of Sunset Boulevard and Vine Street across from what was then Wallich's Music City, an amazing store. Let me describe Wallich's for you: They sold all kinds of music there—45s, LPs, sheet music, books about music—and in a little shop upstairs guitars and other instruments were displayed. There were also listening booths where you could hear singles on headphones and see if you wanted to buy them. I spent a lot of time there. Of course, the place was crawling with flower children and beautiful hippie girls.

Anyway, like I said, upstairs at Wallich's there was a great guitar department. Martins, Gibsons, all manner of electric and very nice old acoustic guitars were there. This was around the time the Springfield was happening; we were playing at the Whisky a Go Go, about a mile down Sunset toward Beverly Hills. Stills and I went to Wallich's a lot and tried out Martins together. Stephen

Buffalo Springfield near my Laurel Canyon cabin, 1967. Left to right, Dewey Martin, me, Richie Furay, Jim Fielder (replacing Bruce Palmer), Stephen Stills.

was fast becoming an excellent player and had surpassed me in his knowledge of voicings, and he was always playing rhythms naturally that blew my mind.

One day, I was there at Teen Fair with a few friends, looking around, taking in the sights, the sounds, the girls, the crowds, an overwhelming chaos of inputs, when the sky started to spin a little and I felt a bit sick to my stomach. I started to fall. The sky was getting dark and the sounds were all echoing, a hollow reverberation inside my head. Lying on my back on the pavement, I saw the faces looking down on me. It was like I had just been born, and I recognized no one. I didn't really even know my own name. I was hot and sweating.

"Neil, Neil! Are you okay? Are you all right?"

I didn't know the answer to that question, but I was becoming aware that my name was Neil and that I was in a crowd of people lying down somewhere. I did feel strangely reborn. On the other hand, I was being helped up and people were all dispersing and walking away. Someone must have taken me home, back to Barry's, and later I fell asleep, I guess.

From that moment on, for years, I lived in constant fear that it was going to happen again. I could feel it in my stomach, and then I would get really scared and withdrawn until it went away. I felt it onstage, I felt it in crowds, I felt it in grocery stores, this unreasonable anxiety all the time waiting in the wings to come out and envelop me. It had an effect. Eventually I could not even go to the Laurel Canyon Country Store, which was near my place, to buy food. There were too many aisles and too much produce, too many choices for me.

The Canyon Country Store was just two blocks from where I had been living in the hearse less than a year before. I now had a house/cabin at the top of Ridpath Avenue near Utica Drive, way up at the end of the road at the top of Laurel Canyon. It was a crazy place up there, with a main house, a garage, and a little cabin. The shingles were all curved and mystical like a witch's castle. Wonderful. I was renting a cabin at the top of a flight of stairs, maybe one to two hundred–plus steps. Below it, the garage was down on Utica, and a drummer, John Densmore of the Doors, lived there. The garage was constructed with the same mystical shingle work. An astrologer, Kiyo Hodel, was my landlord. She lived in the main house of the whole compound and was very cosmic. The little cabin was made of knotty pine, very rustic, and I loved it. I had a llama rug on the floor. A lot happened to me up there. I brought a lot of girls up there to my little shack and we had good times, although I was not very confident in myself and probably not an impressive lover to be sure. We could call it performance anxiety.

I was kind of lost in that area and worked on that for a long, long time. Learning how to open up and give myself to another person, learning the depths of intimacy as more than sex. It has become the journey of a lifetime, one of the great revelations. I never did get much advice from my father and growing up missed his presence to quite a degree. I'm uncomfortable talking about that, but I feel a lot better about myself now than I did in my earlier days.

One day Dennis Hopper, who Stephen had met through Peter Fonda, came and took some pictures of the Springfield behind my little cabin. It was very simple, with only two rooms, a bedroom and a bathroom, and a little add-on porch where I kept my fridge.

Who knows what I put in that fridge? It was certainly not much. I think I had a hot plate, too. I used it for pork and beans . . . probably.

Once, when I had been on the road for a week or so, I stopped on Sunset at the Whisky before going home to the cabin. I met the daughter of one of the Rat Pack there that night and brought her up to show her my place. She was very nice. We went back to the cabin late that night without me having a chance to get there first. Somehow I had closed my cat in there for a week. The cabin was full of cat shit! Wow! I've never seen a girl get out of anyplace faster than she did. I did not make a very good impression on her.

In that little cabin, I wrote "Mr. Soul," "Expecting to Fly," "Broken Arrow," and a few other songs. I would listen to acetates of the mixes with my friends often there, too. (Acetates were records that you could make fast and play only a few times before they wore out and lost their sound. They would make them to take home and listen to right after we cut a song at Gold Star Studios in a little room where a lathe was set up. I still remember that acetate smell. The acetate would go in a little record sleeve and a Gold Star label would be typed up and stuck on it. I heard the first Buffalo Springfield album for the first time on my KLH record player and speakers in that little room.) We would hang and play records for hours, sitting on the llama rug in front of the speakers, listening to tracks like "A Day in the Life" by the Beatles over and over. The sound was so good, you could never get enough of it. I really feel sorry for kids with their MP3s today who can't hear music the way we did then. What a bummer. I can't imagine that. It really bothers me.

Now, I didn't get this cabin until the Springfield was happening, months after my first episode at Teen Fair, but somehow we got around to the subject, so here we are. The Canyon Country Store was where I bought food. Not that I bought much food. I would go down there and stand in the parking lot, working up the nerve to go in, hoping I would not get anxious and paranoid and freak out, leaving whatever I had chosen to buy inside and bolting for the door. This anxious feeling was similar to a seizure feeling in my stomach, and I couldn't tell the difference, so I just panicked.

Somewhere along the line, our managers, Charlie Greene and Brian Stone, who we hired in 1966, set up an appointment for me with a doctor at UCLA Medical Center to do some tests. April Full, Greene and Stone's secretary, took me down there. First they stuck a bunch of things on my head and gave me a little liquid in a cup and told me to go in this dark room and lie down. Then they wired all the things up, and while I was lying there I could feel these little flashes. I still feel those today, kind of like little rushes of something, gusts of cosmic wind in my head. My hearing changes for an instant, and it's hard to describe. Anyway. I live with that, and it's nothing. But it is somehow related to the feeling I used to get going up and down steep hills in my car. After that test, which revealed nothing to my knowledge, I went back to April's house. April chose that moment to explain to me what turned a woman on, demonstrating what would be physically stimulating for me to do as an education for me to apply later in life, say five or ten minutes later at the most.

It was not long afterward that suddenly I realized I had the clap. There were a lot of hippie girls, and we saw them at the

Whisky all the time. After the show it was time to go to the International House of Pancakes on Sunset Boulevard. I remember those German pancakes. They were delicious. How much sugar can one person eat? After that we paired off and went back to our shacks for some fun. Anyway, I had the clap and I had to go to the clinic. The doctor said he wanted to draw some blood. I said okay. I was on a metal table. He drew my blood. I crashed and had another full-on seizure on the spot. The same feeling. The room spinning slowly, the echoes, the darkness creeping in, and finally the doctor and nurses trying to get me back on the table, shoving a piece of wood in my mouth so I wouldn't bite off my own tongue. Then remembering my name, starting over. Getting a grip on my identity, where I lived, etc. It would all come back in a semi-orderly fashion, like a reboot. Eventually, I had to take another test with Dr. Morton K. Rubenstein. I DO NOT RECOMMEND THIS TEST. It is barbaric. It was called a pneumoencephalogram.

Pneumoencephalography (sometimes abbreviated PEG) is a medical procedure in which most of the cerebrospinal fluid is drained from around the brain and replaced with air, oxygen, or helium to allow the structure of the brain to show up more clearly on an X-ray image. It is derived from ventriculography, an earlier and more primitive method where the air is injected through holes drilled in the skull.

The procedure was introduced in 1919 by the American neurosurgeon Walter Dandy.

Pneumoencephalography was performed extensively throughout the early twentieth century, but it was extremely painful. The test was generally not well tolerated by patients. Headaches and severe vomiting were common side effects. Replacement of the drained spinal fluid is by slow natural production, and therefore required recovery for as long as two to three months before normal fluid volumes were restored . . . Modern imaging techniques such as MRI and computed tomography have rendered pneumoencephalography obsolete. Today, pneumoencephalography is limited to the research field and is used under rare circumstances.

Thanks, Wiki.

It is the most painful thing I have ever been through. Pure torture, where they tie you into a big device, stick a needle in you, and inject radioactive dye into your spinal column. Then they track its progress through your brain. Of course, being man-made, it is flawed, and bubbles sometimes get in there with the radioactive dye. These fucking bubbles are the worst pain ever in the universe. I took a long time to recover from that shit, and they learned *nothing.* I am still pissed about that. Of course, medical professionals don't do that test anymore. It's too barbaric. I am even more pissed now to realize that they *knew* they were injecting gas into my brain, then they had the nerve to tell me some bubbles *might* have gotten in there with the dye. I am pissed. I am over it. None of these tests revealed any new information about my condition. There was no conclusion. The doctor's recommendations were that I not take any LSD. Prior to that I had never had a doctor recommend that I take LSD. I had never taken acid. I never wanted to, anyway. I hallucinate enough on my own and can't control that.

In my life I have had various health threats: polio, seizures, a brain aneurysm. None of these things has really changed me much, although it is hard to say for sure. These are events that are part of my life. They make me who I am. I am thankful for them. They are scary.

Chapter Twenty-One

H ave you ever wondered what goes into writing a song? I wish I could tell you the exact ingredients, but there is nothing specific that comes to mind. It seems to me that songs are a product of experience and a cosmic alignment of circumstance. That is, who you are and how you feel at a certain time.

I have written a lot of songs. Some of them suck. Some of them are brilliant, and some are just okay. Those are all other people's opinions. To me, they are like children. They are born and raised and sent out into the world to fend for themselves. It's not an easy place to be, the world, for a song. You might find yourself on a tape in the garbage, or on a CD someone threw out, or you may even be in the bargain bin. You may be a forgotten song languishing on a vinyl record in the dump or, more hopefully, in an independent record store rack. In one of the worst cases, you may be relegated to being nothing more than another MP3 file with less than five

With Joni Mitchell, doing her song "Raised on Robbery"
at Studio Instrument Rentals in Los Angeles, where the album
Tonight's the Night *was recorded in 1973.*

percent of your original sound. However, someone had to create you, and that is our subject for now.

I have not written one song since I stopped smoking weed in January 2011, so we are currently in the midst of a great chemical experiment.

When I write a song, it starts with a feeling. I can hear something in my head or feel it in my heart. It may be that I just picked up the guitar and mindlessly started playing. That's the way a lot of songs begin. When you do that, you are not thinking. Thinking is the worst thing for writing a song. So you just start playing and something new comes out. Where does it come from? Who cares? Just keep it and go with it. That's what I do. I never judge it. I believe it. It came as a gift when I picked up my musical instrument and it came through me playing with the instrument. The chords and melody just appeared. Now is not the time for interrogation or analysis. Now is the time to get to know the song, not change it before you even know it. It is like a wild animal, a living thing. Be careful not to scare it away. That's my method, or one of my methods, at least.

I was just thinking that I am putting a lot of pressure on myself to write a song. That never works. Songs are like rabbits and they like to come out of their holes when you're not looking, so if you stand there waiting they will just burrow down and come out somewhere far away, a new place where you can't see them. So I feel like I am standing over a song hole. That will never result in success. The more we talk about this, the worse it will get. So that is why we are changing the subject.

The Black Queen is a 1947 Buick Roadmaster sedanette fast-back. Originally the Black Queen was found in Idaho in a church parking lot by a friend of mine who purchased it for $650. That was a great deal. I used this car exclusively during the recording of *Tonight's the Night*. This is a beautiful car that is out of Feelgood's right now, getting some work done on the transmission. *Tonight's the Night* is an LP that centers in on the lives and deaths of Bruce Berry and Danny Whitten. Both tragic deaths were drug-related. There was an epidemic of these events going on in the early seventies, and I was not interested in referring to it directly. I did not want to be specific. These were just my friends. Actually, *Tonight's the Night* centers in on the aftermath of those deaths. It is a wake of sorts.

Anyway, the *Tonight's the Night* sessions, recorded on the Green Board by David Briggs, were done at SIR, Studio Instrument Rentals. Jan Berry of Jan & Dean, the surf legends, was an owner of SIR and the older brother of Bruce, one of CSNY's roadies. So memorializing Bruce Berry, the little brother of Jan, at those sessions was particularly close to home. Danny Whitten, the original Crazy Horse guitarist and singer, was the spirit of the album, as was Bruce. The songs were all pretty down. Both Bruce and Danny had OD'd on heroin.

It was an LP recorded in audio vérité, if you will, while completely intoxicated on Jose Cuervo tequila. We would not start recording until midnight, when we were so fucked up we could hardly walk. One night Joni Mitchell came in and did "Raised on Robbery" in the most sexy and revealing version that song ever had. She still refuses to let me release it. I don't know what the hell she was thinking when she joined us and sang the song. It kicks ass. What the fuck was that about? It was funkier than anything she has ever cut. A total gem!

I drove to SIR and home from SIR in the Black Queen nightly. The album was risky and real. It was a real mess of a recording, with no respect given to technical issues, although it sounds like God when played loud, under the able production of David Briggs. The original roughs were never remixed to our satisfaction, and the album was held up for more than a year, and released after one or two other albums were already done. Zeke Young used to use the rough masters on his toy tape recorder, practicing threading, winding, and rewinding the tapes for when he would grow up and be a big-time recording engineer.

This album survived a memorable production cycle unparalleled in my history, from the great David Briggs to my three-year-old son Zeke, all having their way with those rough master tapes. Those original roughs were used in the final release.

Homegrown had been recorded and *On the Beach* had already been released when Ben Keith and I played the tapes one midnight in what is now known as the Belushi bungalow of Hollywood's Chateau Marmont Hotel for Rick Danko of The Band and some other musicians. Rick said after hearing *Homegrown* and then *Tonight's the Night*, "You ought to put THAT out! What the hell is THAT?" So we did. It was Rick Danko who brought it back. *Home-*

grown, which I think is a great album, is still unreleased to this day. (It will come out, though, and we are preparing it now.)

When I played *Tonight's the Night* for Mo Ostin and Lenny Waronker at Reprise, as was always my habit to do when I handed a record in, Mo asked, "Neil, are you sure you want to put THAT out? It is really rough, and it may not be received well." I said yes. He understood why, which makes him one of the greatest record men of all time, along with Ahmet Ertegun and Clive Davis. Then we got in the Black Queen and rode home to the ranch, at least a full year after *Tonight's the Night* had been originally recorded. The car was there for every event tied to that record. Every night after those sessions, we rode the Black Queen home to the Sunset Marquis on Alta Loma in Hollywood, weaving down Santa Monica Boulevard at three or four in the morning, completely wrecked on tequila, and we made it, so there is a God.

When I first went to Topanga, I still didn't have a California driver's license, because I was in the country illegally. I had no Social Security number. I had recently gone to Santa Ana and purchased the 1951 Willys Jeepster that I have told you about already.

One fine summer day Briggs and I were out by Mulholland Drive, cruising in the hills, smoking a joint. It was a nice sunny day and we were grooving with the top down. California really is beautiful if you've never been there. It's worth a visit for sure. Anyway,

*The Black Queen leaving the Sunset Marquis Hotel parking garage
en route to the Roxy nightclub to debut* Tonight's the Night *live
in West Hollywood, 1973.*

we were driving along, Briggs, Danny Tucker (another good To-panga friend), and I, when a cop went by going the other way. He turned around and started following us. Briggs reached into his pocket and slipped me his license.

The cop pulled us over and asked me for my driver's license, looked at it, looked at me, and said, "I'm going to have to cite you for no brake lights. Get that fixed."

"Thanks, Officer," I said as coolly as I could.

I was scared shitless. Something happened later where I fucked up and Briggs was left holding the bag. I am not sure exactly what it was or how it was resolved, but I do remember Briggs saying that I had to get those lights fixed so the cops wouldn't be coming after him . . . Anyway, that was just another Briggs story, and there are a million of 'em. Point is, Briggs and I were brothers. He saw that cop coming and just slipped me his wallet without saying a thing. He was my best friend. Nobody can take that away from me. I always try to pay him back in any way I can. When he died years later, I did exactly what he asked me to do after he was gone, just like he asked me to do, some personal things that I know he would not want me to share with you. They had to do with how he felt about some people and how they should be dealt with.

As I said, I didn't have a California driver's license for a long time. I couldn't get one. I was illegal. I needed a green card. I couldn't even leave the country without a green card, because I would have to sneak back in if I did. Remember? The "United States has better roads" story?

Thank God capitalism saved me, and I was able to *buy* a green card. A real one! Through my lawyer! It took a long time to find the right lawyer in New York with the correct connections in the INS, but by the end of the sixties, I had a real green card! America is great, and capitalism rocks! Most folks don't know how hard it is to get one of those cards. An American could do the job I am doing. There are plenty of other guitar players. I don't really know how the lawyer did it, but it cost $5,000. I don't know if that was his fee or whether he did it for nothing and the money was paid to someone else. But it was capitalism at work, I can tell you that. I can't tell you how good it felt to be free in the USA without worrying about being deported at that time!

I felt so free when I got my first driver's license in California that I was floating on air! Not looking around for cops all the time, not hoping I didn't get stopped and busted, deported. I was one paranoid person before I got my license. That was two or three years of looking over my shoulder. FREEDOM ROCKS! Hey. Is that a song or what? I might be having a breakthrough moment . . .

Chapter Twenty-Two

A Note About Ronald Reagan

L et's have a word or two about Ronald Reagan, President of the United States of America. I don't know what you think of him, and it doesn't matter that much, really. What matters to me, though, is when people get an attitude about somebody and paint that person all one color.

I was sitting on my bus in New Orleans, backstage at a concert in the mid-eighties, recording what turned out to be *A Treasure*. We were playing music that I was getting sued for because it was deemed "uncharacteristic of Neil Young" by my new record company. My new record company was run by people who liked to get their way. Success was measured in sales. My first record for them, *Trans*, was a bit of a departure from what they expected. First off, the owner of the record company, David Geffen, listened to the record *Island in the Sun*, which I thought was done, and told me to do more. I wanted to get started on a good foot, so I added another dimension, vocoded (electronically synthesized) voices, that made it into *Trans*.

Logically to me that would have been my second record for them, but they didn't want the first record I gave them, which was a fucking great record. I knew it was a great record, but then I wouldn't have wanted to release it if I didn't like it. I was used to Mo Ostin, who understood art. My new record company wanted me to make a hit as big as *Harvest* and thought that I had ripped them off by not repeating myself and making them look like a great record company. I have never thought it was my job to make a record company look great. I thought it was the other way around. The record company has to recognize when something is a statement by the artist or whether it is commercial enough to be a hit and do a good job of presenting either option to maximize the release.

Not every record made by me is designed to be a hit. Some are expressions in an artist's life. They tried telling me what to do so they could have their hit. They told me they wanted rock and roll, so I gave them *Everybody's Rockin'* by Neil and the Shocking Pinks! Then they tried canceling my sessions and interrupting my creative flow to show me they meant business. Then, in their apparent frustration, not being able to have their own way, they decided I was purposefully making records that made them look like losers. Then they sued me for making records that were "uncharacteristic of Neil Young."

This, of course, made me look like a hero.

Anyway, in that climate, a pair of AP reporters came to my bus to interview me. I did quite a few interviews during that tour. Elliot had set up another one. These guys were supposed to be good. They came on the bus and started right off making derogatory remarks about Reagan. They were presumptuous; I could see they thought they had me all figured out. I was that hippie who wrote "Ohio" and "Southern Man" and sang with that group CSNY. The more they said to ingratiate themselves, the more I didn't like them. I asked them if they'd ever met Reagan. They hadn't. Neither had I, I reasoned. I told them I did not believe in painting someone with one brush, that there must be more to a person than that, and I liked Reagan for some things he had said. Reagan had talked about the need for communities to come together to help themselves in ways that I thought were reasonable, and I told them that I did not believe that he was the villain so many had painted him to be. Just because you don't believe in some things a man says does not make him a bad man. There is good to be found in most people.

I also said that the guy is the president, so *someone* must think he is all right. Not everyone is against him.

I could tell they weren't buying it. Reagan was an asshole as far as they were concerned. So they wrote a story that made it sound like I was some all-out Reagan supporter, and I heard about it everywhere I went. One of my peers, who I respect, was calling me a buffoon, saying I didn't know what I was talking about and raving away about Guatemala.

Since the moment I met those two AP jerks, I have been trying to straighten out what they said. What they said *I* said. So in the end, I hate interviews, although I still do them every once in a while. I want people to know what I am up to if it supports my music in some way and brings awareness that a new recording exists. Sometimes that is the only way to get it out there. That certainly was the case in the eighties, although I don't think it is now. Things are better now, because we have tools to get information out there, and if you're smart enough, you don't have to talk to two dickheads on a bus anymore. And that's all I have to say about Ronald Reagan.

## Chapter Twenty-Three

Danny and the Memories was the band at the root of Crazy Horse. They were a vocal group with Danny Whitten, Ralphie, Billy, and a guy named Ben Rocco. When I recently saw their old video of "Land of a Thousand Dances" on YouTube, I realized that is truly the shit. You know, I looked at it maybe twenty times in a row. Even though Danny was amazing and he held the Horse together in the early days, I did not know how great Danny was until I saw this! The moves! What an amazing dancer he was. His presence on that performance is elevating! He is gone, and no one can change that. We will never see and hear where he was going. I am telling you, the world missed one of the greatest when Danny and the Memories did not have a NUMBER ONE smash record back in the day. They were so musical, with great harmonies, and Danny was a total knockout! I am so moved by this that it could make me cry at any time. This is one of those many times when words can't describe music.

Original Crazy Horse guitarist/vocalist Danny Whitten backstage at the Electric Factory in Philadelphia, where I performed with Crazy Horse, February 1970.

Danny and the Memories eventually transformed into the Rockets; they were playing in this old house in Laurel Canyon, and I somehow connected with them while Buffalo Springfield was at the Whisky. We had a lot of pot jams in that house. Later on I saw Danny and the guys at somebody's house in Topanga. After that I asked if Danny, Billy, and Ralphie would play on a record with me. We did one day, practicing in my Topanga house, and it sounded great. I named the band Crazy Horse and away we went. The Rockets were still together, but this was a different deal.

At that time, I thought Danny was a great guitarist and singer. I had no idea *how* great, though. I just was too full of myself to see it. *Now* I see it clearly. I wish I could do that again, because more of Danny would be there.

I have made an *Early Daze* record of the Horse, and you can hear a different vocal of "Cinnamon Girl" featuring more of Danny. He was singing the high part, and it came through big-time. I changed it so I sang the high part and put that out. That was a big mistake. I fucked up. I did not know who Danny was. He was better than me. I didn't see it. I was strong, and maybe I helped destroy something sacred by not seeing it. He was never pissed off about it. It wasn't like that. I was young, and maybe I didn't know what I was doing. Some things you wish never happened. But we got what we got.

I never really saw him sing and move until I saw that "Land of a Thousand Dances" video. I could watch it over and over. I can't believe it. It's just one of those things. My heart aches for what happened to him. These memories are what make Crazy Horse great today. And now we don't have Briggs, either, for the next record, but we have the spirit and the heart to go on. And we have John Hanlon, taught by Briggs, to engineer this sucker. It will rock and cry. Please let's get to this before life comes knocking again.

So we are getting into this now. There may have to be more than one book. I read up on this sort of thing, and the worst thing you can have is a book that is too long. That doesn't help the publisher. There is a lot here to cover, and I have never done this before. Also, I am not interested in form for form's sake. So if you are having trouble reading this, give it to someone else. End of chapter.

## Chapter Twenty-Four

Pains

A long the way, I have encountered many doctors. One of my favorites is Dr. Petter Lindstrom, who was well-known for performing laminectomies. He came to me highly recommended and coincidentally was a former husband of Ingrid Bergman.

I had a double laminectomy by him in 1971.

But let me back up.

I had just signed with Reprise as a solo artist and got a big enough advance to buy my first house in Topanga Canyon. 611 Skyline Trail was all mine, a really wonderful redwood house built with a view of the whole canyon.

I used to go to the Canyon Kitchen every morning for breakfast. Susan Acevedo, the beautiful Sicilian hostess/owner, would bring me a one-eye and bacon. I got to look at Susan Acevedo every day at breakfast! Morning on the deck began with coffee overlooking the canyon, watching everything start to move below as the day unfolded. The scene in there was always stimulating, full of the color of the canyon, with the artists and other local characters, drug dealers and beautiful hippie girls, and I really enjoyed my breakfasts.

Eventually I met Tia, Susan's daughter. She was a cute little girl about five or six years old with a pretty little round face. Although Susan was a little older than I was, I found myself becoming more and more attracted to her. Eventually we fell in love. Susan introduced me to a lot of great artists in the canyon: Wallace Berman, Roland Diehl (who painted my first album cover), George Herms, Dean Stockwell, Russell Tamblyn, Kiel Martin, to name just a few. Susan was active in the Topanga Players, a local theater group, and I remember going to see George Herms's play *Egg of Night* and many other theater presentations there with her. She made all of my patchwork clothes, creating a style that spoke to the times, really the only time I was anywhere near fashionable. That was all Susan's doing, and it was so beautiful.

Susan and I were married in my new Topanga house, perched on the top of Skyline Trail, overlooking the canyon, and George Herms performed the ceremony. Our house was on a steep hill with the garage at the lowest point on a steep drive. One time Susan loaded my Mini Cooper with pies in the garage, preparing for a catering job she was doing with her company, Scuzzy Catering. Somehow after the pies were fully loaded, the emergency brake came loose and the Mini and its pies rolled down the hill and straight into the neighbor's garage, knocking out the support posts for his house. Pies were splattered all over the inside of the Mini. The neighbor, a gay man, was yelling at Susan, and she was going right back at him. It was quite a moment, full of expletives. Susan was quite a spirited lady, and I don't think the poor guy knew what he was in for!

Sadly, I was not mature enough to be a very good father to Tia, and I regret that I missed the boat there, but she sure was a sweet girl. Eventually Susan and I broke up. I don't think I was mature enough for her, either. The instant fame that came with *After the Gold Rush* and CSNY were too much for us. I have a lot of respect for Susan. She never asked for anything from me that was unreasonable, and she gave all she had to our short marriage. I was too young, and the pressures were too great for who I was at that time. The marriage lasted about a year. Sometimes I hear little tidbits about her, and I am always hoping she is doing well with her life. She was seen in Mexico recently and looking very good, was my last report. Love you, Susan. Thanks. You, too, Tia. Maybe we will meet again someday.

One day in early '70, still living in Topanga with Susan, I was working with a hoe in the brush on the hillside outside the house. I don't know what I was doing. I had thrown a portable TV off the deck and I could see it down there. I may have been preparing for a garden. Anyway, the next day I was in my car and I went to put my left foot on the clutch and my foot wouldn't come up. It just wouldn't move. So I went to a chiropractor Susan knew, and he did an adjustment on my back. After that my movement came back pretty much like it was before, but there was a little pain in my leg. That was the end of that.

In September of that year, Susan and I had split up and I was living on Broken Arrow Ranch, tearing my new house apart. At

Crosby's advice, I went to Berkeley to a hardwood dealer and saw some amazing huge slabs of California walnut. There were six big ones. I mean nine-footers, three feet wide and two to three inches thick. I bought them all and wanted to do the walls of my dining room with them. I was so excited that I tried to put them up myself. Doing that, I injured my back again. But the symptoms were worse: My leg didn't work, and it hurt all up and down the front. So I went to LA to see the doctor there that Elliot had, a Dr. Lipshutz. Walking through the airport to catch a plane to fly to LA was very painful, and I was sweating profusely when the sexy go-go stewardess brought me a Coke on PSA.

Things get blurry now in the memory department. I was told by the doctor to take Soma Compound (a muscle relaxant) and rest in bed so that the swelling would go down. There was no mention of surgery at that time, and I was thinking that if I just mellowed out while taking this Soma and stayed in the hospital bed they had moved into my room at the Chateau Marmont that everything would work itself out.

So there I was in the hospital bed at the Chateau, and it was there and then I first met Carrie Snodgress. After reading a story about her in *Newsweek* or *Time*, I had found her number and called her up, introducing myself and inviting her down to the Chateau. She was very attractive to me. What a way to meet. I was taking so much of the Soma Compound that I could hardly move. I liked her right away.

A few days after that, I returned to the ranch on doctor's orders to rest in a hospital bed that had been moved into my house there. Lying in bed, taking Soma at Broken Arrow, I found out that

Michelob and Soma Compound are a great combination—and eventually I landed in traction at Cedars-Sinai on Melrose Avenue back in LA. The doctors were hoping that traction would solve the problem and there would be no need for surgery.

Anyway, Cedars back then was an old hospital. I was in traction, with wires and weights pulling on my feet to relieve the pressure on discs in my back. (While I was there, I listened a lot to a cassette tape I had from the Cellar Door in Washington, D.C. It was a live tape I had recently recorded with Henry Lewy. It was real good, and I made some notes for an album, and I will eventually release a very cool record of those times. (Now, these years later, I am still finishing some things and looking for closure.) A lot of folks visited me in the hospital. I had friends from Hollywood, and some of them were beautiful ladies. I had a pretty good stay in that hospital!

When I finally got out and went home, I was wearing a back brace. It was still painful, but not too bad. Back at the ranch, I tried to walk up the hill behind my house toward the site of my new pool, but I couldn't make it. That really depressed me. Two weeks later, I went on the road across Canada with the brace. That was in early January.

I was corresponding with Carrie and writing songs. A lot of songs, like "Old Man," "Heart of Gold," "Needle and the Damage Done," and "Bad Fog of Loneliness." During that tour, I recorded at Massey Hall, and that came out as a record years later. Briggs was living in Toronto then and produced that. He had gone up there to live and had started a studio called Thunder Sound. The live Massey Hall record is David's live mix to 7.5 ips analog. You can see the brace and my hunkered-over posture in the Massey Hall video—which is actually a Stratford, Connecticut, picture from a few days earlier with Massey Hall's sound synched up. I used the sound from one place and the picture from another. "A cheap Hollywood trick," as Larry Johnson used to say.

I went on to Nashville at the end of the tour to do the Johnny Cash television show, which was new and really hot at the time. Bob Dylan had just done the first one, and everyone wanted to do it. James Taylor and Linda Ronstadt were doing the second show, and so was I. Everyone loved Johnny Cash; he was the real thing. The show was all about music, and it was cool, very real.

While I was there I met Elliot Mazer, the record producer, and we went into the studio to try some studio versions of all my new songs. Tim Drummond was there, and he put together a great band, with Kenny Buttrey, John Harris, Ben Keith, and another guitarist who played some tasty things like the harmonics on "Heart of Gold." This was a great-sounding band. James and Linda came in and added some vocals; James even played banjo on "Old Man." That session was a solid beginning for *Harvest*. Then, a few weeks later, I was in London and recorded "A Man Needs a Maid" and "There's a World" with the London Symphony Orchestra, produced and arranged by Jack Nitzsche. After hearing the playback in Glyn Johns's truck, where the pieces were recorded outside the Barking Town Hall, Jack said, "I think it's a bit overblown." We knew it was over-the-top, but we had done it and we loved it.

Later, when Carrie and I were seriously getting together and she was moving to the ranch, I wrote the rest of *Harvest*, and we went back to Nashville for another session. We did "Out on the

Weekend," "Journey Through the Past," and a few other ones, including "Harvest" itself. Then I asked the band to fly out to the ranch with Elliot Mazer to record a little in my barn. That was where we got "Alabama," "Are You Ready for the Country?" and "Words."

"Words" is the first song that reveals a little of my early doubts of being in a long-term relationship with Carrie. It was a new relationship. There were so many people around all the time, talking and talking, sitting in a circle smoking cigarettes in my living room. It had never been like that before. I am a very quiet and private person. The peace was going away. It was changing too fast. I remember actually jumping out the living room window onto the lawn to get out of there—I couldn't wait long enough to use the door! Words—too many of them, it seemed to me. I was young and not ready for what I had gotten myself into. I became paranoid and aware of mind games others were trying to play on me. I had never even thought of that before. That was how we did *Harvest*, in love in the beginning and with some doubts at the end.

The album was received well, and I suppose that was my commercial peak, at least my first and biggest one, although I didn't do the math. Some people liked it a lot and it was a big thing for them in their lives. It was for me. But my Crazy Horse fans were not knocked out. There is a line there. I suppose it matters to them, but it doesn't matter to me. I just like to make all kinds of music and do what is coming naturally to me. Nobody told me to make *Harvest*. No record company told me what to do until a lot later—and that didn't work.

But this was not the end of my back problem.

Eventually surgery was required. My left side was chronically weak from my childhood polio, and I was too active for the sort of long careful recovery that limited my movement for the rest of time without surgery.

I met with Dr. Lindstrom, who advised me that surgery was the only option and I should get ready to leave my pain behind. He came to see me in the hospital in San Francisco. He asked me how I was feeling, and I told him, "Not too good." Then he looked at me and said that after the surgery, he would come back and get me out of bed to walk around the room without the brace and the pain.

I said, "Really?"

He said, "Yes, but first we have to do the operation, and that will be tomorrow morning at six."

The next day I went to surgery. All I remember is lying on the gurney, the ceiling rolling by on my way to the operating room. And the next thing I knew, there he was, asking me to get up and walk around my room. I did it. He thanked me and said he would check in on me regularly for a few days and then I could go home. He was an amazing doctor. He told me to swim and exercise and do everything gently for a while. No football or hockey, he laughed. Then he made some graceful moves imitating a tennis player in slow motion. Nothing too fast, he said. Forty-two years later, I am still fine. Thank you, Dr. Lindstrom; what a gift.

Maybe the combination of Michelob and Soma was such that my thoughts were completely jumbled—and perhaps my love affair with Carrie was part of that process. I was never really happy during it, with the excessive amount of analysis and psychodrama that was spawned. And I have never been in that type of relationship before or after, so there is just something about my time with Carrie that I am unsettled about.

It is important for me to say that I initiated our relationship based on an article about her I read in *Newsweek* or *Time* and a beautiful picture the magazine ran. Falling in love from a picture in a magazine, however, is not a very calculated thing; nor are the effects of loneliness on one's decision making. It is a great thing to write a song about, though. I am just trying to make sense of the thought process and emotional landscape that resulted, and I suppose that would be a fruitless endeavor at this point, an emotional Band-Aid.

Carrie had a lot to give, but it didn't work with me for very long. I can take the blame for that. A lot of people were telling me that I had ruined her acting career by taking her to the seclusion of the ranch. That may be true. Because of Carrie, I have my wonderful son Zeke Young, who I love. So I would never change what happened. About eighteen months after *Harvest* was released, Carrie and I broke up and started sharing Zeke.

## Chapter Twenty-Five

Religion

Religion is not one of my high points. I really don't subscribe to the stories surrounding each one, because they are just stories, remembered by men. I do feel the Great Spirit in all that is around me, and I am humbled. I do pray with others if that is what they do. I don't judge them for that. That is their way. I join them. Then I move on. The moon means a lot to me, as does the forest. All things natural speak to me with a rhythm that I feel. It is this that probably makes me a pagan.

I think pagans have taken a bad rap from Christians. I feel, although I was not present when it started, that the Christians were threatened by the pagan beliefs and lashed out at them, attacking them and striking them down as witchcraft or something bad and evil. I suppose evil is necessary to justify the existence of organized religion. It seems to be the focus of a lot of sermonizing and preaching.

There is no evil in the forest or the moon. Or if there is, I don't see it. Somehow these things, the moon and the forest, move through space or survive on their own. I read a book called *The Mists of Avalon* by Marion Zimmer Bradley, which retells the Arthurian legends from the perspective of the female characters, especially Morgan le Fay, who fought to save her Celtic culture from the encroaching Christianity. There is a lot in that book that I relate to personally. Being alive may just be part of God, but not all. The Great Spirit, as I like to call her, is in us all and in everything that lives or used to live, in everything that exists or used to exist. So I have no story to tell that proves anything, but I think it was Pegi who gave me that book.

## Chapter Twenty-Six

Stories from Topanga

When I came to Topanga Canyon to live, I think I was still in Buffalo Springfield, but it was near the end. There was a lady, Linda Stevens, who was a friend of mine who put me up in her house. She knew both Stephen and me. It was 1968, because I remember during the time I was there at her house, my dad came down to cover the aftermath of the assassination of Robert Kennedy at the Ambassador Hotel in Los Angeles. My dad was working as a columnist for *The Globe and Mail* in Toronto, and the paper sent him down on special assignment.

I went into town to see him, and we hung for a few hours; then he went back to work. It was nice to see his face. That may have been the first time I saw him since I left Toronto two years before. We talked and may have shared a meal. He was just as shy as I am, so there wasn't a lot of heavy communication. Just being together and seeing each other was enough for both of us.

Anyway, it was pleasant living in Topanga with Linda and her daughter. My cats from Laurel Canyon were there. They were two orange kitties, and one of them was named Duck Egg and the other

Orange Julius, for the beverage. There were a lot of Orange Julius stands in LA at the time. Orange Julius was a mixture of OJ and an egg, whipped to a frothy liquid with some ice. It was pretty nourishing and quite good. I don't know what happened to that franchise. Now I have a distinct memory with a taste and smell, of no interest to anyone but me. It is a memory of that era that is unique to me because it has a taste associated with it, along with the smell of LA air at that time in history. It was sometime around then when I was busted for pot in Stills's house in Topanga. That house, which Stephen called the Old Topanga Ranch, was an old rock structure with a barn of sorts behind it. There were a lot of people there, and it was a big party. Eric Clapton was there with Stephen, and we were all smoking pot, which was odd because Stephen has never been a big pot smoker. Linda Stevens was there, and so was Susan Haffey, one of Stephen's girlfriends from his days hanging with Peter Tork (Thorkelson) of the Monkees.

I was in a bedroom by myself, not being very social at the time, because I probably had smoked too much weed and was paranoid. Things got pretty quiet, and Stephen suddenly came through the room I was in and went out the window! I am not sure he saw me there. The cops had come in, and everyone was arrested and taken to jail. We were all in the *LA Times* the next morning; it was a big deal because Clapton was a pretty famous musician already. I don't know how we got off, but it had something to do with our managers, Greene and Stone.

I recently spoke to Stephen about this, and he remembers it differently. He says we both were sitting on the bed together because we had smoked too much weed and were too paranoid, so we were talking each other down. We heard something change in the room where the party was. It got quiet. I bolted out there to see what was wrong. He heard what he thought was a cop's voice and reached out to stop me, but he caught air. I was gone. Stephen went out the window and went next door to call Ahmet Ertegun, our friend and the president of Atlantic, our record company, to get help from some lawyers, so he escaped and I got busted. Ahmet told him maybe his actions would be misunderstood by everyone else who got caught when he didn't. So he says he has reflected on that.

Soon after, but not for any reason connected to the bust, the Springfield broke up. The success and legendary impact of the Springfield was not really apparent at the time. We were beginning to go our separate ways. Everyone was moving out to Topanga from Hollywood. Topanga was like an art colony. Art was everywhere, and the place was crawling with musicians, rebel actors, and associated culture. A few months later, one morning I was walking into town to the Topanga Village Shopping Center. I was just walking along, and this army truck pulled along beside me. It looked like a personnel carrier or something. A couple of guys were in it wearing hippie/army clothes. They stopped and picked me up. I guess there was a kind of hippie camaraderie that existed then and is nowhere to be found in today's culture. They may have picked me up because I looked like "one of them"; I don't think I was hitchhiking.

We went to the Topanga Center, and I remember we liked one another, 'cause they invited me back to the place they were staying. One of them was named David Briggs. David took me back to their house, and it turned out to be the Old Topanga Ranch where Stephen had lived and we had been busted! David and his wife, Shannon, were living there. Briggs and I became great friends, and I immediately learned he was a record producer. He had just finished making a comedy record with Murray Roman and he was producing some of the guys from Spirit in a new band. He was wonderful to hang with, with an extensive and interesting vocabulary. (I had never heard the word *nomenclature* before.) We really got along well, and it was the beginning of a deep friendship that lasted many years. Not to mention the records we made together.

The Topanga Center was a real melting pot of hippie and art activity, a cultural center for art and music in the sixties. In the very center of the Center was the Canyon Kitchen, a small restaurant that served food all day but specialized in great breakfasts. That's where, as I mentioned, I first met Susan Acevedo, the proprietress I was soon to marry.

I remember once I was at Topanga Days, a fair that happened annually. A flatbed truck was parked in the parking lot with Canned Heat jammin' along at their peak on the back of the truck. Al Wilson was holding down the vocals. The whole band was classic. It didn't get any better than that. The bass player, Larry Taylor, was crazy good, holding down a huge groove. Later he played with Bob and was still masterful. That was so cool! What a great band! Next up there was Taj Mahal playing with Jesse Ed Davis right there in the Topanga Center on the back of that truck. I still remember Jesse Ed Davis, the amazing guitarist, with his Telecaster, so slinky and bad.

People were everywhere. Local art was on display. Artisans sold their wares. Lance Sterling, a leatherworker Susan knew and introduced me to, was often there with his gypsy wagon and female apprentices making leather sandals and bags. I still have my bag. I got it at that time and it goes everywhere with me; I think Susan gave it to me. That was a wonderful time in my life. All was good. I was about to start my solo career after the Springfield, which had been a long time coming. My need to make solo records was one of the big contributing factors to the breakup of Buffalo Springfield, along with a need to be more independent and sing more of my own songs. I had so many of them.

I had met Briggs, and we were planning my first solo record.

The songs were gathered from the past and the future, mostly dreams, nothing concrete; they were mostly created as vehicles for record-making, like "Here We Are in the Years," or personal expression and longing, such as "I've Been Waiting for You." Some of them were stream-of-consciousness, like "The Last Trip to Tulsa," with no preconceived thought behind them. They were just songs. There was no big pressure on me at that time to top anything I had already done. That came later. The sky was the limit. I had no idea what was coming my way.

One more note on this period.

Elliot Roberts, my manager, was planning my first solo tour and coffeehouse gigs. I first met Elliot with Joni Mitchell at Sunset Sound. I already knew Joni from Canada; Elliot was managing her now. He wanted to manage the Springfield, and had actually just started. He had accompanied us to a gig in San Diego we were playing with the Turtles and some other groups. The Turtles were at their peak. It was a huge show for us. I was sick in the hotel room with the flu and wanted something. Elliot was gone, playing golf with somebody. I decided at that moment he was never going to work as our manager and insisted we fire him. I was a spoiled brat! But what did I know? So we fired Elliot. The next week I quit the Springfield for good.

A few days later I called Elliot and asked him to manage me. Was I making sense or what? That is the weirdest sequence of events I can imagine. I was totally committed every step of the way and had no idea what I would be thinking the next day. This was *not* planned. I was just completely crazy and fluid, changing from day to day, adapting to my feelings and acting on them immediately. Much of what I did then is the foundation for where I am today.

He took me on. We got started, and he negotiated a great deal for me at Reprise Records, where I still record today. I am a Warner Brothers artist. Reprise is a Warner label. I will probably always be on Warner-Reprise as long as it exists. And Elliot will be representing me as long as we both live. That is the plan. It makes me sad to think this could all end, so I hope it doesn't. I love my life and the people around me. But as you know, nothing lasts forever. We know life, don't we? Maybe that is why people need religion (please see previous chapter). That might be it. I just might have figured it out.

## Chapter Twenty-Seven

And Now, Another Word from
Our Sponsor, PureTone

I t has come to my attention that a lot of the people we are reaching out to in the PureTone project are scared of Apple and what would happen to their businesses if we were to provoke Apple in some way. It is disconcerting to feel the fear in others that what I am trying to do would somehow provoke Apple into a destructive action against someone trying to serve a quality product. I have consistently reached out to try to assist Apple with true audio quality, and I have even shared my high-resolution masters with them so that they could show me what they could do with them to make their iPod sound great. I guess there would be an area of concern if what they think is great is not great in my opinion, yet they wanted to market it as studio quality or master quality while it contained only five percent of the data of some original hi-res digital recordings I and others have made.

In the end, the record companies have the power to control the quality that is served online. Online service has been problematic in that it actively or discreetly promotes trading and duplication of music. It is not offensive to me that the MP3-quality sound is traded around. It is, in my opinion, the new radio and serves a great purpose: making music lovers aware of the content that is out there to buy. If the consumers want it, let them take it, whatever quality they prefer. Ultimately, nothing can stop absolute quality from making a big comeback. The stage is well set. I believe in what I am trying to do and that good karma will come from it.

It is just a matter of time.

## Chapter Twenty-Eight

When Zeke Young was born on September 8, 1972, Carrie and I had been together for about a year and a half. We had been going to Lamaze classes for a few weeks and (mistakenly) felt pretty prepared. Our neighbor Beverly Oaks was going to be the midwife. Our doctor had told us everything was going to be fine, and we were gung-ho to do a natural childbirth.

On the ranch on the morning when Carrie's water broke, Bev said we should go to the hospital because she thought something was going wrong, or at least differently from what she expected. So we got in a car and headed down to the hospital, forty minutes away.

Zeke was born that day, and we needed forceps to help the delivery, so it was a good thing we followed Bev's advice. He was a beautiful baby boy, and I was as high as I have ever been in my life! What a feeling! We brought him home and put him in our little bed; then he graduated to a handmade cradle that one of our carpenter friends, Larry Christiani, had made especially for us.

As Zeke grew, we noticed that his right foot seemed extended and he could not straighten out his ankle. His right hand was also held in a different position from his left, and he did not have the same control of it. He was a cool kid, really happy and beautiful, and we were really young and innocent. We talked to doctors and sought advice on what might be happening and what to do. There was some strain developing between Carrie and me as the dream of an idyllic life with few responsibilities came shattering down around us. We knew we had to do something, and felt like we were running out of time, not knowing what was the matter with Zeke, not knowing it was a condition of life, not something that could be cured.

Eventually we got a brace for Zeke, and he started to get picked on by the other kids. This was the beginning of a rough time for him, and he lashed out at other kids and had a lot of anger that he was expressing. At the same time, Carrie and I were not doing well together. We were breaking up, and it was a nightmare. Not fights, but distance. Not screaming, but pain. Everything was coming apart.

Then I got a call from Carrie that Zeke had experienced a grand mal seizure. The doctor thought he might be epileptic or have some other condition. Eventually it was decided that Zeke had cerebral palsy.

Zeke was going from school to school, getting in trouble at all of them. He was living with me in Malibu on weekends, and one day he came home from playing with the other kids and had taken off his brace. His foot was bleeding from direct exposure to the asphalt on the road where they had been playing some game. I remember how I felt the unfairness of it all, that he had to contend with this and the other kids didn't, but now when I look at him, I admire him for the wonderful man he has grown up to be, handling himself so beautifully, and I feel very proud.

Sometimes he was with me and sometimes with his mom. Mostly he was with his mom. Somewhere along the line she did an interview with *People* magazine. They went to the house in Hancock Park, a beautiful old residential area, that I had bought for Carrie and Zeke, and took pictures, etc. The magazines love this kind of thing. So a big story came out that was all slanted and crazy, making me look like a villain. I have never talked to that magazine since and don't plan on it.

Pegi and I were together by then, and Zeke would come to visit us. He had to be a member of the "Clean Plate Club" to leave the table! We had a lot of love and structure in our home, and it was always that way with Pegi. That is the important thing. Zeke loved both Pegi and his mother.

Back and forth and back and forth he went between homes. That was our life until, in a great stroke, Carrie found a school in Idyllwild, California, that was specifically for kids who were having problems adjusting. Carrie and I placed Zeke in that school. Working together, we did something really good. There was a man there who ran the Morning Sky School, and his name was Jack Weaver. I went and met him, and he saw Zeke. I felt really good about what Carrie had found for us. Zeke came out of there a changed young man. They really helped him, and he attributes it all to Jack, who he loved. Jack unfortunately died a few years later of an asthma attack, or I am sure we would still be visiting him today just to keep in touch and tell him how much we loved him for what he did for our family. He was a saint.

Today, Zeke and I are very close.

## Chapter Twenty-Nine

The surf is coming up. It has been quiet here in Hawaii for about five days, and just a minute ago a wave broke on the seawall and put a slight tremble in the ground. The rhythm of the ocean is such a gift, and this is the perfect place to enjoy it. I don't expect to have another ocean place as cool and cosmic as this one is in my lifetime, so I am eternally thankful for it now.

Back when I was living in Coconut Grove in Florida in the mid-seventies, there was a houseboat that I slept in that was owned by a lady named Heather. We were recording the Stills-Young Band's *Long May You Run* at Criteria Recording Studios, and it was quite a trip from the studio in Fort Lauderdale back to the Grove every night—and I was usually pretty high on the way home. I had a '57 Jensen 541 that I drove regularly to and from the studio.

Heather's houseboat was way out on the end of the docks. Every night after the studio, I would end up in the houseboat and Heather would be there, welcoming me back. She was really kind to me, and I always was happy to get back there. We had a

With Zeke Young in a dinghy off the WN Ragland, *1978.*

good relationship. The water was right there, and it was soothing to rock in the boat as dawn came up on the bay.

The Grove was intoxicating, and I stayed there on and off for years. I had a suite in a local hotel called the Rangoon. There were a lot of high rollers in and out of the hotel all the time. Fred Neil, the great folksinger/songwriter who wrote "Everybody's Talkin'," which was eventually used in the movie *Midnight Cowboy*, was there hanging out at the dock a lot with some of his friends. (It is ironic to me that someone as seminal and influential as Freddy Neil would become more known for a movie song than the influence he had on a generation of musicians, including Stephen Stills, but that's the way it goes.)

The high rollers always seemed entertained by my comings and goings, like I was just some inexperienced kid. I did not feel that inexperienced. Eventually I bought my own boat in Fort Lauderdale and brought it back to the Grove. It was an old Trumpy yacht that I called *The Evening Coconut*. I was in the habit of taking it out for cruises, and I was known for sometimes crashing it into the dock. The engine kept failing on my approach. I had a lot of fun times on the *Coconut* and met a guy there in the Grove named Andre Prest.

He was charged with finding me a sailboat that I could buy and sail around the world. It seemed like a simple enough task, and soon we found the boat. It was in Saint Vincent and the Grenadines, on an island called Bequia. We went way down there and saw the boat. It was a huge Baltic Trader, and it needed some work on the deck. When I first saw the boat it was in a bay, looking like a dream. We needed to take a skiff out to it. Cruising out to get on board, we saw a lot of sharks in the water. I was very happy to get off the small boat and onto *Lilli*, as she was called then.

After the purchase, we sailed to Grenada and had some deck work done, Captain Andre Prest in command. The good captain had hired a first mate named Roger Katz. It turned out that Andre knew nothing about being captain of a boat or sailing, so quite soon it became obvious that Roger Katz was the de facto captain. We got the boat to Saint Thomas somehow, even though we were seasick. We sat at the dock with the generator running and choked out half of the marina.

I flew back from there to my ranch to do some recording, and they managed to get the *Lilli* back to Fort Lauderdale, where Captain Katz took over officially and took charge of the rebuild. We renamed her *WN Ragland* in honor of my grandfather, Bill Ragland, a southerner who came north to Winnipeg from South Carolina and started his family there, giving birth to my mother, Rassy, and her sisters, Snooky and Toots. Naming my boat after him felt good. We took her to Rogers Marina in Fort Lauderdale, and many dollars were put into rebuilding the boat over a year or so.

Zeke came out and visited us there at Rogers Marina while we were working on the boat. Ellen Talbot, a friend of Carrie's and the wife of Johnny Talbot, who was my roadie with Crazy Horse at the time, brought him to Fort Lauderdale from his mother's house. He was a child with two homes: my house wherever I was, and his mother's house wherever it was. He was about five years old and as cute as could be. He went to a Montessori-type school while he was there, which he got kicked out of for being too rowdy. He had his brace on and was pretty angry with the other kids. He was a real handful.

But when we were together he was just a happy, sweet little guy who I loved and who loved me. We used to go for rides in our yellow rubber dinghy that he loved tremendously. It had a Mercury outboard and really went fast. It had a steering wheel, and he loved that, too. We really had a great time together and both remember those times very fondly, racing up and down the New River in Fort Lauderdale. Those boat rides are some of our happiest early memories.

One of the scariest was when he fell in the river getting on *The Evening Coconut*. It was tied at a dock and was out of the water for hull repairs. Zeke was fearless, and one day he just tried to get on board from the dock himself, even though we were always around to guide him and told him to always be with someone. While I was at the work site, Zeke, with his heavy brace on, fell into the water. Dennis Buford, one of the shipwrights working on the boat, rescued Zeke! Thank you, Dennis! You probably saved my son's life!

A great tradition was payday. Every Friday we got together for some Jose Cuervo on *The Evening Coconut*, where Roger would hand out the checks to the shipbuilders, who were a motley crew just like us, and then we would go out partying. We eventually moved the *Ragland* to another place on the New River to get her finished and rigged with sails. So there she was in Fort Lauderdale on the New River, tied alongside an empty lot where the workers parked their cars and eventually I brought Pocahontas, my bus, to live in. I parked the bus right alongside the boat. At first, I slept on the boat in the construction zone of my cabin on my cot with sawdust everywhere, and then I moved to Pocahontas. It was fun.

On Valentine's Day I asked Pegi, who I was just beginning to hang out with, to come out and see my new boat. That was our first big outing, the first time we traveled together as a couple. We flew out to Fort Lauderdale together and stayed for a while. She was game, but obviously the place was not ready for us yet, with carpenters crawling all over the boat at seven A.M. This was a remarkably good time, full of memories of Pegi and me together, rebuilding this beautiful old boat and getting ready for the first sail. We had a crew of about thirty people working on the project, and as I've said, I always love that kind of thing, building things.

We went into Miami, Roger, Pegi, and I, to see a place called Stoneage Antiques. Stoneage was owned and run by Milton Stone, a great and unforgettable character, and it housed a rich collection of marine antiques and a host of other things, among them a beautiful classic nineteenth-century nine-foot Steinway grand piano I bought and shipped to the ranch. It was restored, and I still enjoy it today. I love things with memories attached. It's nice to think that it was one of the first times Pegi and I were together when I found that old piano, which is now restored and in our hallway. We also purchased a collection of wood from the dance floor of the Essex House hotel in New York City to use as bulkhead finish on the interior of the *WN Ragland*.

There is another part of the boat story. It is the hurt part, the emotional-impact part.

Sometime in 1973 before I bought the *Ragland*, the touring and constant womanizing finally caught up with me. I was growing further and further from Carrie. During the recording of *On the Beach* I did a song called "Motion Pictures." I did the recording with Ben Keith and Rusty Kershaw and we were all high on "honey slides," a little concoction that Rusty's wife, Julie, cooked up. Honey slides were made with grass and honey cooked together and stirred in a frying pan until a black gooey substance was left in the pan. A couple of spoonfuls of that and you would be laid-back into the middle of next week. The record was slow and dreamy, kind of underwater without bubbles.

Motion pictures on my TV screen,
A home away from home, and I'm livin' in between
But I hear some people have got their dream.
I've got mine.

I hear the mountains are doin' fine,
Mornin' glory is on the vine,
And the dew is fallin', the ducks are callin'.
Yes, I've got mine.

Well, all those people, they think they got it made
But I wouldn't buy, sell, borrow or trade

Anything I have to be like one of them.
I'd rather start all over again.

Well, all those headlines, they just bore me now
I'm deep inside myself, but I'll get out somehow,
And I'll stand before you, and I'll bring a smile to your eyes.
Motion pictures, motion pictures.

I asked Larry Johnson what he thought of it. He told me, "It scares me." Carrie was in Hawaii with Zeke at the time, and I was in the studio. When the recording was over, I drove Hank to the ranch and jumped on a plane to Maui. I was too late for one thing and just in time for another. When I got there, I went looking for Carrie at the Pioneer Hotel, where she was staying. I found out she was out on a sailboat with Zeke and a guy I had heard of, a friend of Crosby's, and she'd been gone for a number of days.

I realized right there that it was probably over, and went off the deep end, drinking a lot of tequila and drowning myself in sorrow. Of course, I was as guilty as hell myself, but that did not take away the pain. The thought that my family was irreparably harmed was inescapable. There were too many disconnects between Carrie and me, aside from the infidelities. I was so drunk that I went to the Chart House and played a solo set in front of a few tourists. Who knows? I was really getting the meaning of "What goes around, comes around."

In this frame of mind, I wrote about twenty songs I recorded in one form or another. Tapes of this are in a shambles, still being sorted out and readied for *The Archives Volume 2*. There was a lot of traveling around, soul-searching, and the like, crossing over to Europe and Canada and Hawaii, just moving for the sake of moving. That is when I started looking for a boat, my own boat. In some sort of balancing act inside my own head and heart, I decided to buy a boat and sail around the world, which never happened in the end. I did not sail around the world.

It was also around that time I first saw Pegi Morton. She was the hostess at Alex's, a bar/restaurant up on the mountain above the ranch. I first met Pegi in 1974. I loved her instantly, but was very nervous about repeating my past and not being able to hold the relationship together. I remember thinking Pegi would always be a beautiful girl, even when she was a hundred years old. Time passed. It was a different kind of love, infatuating like Carrie, but I felt this much deeper. Pegi's blue eyes are like crystals. They are so deep and true. Too good for me? In those eyes I saw myself and a life I hoped I would be able to hold together.

Time passed, and Pegi and I visited the boat a few times and made a few trips. On one of the early ones, Pegi was pregnant with Ben Young. We both got so seasick. We returned to California and the ranch. Then Ben Young was born on November 28, 1978, at Stanford Hospital in Palo Alto. He was premature, and we had to keep him in the hospital for a while. Pegi remembers the day after we got little Ben home—we took him on a blue-jeep ride in the pasture near our house. She had him all bundled up like the wonderful mother she is, and was so protective. We sat there in the sun for a while and took it all in.

Things had moved pretty fast with us, and we were reeling a

little. We were deeply in love. Our family was starting. We kept on moving with our young lives shortly afterward and took Ben Young with us everywhere. But pretty soon Pegi started noticing that Ben was not doing the things some other babies were doing. Pegi was wondering if something was wrong. She was young, and nothing had ever gone wrong in her life. People told us kids grow at different rates and do things at different times.

But as Ben reached six months old, we found ourselves sitting in a doctor's office. He glanced at us and offhandedly said, "Of course Ben has cerebral palsy."

I was in shock. I walked around in a fog for weeks. I couldn't fathom how I had fathered two children with a rare condition that was not supposed to be hereditary, with two different mothers. I was so angry and confused inside, projecting scenarios in my mind where people said something bad about Ben or Zeke and I would just attack them, going wild. Luckily that never did happen, but there was a root of instability inside me for a while. Although it mellowed with time, I carried that feeling around for years.

Eventually Pegi and I, wanting to have another child after Ben, went to see an expert on the subject. That was Pegi's idea. Always organized and methodical in her approach to problems, Pegi planned an approach to our dilemma with her very high intelligence. We both loved children but were a little gun-shy about having another, to say the least. After evaluating our situation and our children, the doctor told us that probably Zeke did not actually have CP—he likely had suffered a stroke in utero. The symptoms are very similar. Pegi and I weighed this information. To know someone like her and to make a decision about a subject as important as this with her was a gift beyond anything I have ever experienced. It was her idea, and she had guided us to this point. We made a decision together to go forward and have another child.

W e tried being on the boat with Ben, but it was not in the cards. Ben was a handful, and neither Pegi nor I was truly a sailor. The boat went around the world more or less, but we didn't. That dream didn't come true. There was something more important to me than that: my family. My Pegi and Ben.

Zeke was coming to the ranch for weekends, and Pegi was becoming a strong mother figure for him, too, building a strong family foundation, stability, and security for the kids. So we would fly out and meet the *Ragland* at different locations around the world. Acapulco, Alaska, Panama, Bora-Bora, Papeete, Huahine, Mooréa, the Virgin Islands, the Bahamas—we did have some really good times! Now that Ben is so big, it is largely impossible for us to travel on the *Ragland* as a family, and we *are* a family, so we have been trying to sell her for a few years. Eventually it will happen, and that chapter will close. But these memories will live forever.

## Chapter Thirty

A fter Ben Young was born, Pegi and I headed south to Los Angeles to begin filming *Human Highway* on a soundstage in Hollywood. I needed to do something besides music to keep fresh and have a musical perspective. Have you ever heard the expression "How can you miss me if I don't go away?" That expression defines why I do other things. I love the variety, and the projects are all interrelated anyway. There is no reason to just repeat oneself until further notice. When we got to LA, we set up house at a hotel we really liked at the time called L'Hermitage, not to be confused with my favorite hotel in Nashville, the Hermitage.

Like movies made a long time ago in Hollywood, we used sets that were made to look like the real world. That's how a storybook quality can be created, and I was trying to get that look. It's harder to do that storybook quality, if not impossible, when you use real-life scenes and go outdoors. The *Human Highway* con-

Ben Young on my lap, David Myers, Pegi Young, and John Thompson on the Human Highway *set, 1980.*

cept was for us to film on an indoor set that looked like a corner gas station in a fictional place called Linear Valley. Megapolitan City was visible in the distance, and a nuclear power plant was about a mile away in the background. We had a set designed and constructed that had a train track and a train that passed by occasionally. The action focused on the folks at the gas station and attached café, which was a caboose.

Three waitresses, played by Geraldine Baron, Sally Kirkland, and Charlotte Stewart, worked in the café. The part of the café cook was played by Dennis Hopper. Dean Stockwell, codirecting with me, played the proprietor. I played Lionel, a very dorky (think Jerry Lewis) mechanic working at the station, and Russell Tamblyn played Fred, a friend of Lionel's who wanted a job. Pegi had a small part as a biker girl. David Myers was our director of photography, with Larry Johnson as assistant director and Jeanne Field in production. It was a sort of day-in-the-life concept, all taking place in one day, just a regular day, the day the earth suddenly ended in a world war. It was a comedy.

Every day we began with shooting the script we had come up with the night before. What a blast! We did some really crazy and fun things, riding bikes and using rear-screen projection—really old-time techniques. We came up with new wacky things to do every day. Some of the ideas were really old-school, and some of them were just plain dorky. There was a lot of improvising, and the set was very alive. It was purposefully made to look like a set, not real.

It was a big family, and we shot for six weeks. I financed the whole thing myself because we couldn't get anyone to back the way we were approaching the film. It was a typical Shakey Pictures production! It was a definite high point for Larry, David Myers, and me. Pegi brought Ben Young down to the set on occasion to share the fun, and we were all having such a great time.

After we finished shooting, the film went through several versions in editing. We had a screening in San Diego and passed out info cards for people to comment on the film. It was a disaster, but a really funny one. People were outraged that I was playing such a dorky character, and some were advising me that we bury the picture because it would kill my career. I took that positively—it was a good sign that my character was getting a strong reaction. I felt strangely good about it.

It was my feeling that the film was what I wanted it to be, but the main area of concern for me was a dream sequence that was not quite what I had intended. Several versions of the film were edited and one was even put out on Pioneer LaserDisc. I still like the first cut, the director's cut that I did, and today we are preparing it for a release as part of the Shakey Pictures collection on Netflix. I am going back in to edit and finalize that dream sequence when I get back to the mainland.

Larry's great talent in filmmaking was partly his ability to get emotions from the scene in the editing room. His touch would bring out the soul and magic. He did an edit on the bonfire scene at Puye in *Human Highway* that he cut to my song "Goin' Back." It was magical to me. I think it is the turning point in *Human Highway*, where you forget about everything else and become in the moment with the counterculture, the hippies, the artists, the Indians. Everything in the film revolves around that scene to me. That was Larry. He went into the editing room one day and came out with that. Sheer brilliance. On top of that, he was so positive and energized, keeping everyone on their toes and having fun. His energy was contagious.

When we lost Larry in 2010, he was working with Toshi Onuki on revising *Human Highway*. Toshi is a very creative and important part of the Shakey Pictures team, who spent years with Larry developing the archives. Larry was upset because a piece of film was missing, and he never did get to complete the high-resolution digital version before he died. He wanted to maintain the quality of David Myers's original film. I am less concerned with that than I am with content, although we will try to find the footage, and Toshi and I will hopefully get this done in a way that Larry would have liked once and for all.

It was a wild time. Devo and I were doing "Out of the Blue" in the studio and a lot of stuff from *Trans* on the radio, plus Devo's performance of "Worried Man," the Kingston Trio classic. There was a lot of Devo in *Human Highway*; they contributed three performances. Add to that some of the off-the-wall scoring things we did with Mark Mothersbaugh from Devo and I am sure we will have something very memorable for the sound track.

I will be excited to close the book on *Human Highway*. There is certainly a lot to do to pick up the pieces strewn around from this long life so far, but I have an excellent crew and am confident that we are up to it. Of course, time must be set aside to have fun.

Right near the end of filming at the soundstage, Pegi started having some headaches. They were really bad ones. She was in a lot of very intense pain. At this time I must confess to one of the worst low points I have had. Pegi was in the hospital and they were looking at her brain, giving her some tests to find out why she was having these terrible headaches. The shooting on set was finished for *Human Highway* and we were having a wrap party. I got stoned and way too high to be visiting her in the hospital, but I went anyway. She had been having a bad time there, and her mother was visiting her when I arrived stoned. Pegi knew it right away and threw me out of the room, seeing the shape I was in. I really let her down. She was always there for me, and I had blown a chance to be there for her. Her mother, of course, had no idea why Pegi threw me out. It was just very confusing for her and a real low point for me.

Anyway, we had some tests done and found out that Pegi had a disorder in the veins in her brain called an arteriovenous malformation (AVM), and pressure was building. These AVMs often go undetected until something catastrophic occurs, such as stroke or death. They are also very often inoperable because of their location in the brain. So we were lucky on both counts. It was decided that this area of her brain had to be operated on. Major brain surgery was performed at Stanford University Medical Center. They had to cut off all her beautiful blond hair. I remember her sitting upright in her bed like a little girl, wrapped in a white hospital gown, with her hair all gone. She looked so beautiful and so innocent. I was so scared that something might happen to her in the surgery. It was possible. The brain is a very risky thing to operate on. I tried to show Pegi that everything was going to be fine, but I was really scared. That Pegi might never be the same or might be greatly injured as a result of the operation was a fleeting thought. I quickly pushed it out of my mind. After I left the hospital, I went out with Briggs and got really stoned. When I went back to the hospital the next day, Pegi could see that I was all hungover. It must have been so disappointing for her. I had let her down again.

The time arrived for the surgery, and it was successfully performed. During recovery, which took quite a while, Pegi spoke very slowly; over a period of about three months her speech gradually returned to normal. She used to go out into the garden and sit there, pulling weeds and doing simple things, while the sun rose and set. I was always thinking how much I loved her and how I never wanted to lose her. I can still see her sitting in that garden like a little girl, with her hair so short. I wanted her to get her laugh back. And she did. Her laugh started coming back slowly, and it returned to its full glory in a few months. I was so happy. Day after day. Week after week. She came back. My Pegi and I have been through a lot of life together. I am so thankful for every day.

Whenever I think of Larry Johnson, I am always struck by the amount of time he dedicated to helping others have a good time. He was always doing things for other people. In his work with me, he made sure that everything was ready for me to contribute when I arrived at the scene. Materials were lined up. People were ready. Larry was always looking out for everyone—except Larry. When he started getting tired in the afternoon and needed to take a rest, I should have known something big was wrong, because he was taking time out for himself. If I had really noticed that fully, it would have registered loudly that something was amiss. Of course, I was preoccupied, as is my nature, and I often miss important things going on with others around me. I was focused on something that had to do with me, or one of my creations, which is also my nature. So I missed helping the one person who helped me when he needed it most. That is the nature of life, to learn lessons too late in some instances. People like me learn the hard way. Now I am looking out for these signs in my loved ones more than ever before.

I will never be as giving a person as Larry—at least it is highly unlikely because I am so possessed. But *never* is also a big word, and things do change. Maybe someday I will evolve to a place where I have some of the qualities Larry had. Even the people who got the wrong end of the stick loved Larry. If you offended Larry, you went straight to the penalty box, and it was not easy to get released. If a professional did not do a great job and failed to deliver quality when he was offered an opportunity, that person went straight to the box. If you were focused on something other than your responsibility to Larry and he had given you a good chance, off you went. Some people spent years in that box. Larry had his reasons. But everybody loved him, even those put in the box.

He had more women in more places than anyone I know.

They all loved him dearly and they all understood that there were others. This was not totally comfortable for him, but he would juggle and balance it like a magician. When we held a celebration of Larry's life, the women he loved were all there together, and his most recent girlfriend was snubbed by the others. Somehow that made sense. She had certainly not established herself as being on the same level as Larry's previous ladies; they all knew one another, but they didn't know her.

When we first met, Larry was with Jeanne Field. "Miss Field," as Larry used to call her, was a jewel of a person and still is today. We were all working on *Journey Through the Past* and having a big old time. Miss Field was doing production. Larry had us down in Asheville, North Carolina, interviewing an old black couple, Sandie and Levie, who were a part of his early life. They were recalling the slave days, and Larry was hanging on every word. The footage was beautiful. We have not used it yet.

I am sure it will hold some great meaning for me now. It was like that. Larry did things and much later you would discover why. He often joked about being a redneck cracker. He carried a white kerchief and dabbed the sweat on his forehead, playing the part of a gracious southern gentleman, tipping his hat to lady passersby. I am sure he is doing the same in heaven, or something a lot like heaven.

Larry Johnson editing Journey Through the Past
at the ranch, 1972.

## Chapter Thirty-One

Hawaii

The Big Island's volcano has been active for a long time. It started spewing ash that resulted in a heavy vog around five-plus years ago.

Vog looks like smog, but it isn't. It is natural pollution from the fires inside the earth. Our paradise looks really different now, and our eyes and lungs have started complaining to us. Recently, the vog was coming and going irregularly with the changing winds and unknown other factors contributing. As I write this today, I have been here on the island for six days, and the vog is not around. It looks a lot like it used to back in the day before the vog came, and there is an air of happiness because of this.

We have no control over these things, and they are a good reminder of our helplessness and insignificance in the grand scope of natural events. The vog does remind me of the stupid laws against burning wood in fireplaces in the city because it causes air pollution. Shit! That is ridiculous! These beautiful fireplaces were built in the homes and apartments of New York and San Francisco and all the other big cities with winter for a reason. Thank you for the state law in California forbidding the inclusion of fireplaces in any new homes. What a law! How about the cars? They would not be possible to outlaw because of the economic consequences, so let's go after fireplaces and their evil smoke! Thank you, lawmakers, for your perception and vision in this matter. You are an inspiration to us all.

I am an electric-car fanatic who loves big luxury cars. Lincvolt is in its fourth year now. I can't wait to ride down to LA in Lincvolt. That will be a complete blast. I plan on stopping and staying in my favorite bungalow in a Santa Barbara hotel and lighting a fire in the fireplace. I was just kidding about that law. There really is no law. I might have just made that up, because part of this book is from my memory and I have a big imagination. (News bulletin: In truth, there really *is* a law like that. I just learned about it.)

Anyway, the air is clear as a bell in Hawaii, and I am very happy! Just as there is no way to change the past, there is no way to predict the future. I am sure of that. I have just learned that the vog on the Big Island is about one fiftieth of what it was for the last few years. I am so thankful!

Of course, it could be back tomorrow.

My archive project is a multiedged sword. It is something I love doing, but it raises some questions about my motives in doing it. A writer accused me of building my archives just to further my own legend, whatever that is. I hope you don't believe that. What a shallow existence that would be! I remember reading that article saying that about me. It pissed me off. It's my life, and I am a collector. I collect everything: cars, trains, manuscripts, photographs, tape recordings, records, memories, and clothes, to name a few. The fact that I want to create a chronological history of my recordings and supporting work is proof positive that I am an incurable collector, confronted with an amazingly detailed array of creations that I have painstakingly rat-holed over the years.

Some of them are complete pieces of shit, but they have their place in my chronological obsession. There is nothing we can do about it. I have already done enough good and damage with this book to defeat any number of earlier theories about the order of things and how I should be acting. There is no reason for me to start worrying about what people think now; I have already been worrying for far too long, and it hasn't helped or changed a thing. I do enjoy writing, and I hope someone gets something interesting out of this book. I already have. Now, if I ever have to write a book that is not about me, I may be totally stumped and have writer's block. We will see. Writing is very convenient, has a low expense, and is a great way to pass the time. I highly recommend it to any old rocker who is out of cash and doesn't know what to do next. You could hire someone else to write it for you if you can't write yourself. That doesn't seem to matter. Just don't hire some sweaty hack who asks you questions for years and twists them into his own vision of what is right or wrong. Try to avoid doing that.

I just spoke to Billy Talbot and told him about the plan to use my ranch's White House for a Crazy Horse session, with John Hanlon and Mark Humphreys. Mark is our onstage monitor mixer and loves Crazy Horse. John Hanlon was trained by Briggs to record the sound a certain way and not explain what he is doing. (John talks quite a bit, and Briggs, after listening to him talk too much in the studio, taking up a lot of space in the air, coined the phrase, "Don't explain.") Billy is in. The forces of good are all converging for the rebirth of Crazy Horse in its next incarnation, basically the same as it always was except with more years behind it.

God, I miss Briggs.

It would be so great to be talking to him today. I would like to know what he thinks of the fact that I have not written a song since I stopped smoking. Smoking weed opened up the door for me, and I miss that part, especially when it comes to songs and music.

This is very important. Don't spook the Horse. That is very essential to the success of any ride. The Horse will head for the barn if it is spooked, and the music will continue but not have that magic that the Horse possesses. Any ride on the Horse must not have a destination. History has shown that the best way to spook the Horse is to tell it what to do or where to go or, even worse, how to get there. You must not speak directly to the Horse or ever look the Horse in the eyes until the ride is over and the Horse is secured in the barn. It is okay to talk to the Horse directly, but care must be taken to have respect for the muse when discussing anything with the Horse. The Horse and the muse are very good friends. Disrespect for the muse will piss off the Horse, and possibly vice versa, although that is hard to prove. The Horse has met no equal, although there undoubtedly is an equal to the Horse out there somewhere. The Horse knows this well and will not tolerate anyone who is overly complimentary to the point of excluding other friends of the muse in a misguided attempt to gain the Horse's favor. That is absolutely not the thing to do, as it makes the Horse think, and that has a bad effect generally. The Horse has a voracious appetite. The songs the Horse likes to consume are always heartfelt and do not need to have anything fancy associated with them. The Horse is very suspicious of tricks. Keeping these simple guidelines in place is always a good idea when approaching the Horse for any reason.

One day Bob Dylan called me, which was a surprise. He doesn't typically call. It was after Hurricane Katrina destroyed New Orleans and I had done some TV with many other artists to help raise funds for the victims. New Orleans music is sacred. I was playing on the Nashville Network, and he heard us do "Walking to New Orleans" and wanted to tell me what a good performance it was. That was really cool, and it meant a lot to me.

I was in New York doing something, walking on the street, and it was a real surprise to hear from him out of the blue. He was also pointing out what a cool hat I had on during the telecast and that I looked good. Bob is always looking sharp when he performs. Once, we had Bob and Elliot for dinner at the ranch house, and he and Pegi had a conversation about my look. "Comfy" was one word that came up! So I think I made a big advance there.

It is always a struggle for me to get dressed up to play with the Horse. It seems incongruous with the music to me for some reason. Who knows, possibly the next time we play it will be the "Clothes Horse."

My love for plaid shirts goes back a long way. Susan, my first wife, made all those cool patches I wore back in the day when even I was fashionable. The pants on the back cover of *After the Gold Rush* were Susan's work. She was very artistic and put so much of her love into it. She even made me a beautiful patchwork vest with a blue velvet back. She sewed the patches on with some strands of her own hair. After we broke up, I wanted to keep it carefully tucked away forever. It was beautiful. I wanted to always remember her by it. One day I came home and Carrie had taken it apart and used the patches to cover holes in a pair of my jeans that I never wore. That was pretty numbing. I am not sure I am over that. Clothes make the man.

## Chapter Thirty-Two

I like bands for different reasons, and the reasons are not consistent.

Pearl Jam is a band I have a lot of respect for. Nirvana and Sonic Youth I feel the same way about. Mumford & Sons, My Morning Jacket, Wilco, Givers, and Foo Fighters are just some of my favorites. I respect bands that give me something of themselves that I can feel. ("Posing" bands turn me off, generally speaking.) It all has to do with a feeling I have about them. That is what music is to me, a feeling. It's similar with people, too.

In 1995, I went to Seattle to record with Pearl Jam, minus Eddie, just after I was inducted into the Rock and Roll Hall of Fame. I knew I had a small window to get a record done because of their availability and mine—and I like working like that. When I got there, I wrote a song every night in the hotel so I would always have new material for each session. I still sometimes think Briggs should have been involved, but he wasn't, because I thought at the

Pegi Young, with Larry Johnson in the background. In partial view on the left is Eric Johnson; on the right is Keith Wissmar (both part of my team).

time that he might be too abrasive a producer for PJ. We used their producer, Brendan O'Brien, who was a fast-moving guy and who played keys on some of the tunes. We just kept rolling along, and soon *Mirror Ball* was recorded. We did an impromptu gig in a Seattle nightspot where local bands played.

Pulling up outside the place, I noticed an alert-looking guy standing on the loading dock who seemed to be in a leadership role. Later, I met him and found out he was working for PJ as a road manager. We got along well, and my enduring relationship with Eric Johnson began. After that PJ was not working for a while, so Eric came with us and ultimately stayed. It was not a rocky change where I stole somebody, although I did steal him, I suppose. It just seemed so right we all just fell into it. Eric still has deep feelings for PJ, and if they needed him, he would be free to go. But I need someone like him to go with me and make sure I am secure when I travel.

Times have changed. I can't go to public airports like I used to. Now when I arrive at an airport, there are professional autograph people all over me. I don't know how the hell they know what I am doing seemingly before I do, but there they are, bugging me in the security line and at the curb.

It costs me to avoid them, but so be it. They bother me. They pose as real fans and try to make me feel guilty if I don't sign something. They are so obvious and deceptive, feeding on my love for my real fans. I think either the travel agency or the hotels notify the autograph hounds' representatives when I am coming to town.

Eric tries to filter through them to get to the real fans so I can sign for them. He tries to get me nice rooms when I stay somewhere, books a lot of charters, coordinates the ins and outs of my appearances. I have also used his artistic talents extensively. He played the Devil in my stage and film productions of *Greendale*. He was the Painter in *Trunk Show*. Eric is my go-to guy for everything on the road. He is the "artist in residence" on my tours, does all the associated design that I ask him to do, from T-shirts to programs, anything having to do with art. He is always drawing on napkins and leaving them behind. I grab them up and Pegi and I save them.

When our dog Bear was really old, Eric would carry him through hotel lobbies to get to the elevator so Bear's feet wouldn't slip on the polished marble floors. Eric calls ahead so everything is ready for Pegi and me when we arrive somewhere. We are not exposed in the lobby, waiting for anything. He is a great artist and a fine person. I am proud to call him my friend. Plus, he is one of the funniest people I have ever met, along with Elliot, of course, who is the master.

## Chapter Thirty-Three

In 1969, when I joined CSN and it became CSNY for a while, I was at an interesting point in my life. I was working with two bands at the same time, recording with Crazy Horse and rehearsing with CSNY. David, Stephen, and Graham had their own sound, and I was brought in by Ahmet and Stephen to add something else to the mix for live appearances, more rock and roll, I guess.

For a while at the beginning, there was a short debate among some about whether I should be included, i.e., whether to add my Y to CSN or not. Thankfully, that never became an issue. Elliot was there and everything worked out fine. Stephen and I were happy to be playing together again and picked up right where we had left off. CSN had a big hit with their first record—they sounded like a new car coming off the assembly line!—and I had *Everybody Knows This Is Nowhere* with Crazy Horse, which stayed on the charts for two years.

Graham Nash, Stephen Stills, David Crosby, and me, with Elliot Roberts in the background, backstage before a CSNY show in Denver, 1974.

We rehearsed together at Stephen's house in Laurel Canyon, trying out different bass players, including Bruce Palmer. Bruce, who was great as usual, had gotten back into the States from Canada somehow, and Stephen and I were very high on playing with him again. He rehearsed with us for a couple of days and was totally on his game. Then he got busted for pot and deported again, just like that. That was one of the last times we ever played together, except for once on the ranch years later when I played with him and Dewey, experimenting with getting the Springfield back together.

So CSNY eventually settled on Greg Reeves on bass and went on the road, where we played the Greek Theatre in LA, Chicago's Auditorium Theatre, the Masonic Temple Theatre in Detroit, and of course, Woodstock. A funny thing happened at Woodstock. I didn't want cameras onstage distracting me while we were playing. I hated the showboating atmosphere that surrounded the filming and thought it distracted from our music. The music was between us and the audience, and anything that got in the way was taboo in my opinion. So if you listen carefully to the band's intro, they say "CSN"—they cut out the Y as payback. On the Woodstock record, Atlantic Records used a song of mine recorded months later at the Fillmore East in New York called "Sea of Madness." That was kind of misleading.

Getting to Woodstock was a lot of fun, though. I remember meeting Jimi Hendrix in a small airport and riding in a pickup truck with Melvin Belli, the famous lawyer, to the gig. We had to take a little charter plane to get close, and then they picked a few of us up and brought us in. CSN were already there. They were anxious to get there early.

There was, of course, a huge crowd, and it was a turning point in rock and roll history. It was so big, it was scary. No one could hear. I was really uncomfortable because everyone was very jacked.

There was one other festival worth mentioning: Altamont. Security onstage was provided by the Hells Angels Motorcycle Club, and there was only one murder at the show. Getting there, starting way in the back, we rode in through the whole crowd in a pickup truck. I was in the cab, and the guys were in the back. Stephen was yelling at the top of his voice, "Crosby, Stills, Nash, and Young!" in an effort to clear a path through the crowd to get to the stage. The pickup crawled along through the crowd. The yelling continued. I was trying to disappear into the glove compartment of the truck's dashboard. It was surreal, and Fellini should have been there to film it. We sucked at the performance. It was one of the worst-feeling gigs I can ever remember. What a monster cocaine-fueled ego trip! The music really sucked air.

I had a sick feeling during that show that I never have forgotten and thankfully have never felt again. I could feel the music dying. There were some really fine CSNY gigs, but they were not in big places, they were in concert halls where we could hear and the band focused on the music instead of superstardom. The live record *4 Way Street* captures some of that. We had some really great musical moments, and Crosby's energy was the catalyst. He was so into it that it was infectious. Stephen and I would trade licks back and forth under his singing and Graham's harmony. Those were some sublime moments. Graham wrote some incredibly vivid songs that suited the harmonies beautifully. It was a great experience I wouldn't trade for anything, although it had its imperfections along the way, like everything else I have done.

One night in San Francisco in the fall of 1969, CSNY was recording the *Déjà Vu* album at Wally Heider/Filmways recording studio. We were playing "Helpless," and I had been going over it with Dallas Taylor, Greg Reeves, and Stephen for hours. Although it is a simple song, it requires laying back, which was not really in Dallas Taylor's musical vocabulary that night. I just kept doing it over and over, waiting for him to settle down on drums and stop playing accents and fills everywhere. It really was a case of wearing him out to the point where he would play it slowly, without pushing it, and without adding little riffs that meant nothing to the song. It was an arduous task.

Stephen played beautiful piano on the track while I sang it live. I was just starting to sing live in the studio; that was one of the first times. Greg, on bass, was always in the pocket, although he played a lot of notes, so getting everyone to relax and just support the song took a while. It got to be the wee hours, and after many tries, we finally got *the* take. It was worth it. In the end, everyone played a really good performance. Sometimes you just have to stay with it.

The next session, Stephen added a guitar with a volume pedal, and it was really a fine part. Graham stayed with us all night in the control room, adding his support on the night of the original session with Bill Halverson at the console. Graham always stayed no matter what. He was always there providing a steady hand and positive constructive vibe, even if he wasn't playing. He was making up background and chorus harmony parts as we recorded and was ready with ideas when it came time to overdub with Crosby the next day. Crosby always had great harmonies that he came up with on the spot.

For some reason I have a vivid memory of that group of sessions. One day after CSN had cut "Teach Your Children," which they sang perfectly without me, I was in the control room and Jerry Garcia came in and played a steel guitar part on it. It was actually on a regular guitar with a slide, as I remember it. He just sat down with it on his lap in the control room down under the speakers and put that part on. I remember that every time I hear that song, which is one of CSNY's greatest. I am proud to have my name on it, although I didn't play or sing a note.

While we were recording in San Francisco, I was staying at a motel called the Caravan Motor Inn just down the street. No one else was staying there but me. I don't really know where everyone else was. (Stephen was probably at a nicer place. He always finds nice places to stay. Nash had a house there already, I think, or was just moving in to one that he later renovated. I don't know where David was staying—he had a lot of friends—probably the Airplane House.) Anyway, I was at the Caravan and I had two pets in my room, Speedy and Harriet. They were bush babies, little primates, which I kept in the bathroom. That was really crazy, but I was alone and wanted some company. They were dirty, and I had to clean up after them every time I came home from a session. I wore a leather glove because when I caught them to put them in their cage they would bite me. Imagine coming home from recording "Helpless" at three o'clock in the morning and cleaning up after bush babies in my bathroom. Is that the life of a star or what? I was not really very social at that point, and some of my behaviors must have been curious at best.

One day I visited Butano Canyon near Pescadero, California, with Crosby. It was 1970, and our CSNY lighting director, Steve Cohen, was living in a place right at the end of Butano Canyon Road. Since it was the last house, there was nothing but canyon to see from the deck of the old redwood home. Most of the houses in this canyon had been constructed as summer residences and were old places built totally with redwood, featuring heat from great stone fireplaces made with stones right from the creek. It was a stunning place. Giant redwoods and the healthy creek running by made for a spectacular view.

Crosby had invited me up there to see the place and hang. Leo Makota, our road manager, was there, too. It was Leo, as I mentioned, who first directed me to what is now Broken Arrow Ranch. Cros really wanted to see me living up north. He loved it up there himself. Cros had also taken me to the Airplane House, where Jefferson Airplane lived. There I met Grace Slick, who was beautiful, sang great, was topless, and blew my mind. That was the first time I met her. The whole San Francisco scene was something I had never seen. It was overwhelming. I remember Paul Kantner driving Cros and me to the airport from the city in his Porsche, demonstrating that the airport was only twenty minutes from Haight-Ashbury now that Interstate 280 had been opened. I was scared shitless with Kantner driving that Porsche at astronomical speeds to demonstrate how easy it was to get there fast! I was really not used to any of this stuff. I was shaking when we got to the airport to get on PSA for $9.95 and be served by stewardesses in short shorts on our way back to LA. Holy shit. Was I green!

So anyway, we're in Butano Canyon at Steve and Leo's place, and the tragedy at Kent State had just happened. *Time* magazine had a picture of the girl, Allison Krause, after the National Guard had killed her and three other victims. We were looking at it together. She was lying there on some pavement with another student kneeling down looking at her, as I remember.

These people were our audience. That's exactly who we were playing for. It was our movement, our culture, our Woodstock generation. We were all one. It was a personal thing, the bond we held between the musicians and the people of the culture: hippies, students, flower children, call them what you will. We were all together.

The weight of that picture cut us to the quick. We had heard and seen the news on TV, but this picture was the first time we had to stop and reflect. It was different before the Internet, before social networking to say the least. So full of this feeling of disbelief and sadness. I picked up my guitar and started to play some chords and immediately wrote "Ohio"; *four dead in Ohio*. The next day, we went into the studio in LA and cut the song. Before a week had passed it was all over the radio. It was really fast for those times; really fast. All the stations played "Ohio." There was no censoring by programmers. Programming services were not even around; DJs

The Kent State shooting, 1970.

played whatever they wanted on the FM stations. We were underground on FM. There was no push-back for criticizing the government. This was America. Freedom of speech was taken very seriously in our era. We were speaking for our generation. We were speaking for ourselves. It rang true. The U.S. government has still not apologized to the families of the fallen four of Ohio.

The band has gotten together for other political causes over the years, and I enjoy it. It's always fun to hear the singing and feel the love and respect, and there is a lot of that. During the Iraq War, when CSNY went on the road singing the songs of my latest album, *Living with War*, and a collection of older songs that reflected politics and American life, we had a sense of the old purpose. But things had changed; we split our audience in half with that music rather than bringing it together. It was a sign of the times. We have been through a lot together: the Summer of Love, hell, distrust, and hurt. Life. When we play now our audience still feels it, like a candle that is flickering, like a sun that is setting. A fog is rolling in. It is really all of our lives together.

That was CSNY to me. The connection with our generation was profound, and we could feel it. I loved all those guys. A lot has changed since those innocent times. We are different today. We were not bound by chemistry the same way as the Springfield was. We were all friends, experiencing a phenomenon together.

Crosby was forever the catalyst, always intense, driving us further and further. Just looking in those eyes made me want to deliver from the heart. He so believed in what we were doing. Graham was the consummate professional, always there with his parts, cheering us on as we jammed, writing the songs we became best known for. Stephen, my brother, always the soulful, conflicted one, was battling unseen demons and many-colored beasts through the days and nights, contributing an edge that was unmistakable.

The combination of that energy all at once—with our audience!—that is what CSNY was to me at its best.

But then came the fame, the drugs, the money, houses, cars, and admirers; then the solo albums. I had to break away. I had so much to give, so many songs in me, so many ideas and sounds in my head. I had to do it. The band didn't break up; it just stopped. It did not regenerate itself. It stopped functioning, like it had a lapse or a heart attack or something. No new songs came forward from anyone. We were all doing our own things. We needed a reason to get together and a purpose behind our music. In the end, we became a celebration of ourselves, and there was no way to keep that going. It doesn't regenerate. We had a golden time, and then we lost our way. Be great or be gone.

I n the aftermath of my breakup with Carrie, Crosby was a really good friend. He kept in touch with me throughout, and we had some really deep conversations about that. He was so supportive; I could not have asked for a better friend. He has since gone through hell and back, and written two books about it with his friend Carl Gottlieb. I would like to read a book that he wrote in his own words because he is masterful with language and very articulate.

When he started to take a dive it was terrible to see. There was nothing we could do to stop him. Once he came to my boat and broke out his pipe to smoke some freebase. He wanted to share some so I could see how it was. As we all sat around, he got it out and started his torch. Then he did it all by himself, forgetting what he was doing completely. That was my experience with freebase, and I came away with a bad impression. He and his wife, Jan, were both into it, but their deep love for each other eventually rescued them from it. They picked up the pieces and moved on with their lives, having a beautiful son and getting the blue sky back finally. They really pulled it out of the jaws of hell and took it back. I still remember "the mighty Cros" visiting the ranch in his van. That van was a rolling laboratory that made Jack Casady's briefcase look like chicken feed. Forget I said that! Was my mic on?

## Chapter Thirty-Four

Pegi and I were at the Hawaii house relaxing from something or other. Conan and Jay Leno were having their moment with NBC, and Conan had walked out on *The Tonight Show*, which turned into a political quagmire when Jay Leno decided he was not going to step down as he had said he would. Conan was left hanging. So Conan's last show was coming up and I was his musical guest. Eric Johnson had come over to Hawaii to fly with me on the United flight to LA that I was taking. When we arrived, he got off the plane and went to make sure everything was ready so I could go straight to a car and to the hotel. Then he came back and said, "I have got some really bad news; Larry Johnson has died." I took that in. Larry was a lifelong friend.

Elliot met us at the LA airport. We hugged. I was in a fog. Tim Foster, my old stage manager, was there, too. We hugged. What

Larry Johnson, me, and David Briggs, playing pool at the ranch, 1978.

can you say? I called Pegi, who was crying like a baby. Larry had died in Ben Young's van. He just slipped behind the wheel to drive Ben to the Sharks' hockey game and let out a last breath. He was gone. Just like that. On the phone, Pegi cried and cried. All I wanted to do was go back to Hawaii and be with her.

I had to go to the hotel, where Dave Matthews and I sat together in my room, learning a song while the time passed. Conan's last show was the next day, and later that night, Dave Matthews and I were doing a thing together for the Haiti Relief Fund; we had to rehearse to get a grip on what we were performing together.

The next day was the Conan show. It was surreal. Conan's shows were always loose and fun. This one was different. As I was singing "Long May You Run," the TV audience must have thought I was singing it for Conan. I was singing it for Larry, too. I barely made it through that performance. I looked over at Conan, and he was watching me with his head in his hands. That guy really got screwed. But he is a survivor. I said good-bye and off we went to the Haiti benefit over in Hollywood. It was the same place we had done the 9/11 Tribute to Heroes, where I sang "Imagine." I think we did a good job. Someone said Kanye West had left a message there for me. I kept seeing Larry in the hallway outside my dressing room. I never got the message.

Pegi came home to California, and we met at the ranch. Pegi cried for six months. She grieved and grieved. Pegi and Larry were very close, and there was nothing I could do but hold her, comfort her, and feel my own thoughts. Life again. (You might notice I refer to my son Ben as Ben Young all the time. Larry always called his son Ben Johnson. I liked the pride with which he would say "Ben Johnson." It is a lingering memory of his great spirit.)

While it's true that Larry Johnson and David Briggs have perhaps played the major roles supporting my endeavors, the others who have worked at my side cannot be underestimated. I have been very lucky to know and create with all of them. Elliot and I are getting older now and can feel the passage of time, but the energy to do what we do is still very much alive. Ben Johnson, Larry's son, and Will Mitchell, who worked beside Larry, are still with me every day, carrying on the work. Hannah Johnson, Larry's daughter, is doing my photography archiving and the preservation/re-creation of manuscripts and art for my current projects. There is a lot of love and caring going on with our whole team. Toshi Onuki, who worked tirelessly with Larry and me, is still with me, helping with UX (user interface) design and film editing. Our work together is so rewarding. Mark Faulkner is editing film for videos in Larry's old Airstream, known affectionately as the "Upstream Airstream." Larry loved those Airstream trailers almost as much as he loved Quonset huts. So although something has been lost, something has been gained along the way, and I am grateful to be working and creating. The Shakey Pictures team lives on in the great space that Larry found and moved us into just before his untimely passing.

I am very proud of the people who have worked with me. Probably my "front of house" sound mixer Tim Mulligan, who has been with me the longest besides Elliot, has withstood the most of my changes in style and content, just riding it out with me. I can always count on Tim to come to the dressing room and tell me how we made out in a show, and not just the good shows. Dave Lohr has been right by Tim's side for years, providing feedback and quality care in tuning the sound in each venue where we play. Honesty, constructive criticism: those things are priceless in this game. I have always had excellent people with me; Joel Bernstein is another one. He is a great photographer and archivist who came along with me for years and tuned my instruments. Now he is working with Graham Nash and others doing a lot of archiving work. In the early years Joel took a lot of pictures that have been priceless in my *Archives* projects.

Recently I visited my brother, Bob, in Ontario. I stayed in his house on the lake with him and his friend Vicky. Dave Toms was there with us, too. Dave is an old friend of me and my dad. We had a really good time together, and it gave me time to reflect on some of the changes in my life. Dave is a big Canadian guy with white hair. I gave him the name SnowBear to go with the character SnowBear in the continuation of the *Greendale* story. If we ever do that movie, Dave will play that part, I'm sure. He has been a traveling companion on the last couple of tours we have done with Lincvolt, sitting in Larry's old seat, and now plays in that story as well. Ben Johnson will be helping with that once I get home and can focus on it again.

Actually, Ben is the one who will be sitting in his dad's seat when we finally take our trip around the country in Lincvolt. Dave will be there, too. There are sure starting to be a lot of loose ends. When we lost Larry Johnson, we had a lot of balls in the air. Maybe too many.

Chapter Thirty-Five

Dustin Cline and Ben Young are on their way here to Hawaii right now and should arrive in a few minutes from the mainland. Dustin, the son of David Cline, who was my road manager and sometime bus driver, was born just about the same time as Ben. He is now one of Ben's main caregivers and the Minister of Fun and Social Activities. Tony Rivera, "Uncle Tony," will be traveling with them as well. We have tried to always have a crew of two with Ben Young to make his comings and goings as safe, fun, and easy as possible, while also taking excellent care of him.

He is completely dependent on others now and is taking nourishment through a feeding tube in his stomach. That is something we implemented a year or so ago, and Ben has responded well, especially now that we prepare our own food for him that is fresh and organic. One of Ben Young's original caregivers, Anne Marie Holmes, a very sweet and kind English lady with an excel-

Performing with Pegi at the 25th Annual Bridge School Benefit Concert at the Shoreline Ampitheatre, Mountain View, California, 2011.

lent sense of humor, has created some nourishing and healthy formulas for Ben. Rather than the canned formula most people like him would have to settle for, Ben is Mr. Gourmet. You are what you eat. And Ben Young is looking good.

Ben has seen a lot in his thirty-three years, including Larry Johnson's passing. We talk about Larry a lot, and Ben is often a part of the memories. Larry was an excellent friend for Ben, taking him everywhere and including him in everything he possibly could. Larry was one of Ben Young's strongest advocates for inclusion in every activity, no matter what logistics were involved.

Ben Young will be rolling up the sidewalk anytime now and into his room for an overhaul before we all take off to the Bamboo in Hawi for our traditional Sunday brunch with friends. Next week, the shift will change and Ben Bourdon will arrive. With him will be Marian Zemla, "Uncle Marian," the senior caregiver who has been with Ben for the longest (except for Anne Marie). Marian, a former practicing doctor from Poland, loves Ben Young very much. I suspect Ben is like a son to Marian and his wife, Teresa. Everyone on Ben's team is top-notch, and we are so blessed that we have this assistance. Pegi and Anne Marie are always looking to have someone "in the wings" so we are never short should something ever happen to one of the team members. Pegi is masterful at organizing this and seeing that Ben Young's staff is organized and running smoothly. That alone is a full-time job. How she does all of that and writes and records a brand-new record that is totally top-notch is incredible to me. She is finally living the dream she had when I first met her. Even with all of the great singers I have sung with, there is nothing like singing with Pegi.

## Chapter Thirty-Six

My daughter, Amber Jean Young, was born May 15, 1984. We brought her home to the ranch from the hospital in a baby-blue 1957 Chevy Bel Air wagon called the Mother Ship. She grew up relatively shy with others and showed a strong interest in art right away, painting first with one hand, then with the other, switching back and forth as she went. Her sense of color is so pleasing to me that I feel it in my heart every time I see one of her works. And now she has an MFA.

Rich with an artist's sentiment, Amber Young today is a beautiful young lady, making her way through life's guesswork and planning her future with grace, style, and conviction. Of course, she would never say that about herself. This is her father talking. I love her. She has been well raised by her mother, who has a natural sense for the art of mothering and nurturing. Amber's art is as complex as it is beautiful, and the textures and boldness she uses speak to me. I get a visceral feeling from her colors, just like great-sounding music gives me. What a pleasure to watch her develop

Pegi and I with Ben and Amber at Willie Nelson's Pedernales Ranch, Spicewood, Texas, June 1984.

her natural talent. She really wants to be an independent artist, making her way with her art and not asking for anything. Amber works at galleries in San Francisco and curates exhibitions.

Looking at the poster for my new Jonathan Demme movie, I am especially proud of my daughter Amber's art. She has done the titles, at Jonathan's request, and the result is so cool. In her strong personality, she is a combination of her mother and my mother, two of my favorite people, plus a little bit of me thrown in there for good measure, along with that indescribably original thing that is just totally her. She is a true original, having created houses built of Ben Young's feeding bags, tubes, and medical devices, heavy-duty construction vehicles made of felt, a wedding cake you can walk inside with beautiful felt roses adorning it, and countless works that hang on walls—works in wax, in paint, and in other mediums I can't adequately describe at the moment.

There is nothing on earth like the feeling of a parent for a child that has matured as Amber Young has. She is my pal, sometimes my confidante—although I am careful not to burden her unnecessarily—and my muse. Named after my granny Jean, an active musician who worked in the copper mines of Flin Flon, Manitoba, during the day, handing out the metal ID tags to the miners before they descended and collecting them back, hanging them on nails in the wall of a little shack, when they finished their shifts, thereby becoming the first to learn of a missing soul in the mine. Then she was partying into the night, singing and playing a barroom piano or producing and playing in the local theater productions she created. She is my daughter, Amber Jean Young. Over the years her mother and I have tried to do our best raising her, and now it is up to her. She is well equipped, soulful and talented, wise and idealistic, and comes fully loaded with the Young/Morton temperament.

I remember once we were having some problems, and she told me I was gone too much when she was growing up and I missed a lot of things. She was so true, so right. Of course I felt terrible, but that was the price I had to pay for my choices. I followed my music and missed her moments. Amber was very honest with me. Who could ask for more? She's my girl.

## Chapter Thirty-Seven

Another Word from PureTone . . .

I think a lot about the music business and how it is reinventing itself. Streaming services like Spotify make ALL music available free instantly or through a subscription and a cool, easy user interface. This is completely different from the way I started, but I am open to it because it gets music to the people in a way that works with today's expectations of the capabilities of technology.

The convenience is fantastic, with instant access to and discovery of the history of recorded sound, but you can't *feel* it like you used to. I don't want to complain and not have a suggestion about how to fix the problem—complaining without a solution is a waste of time. So I have developed a solution. It's just a matter of dealing in the business world and offering people a new way to make money that reintroduces ongoing quality into the equation. I know a way to combine streaming services and PureTone, while improving the sound of streams and making some tracks in playlists available instantly in PureTone-master quality.

I keep thinking about this all the time because I want to make a contribution that lasts. I know I am obsessive about it. Music is an art form compromised by technology; this is not what technology is supposed to do. Maybe the music I make now will not have a huge audience like it once did, and my time in the light may or may not have passed, but I can reach more people than I ever have by helping to bring all kinds of music to them in a way that is superior to anything that has ever been presented in the history of recorded sound. I think *great* digital sound is the future of music, and we are a few steps away from delivering it. It could happen really soon, and that would be a massive sea change for the art of recorded music.

## Chapter Thirty-Eight

M y very first recording session was on July 23, 1963, at CKRC radio in Winnipeg. I was seventeen years old. Harry Taylor was the engineer behind the board, and Bob Bradburn was the producer, a CKRC DJ. The Squires were there to make a record! The first day we played all of our songs so we could hear how they sounded when recorded. It was very exciting, and I was really jacked up. Just before and just after the sessions, we played at the Crescentwood Community Centre and earned $35 the first night and $36 the second night. As you can tell, we were hot.

The CKRC studio had a pair of mono tape recorders, some EQ, some echo, and a control board. The mixing was done live. It was at this session that I first sang on tape. I had a couple of songs, one of which I called "I Wonder." It was the best one that I sang, but we decided, because I had a "different" voice, that the Squires would be an instrumental recording group. I knew that I had to work on my singing, and I knew I felt good when I sang. Those

With book art director and friend Gary Burden,
on the beach in Malibu, 1975.

songs meant something to me. I had written several instrumentals that we were also playing.

The two tunes picked from the audition session were "The Sultan" and "Image in Blue." During the second session we practiced recording these, working on the arrangements. At that time it was decided that "Image in Blue" needed a name change so that Bob Bradburn could say the title at the end of the record in echo. "Aurora" was the new title. They thought of the title and had the idea. I was so young and eager, I didn't complain. I was just happy to be making a record. I did like that a prerecording of a gong was added to "The Sultan" to give it that special sultanesque, desert-tent vibe—we knew all about that in Winnipeg.

After a few long weeks of anticipation, the record was released on V Records, a local company that mainly did polkas but was just getting into rock and roll. We were very excited. Then the big moment came, and we heard "The Sultan" on the radio! I was in my mother's car with my bandmate Ken Koblun, driving somewhere. I felt so good. I am sure I was walking on air for weeks. The Squires were recording artists. My mother was telling everyone she knew. I could hear her on the phone calling all of her friends. She was my biggest fan!

There are a few of these 45 rpm singles available on eBay every once in a while now. I have one signed by the band that Jack Harper, our original drummer, gave to me. The Squires on that record were Ken Koblun on bass, Ken Smyth on drums, Allan Bates on guitar, and Neil Young on guitar. Unreal! Listening to this today, I can say we were pretty good. We needed better equipment, but we played well and it was a good instrumental. What a rush!

Although there was never any art for the Squires' 45, album covers are very important to me. They put a face on the nature of the project. I know albums are viewed as passé by some today, but I am an album artist and I am not ready to give up on my form. I think it has a future and a past. The album cover and liner notes reached out to the music lover, filling them with images and helping to illuminate the story behind the music, the feeling coming from the artist. My first album cover told a lot about me, without words.

I first met Gary Burden while shooting the CSNY cover for *Déjà Vu*, my initial album with CSN. Gary and I became good friends and we immediately worked together on the album cover for *After the Gold Rush*. I loved what he did with the photographs. Gary and I have been working together since that time, and I have done the great majority of my album art, my ads, and my songbooks with him. He is one of my closest compadres. Gary and his wife, Jenice, still work with me on every album cover. We are doing our life's work together.

One of my favorite album covers is *On the Beach*. Of course that was the name of a movie and I stole it for my record, but that doesn't matter. The idea for that cover came like a bolt from the blue. Gary and I traveled around getting all the pieces to put it together. We went to a junkyard in Santa Ana to get the tail fin and fender from a 1959 Cadillac, complete with taillights, and watched them cut it off a Cadillac for us; then we went to a patio supply place to get the umbrella and table. We picked up the bad polyester yellow jacket and white pants at a sleazy men's shop, where we watched a shoplifter getting caught red-handed and busted. Gary and I were stoned on some dynamite weed and stood dumbfounded, watching the bust unfold. This girl was screaming and kicking! Finally we grabbed a local LA paper to use as a prop. It had this amazing headline: SEN. BUCKLEY CALLS FOR NIXON TO RESIGN. Next we took the palm tree I had taken around the world on the Tonight's the Night tour. We then placed all of these pieces carefully in the sand at Santa Monica Beach. Then we shot it. Bob Seidemann was the photographer, the same one who took the famous Blind Faith cover shot of the naked young girl holding an airplane. We used the crazy pattern from the umbrella insides for the inside of the sleeve that held the vinyl recording. That was the creative process at work. We lived for that, Gary and I, and we still do.

Collaborating with Gary has been a joy over the years. We have really maintained a wonderful friendship to this day, no matter where we are on the planet. I hung with him a lot after my breakup with Susan and before I moved north to the ranch. Then I sold my Topanga house to him. A few years ago when Gary married Jenice Heo, an artist he met at Reprise Records, I was his best man.

When CDs came along, it was more of a challenge to present our art. The CD package was about twenty-five percent the size of an album. Everything had to be small. The lyrics were not legible without glasses for anyone over a certain age. So our whole palette was changed by the advent of the CD. Of course, the audio quality also took a dive, with a maximum of fifteen percent of the sound of

On the Beach *LP cover.*

a master, but if you don't know how I feel about that by now, you should put this book down. Go directly to your doctor's office and have your eyes and ears checked.

Now that online music has taken hold with Spotify, Rhapsody, and the other online services, art has become challenged again. Quality has taken another hit, and tactile album art has an unknown future at this point. Things are changing. I have faith that there is a place for tactile art like physical books and album covers and think that we will settle into something new but recognizable. I am not totally sure of this, though. I do think that the future for books is in over-the-top quality printing, paper, photography, and binding. The high price of that quality may enable the survival of the printed and bound hardcover book.

## Chapter Thirty-Nine

Meditations

I was out by the water looking at the shoreline. The waves came in. They receded. The water lapped on the coral when it rushed in, knocking the pieces of coral all around. The lighter pieces got jostled the most, and the pieces that were wedged into other pieces held on and just moved a little, although they got wet. This pattern continued for hours until the tide went out and the water level became lower, causing the waves to not come in as far and to not touch the little pieces of coral I had been watching. The coral pieces dried out and changed color in the sunlight or reflected a little in the moonlight. They were all there together: big ones, little ones, broken ones, ones that looked like little fish.

When the tide returns, it will be higher or lower than it was the last time it came in, and the little pieces will be jostled again. If the waves are particularly big, the coral pieces might get worn down or be broken into smaller pieces, eventually losing their shape completely. If the tide is gentle and the waves are small, very little will happen except to the smallest pieces of coral. It's hard to track the progress of every little piece, but it is predictable that they will eventually be worn down and disappear, to be replaced by other pieces.

This is an example of paganism to me, possibly Buddhism, one of the ways I learn to accept change through nature and the way of things. I am not looking for a story to explain this or a legend to believe in or a place to go where I can learn about this. I am already here. The horizon speaks to me in my time of need, sharing the ultimate story of the moment of change. I accept the horizon for what it is. This is my religion.

When I was a little boy in Omemee, my mom and dad took me to Sunday school. I don't remember much about it, but it didn't last long. I suspect my mom and dad grew tired of taking me down there to the church. My dad always said, "For what we are about to receive, may the Lord make us truly thankful. Amen," before each meal, generally followed by "Neil, get your elbows off the table." I don't even know what religious denomination my mom and dad were.

We had spaghetti a lot. It was really good with my dad's special sauce. Before he poured in the chili peppers, he used to heat it up in a big pot. OMG, it smelled great! Then he would add hamburger meat and let it simmer for hours, covered. Al dente was his preferred way to cook the noodles, and later I got pretty good at that.

My dad's spaghetti sauce recipe is framed and hanging in our kitchen today, back at the ranch. It is so faded that I can barely read it anymore, but it does have his original handwriting. Pegi has made it a few times, and it's great when she does. At least someone

SCOTT YOUNG'S SPAGHETTI RECIPE

Start with two pounds of minced lean beef ~~the best you can afford~~ *for each four servings*

Place this *(over medium hot)* in a large pot with *a 20-oz can of* ~~the contents of a large can of~~ stewed ~~tomatoes~~

tomatoes and ~~a~~ a 4-ounce can or two (depending on taste) of tomato

paste. Add a tablespoon of salt, a half-teaspoon of black pepper,

a tablespoon *(or more)* of curry power , a tablespoon of ~~sugar~~ *honey,* a pinch of rose-

mary, a tablespoon of oregano or pre-mixed italian seasoning, a teaspoon *(or more)*

of cayenne pepper. Crush *several* ~~two to four~~ cloves of garlic in a garlic

press over the pot, and then scrape the crushed buds into the sauce

along with the juices. ~~Chop ...~~

Stir well with a long fork to make the meat break up into a sauce ~~without~~

lumps.

Cut *4 or 5* ~~five~~ medium sized onions (red italian or Bermuda preferred but

cooking onions okay) into the pot. *Chop ... the leaf end of a head of celery*

~~Wash ... mushrooms ...~~ *into smaller pieces, leaves & all, and*

~~add without browning, unless you happen to be~~ a nut on browning

~~mushrooms.~~ Cut a green pepper or two into long strips ~~and hold~~ ready

to add later. *Prepare mushrooms for very high heat cooking at end.*

When the mixture begins to simmer boldly, let it cook for a minimum

of one hour, a maximum of two. About *20* ~~30~~ minutes before you plan

to serve, add the *celery and* green pepper strips and one six or eight-ounce (or so)

smoked sausage for every intended serving (these only need time to heat

through). ~~I use Schneider's.~~

Cook the *pasta* ~~spaghetti~~ itself (I use ~~Lancia~~ *the size called bucatini),* about one-quarter pound per

person) *no more than* ~~about~~ 10 minutes after it begins to boil. (Drain *well* and place on

plates.   On top of each mound of spaghetti, place one sausage, ~~and~~

(+ (optional) mushrooms cooked very fast in butter.

generous portions of the meat sauce, Your table also should have

grated parmesan or romano cheese; cold celery, radishes and dill pickles;

and a ~~the~~ small dish of ground red peppers for customers who like the sauce hotter.

My father Scott Young's spaghetti recipe.

is making it, and that feels good to me. I would like to taste that again. Once, when Crazy Horse was doing what we called the Northern California Coastal Bar Tour in 1975, my daddy was living on the ranch in the little red house and driving my 1950 Plymouth. He came down to the White House and cooked spaghetti for us all one night. His glasses were fogging up while he ate it! It was amazingly great, that meal. A real good memory!

Old memories are wonderful things and should be held on to as long as possible, shared with others, and embellished if need be. Whenever I go back to Canada, my heart is flooded with them—memories, that is. I look forward to seeing my brother, Bob, and Dave Toms up there in Peterborough when I go back for the premiere of Jonathan Demme's new documentary. It will be a great time. (Canadians say *great* a lot, in case you haven't noticed. I know. I have looked up many other words I could have used in the thesaurus, but that is not my style. I prefer to be boring and use the same words over and over, because that is more true to who I really am. That may not work for you if you pride yourself on your great vocabulary.)

Visiting my mom, Rassy Young, in Winnipeg, June 1968.

## Chapter Forty

W hen I arrived back in Toronto from Blind River in the mid-sixties, I visited my dad. I had not seen him much in the few years since our family split up and I moved to Winnipeg with my mother at age twelve or so. He had never shown much interest in my music or supporting it, and he had constantly urged me to improve my grades at school before he would help me with my music in any way. So I was not surprised when he thought I should get a job to support myself while I was looking around for gigs in Yorkville Village, the place where artists and musicians and former beatniks hung out and did their thing.

I got a job at Coles Bookstore on Yonge Street and took a flat nearby at 88 Isabella Street so I could walk to work. I had a hot plate to cook on there. Beans mostly. My job at Coles was described as stock boy. I was the person putting price tags on all the books. I only lasted two weeks. I had no discipline and could not put anything ahead of my music. I spent the days wandering around the

With my dad at the Riverboat club in Toronto, February 1969.

Village, trying to meet other musicians and seeing if I could get a gig or a band going.

Number 88 Isabella Street was filthy, because I never cleaned anything. I was a little pig. But I did write a song called "The Ballad of Peggy Grover" up there. It was pretty good, but not too good. "Peggy Grover" was a play on words for Grover pegs, which were the best tuning pegs you could buy for a guitar.

The way the story goes,
she just ran out of clothes.
This world just wore the peg down.

Then I wrote a song called "Nowadays Clancy Can't Even Sing." That song had a little more depth and was more a stream of consciousness about how it felt to be in my body at the time.

Hey who's that stompin' all over my face?

I was beginning to feel like songwriting was what I was about more than anything else. I wrote a few more songs there and started playing them for people in the Village. Some people said they liked what I was doing.

Then one day I bailed on the flat without paying because I had no money for the rent. I went and slept on the floor at Vicky Taylor's flat above the Night Owl, a club on Avenue Road, just north of the Village. Vicky was a folksinger struggling in the Village, and her parents were paying for the apartment. She was an important part of the scene there with musicians and hippies. She was a magnet. Everybody knew her. She had long, straight, jet-black hair. We were all trying to make it somehow in the music scene. One of the LP records we listened to with Vicky, and I in particular loved, was by Bert Jansch. His singing and guitar playing were masterful. I never forgot that. I learned a lot from him. Vicky was a big fan of Bert, as well.

John Kay, who would later sing "Born to Be Wild" in Steppenwolf, also slept there on the floor in front of the fireplace. We burned anthracite in the fireplace, white coal. We both would be sleeping there, listening to records and crashing. He showed me some cool guitar stuff that helped me to define the way I played. He had been in the Sparrow, a local band that did well. They were really great and had a slippery lead guitar player, Dennis Edmonton. They were the Toronto sound, along with the Hawks, who later became The Band. The Toronto sound featured R&B-based rock, with a Roy Buchanan–influenced Fender Telecaster guitar playing style that Robbie Robertson and Dennis Edmonton, along with Domenic Troiano, were all great at.

One night after hearing me at a hootenanny, Chick Roberts of the Dirty Shames told me he really liked my song "Sugar Mountain"—that made me feel like I was somebody.

Folk clubs and the folk life were burning their way into my psyche. Back in the beginning in Winnipeg, I played with the Squires at a club called the Fourth Dimension. That was one of my first gigs. I was green as could be and played the Hootenanny every weekend, and I would watch the headliners: the Thorns, Sonny Terry and Brownie McGhee, the Dirty Shames, the Allen-Ward Trio, Chuck and Joni Mitchell (who I first met there), Don McLean, Danny Cox, Lisa Kindred, the list goes on and on . . . They came through regularly, a new act every week or couple of weeks.

Joni Mitchell also really loved my song "Sugar Mountain." Later, she wrote "The Circle Game" about "Sugar Mountain." It was a real feeling of recognition that Joni wrote her song to answer mine; I didn't even hear it until she had already been singing it for a year.

Meeting all of these people had an effect on me. I saw myself as a part of it all, the music scene, the writers and performers. I wanted to do just what they did, too—get in a truck after they finished their set and leave.

Eventually that is exactly what I did, taking the Squires to the Flamingo Club in Fort William, Ontario, where to my surprise I discovered *another* Fourth Dimension Club! We played there, too. There was a guy there who played a Fender Telecaster, and he played the shit out of it. He was better than most of the players I had ever heard. He had the Toronto sound, that string-bending Telecaster technique. I don't remember his name or much else about him. He was pretty straight-looking, with really short hair, kind of like a Kingston Trio look. He was there watching the Squires one night when we played "Farmer John." When the instrumental break came along in the song, I just went crazy on the guitar solo. I had just started to do that. One night it just happened, and now I was doing it all the time.

When the set was over, he came up to me.

"What the fuck was that?!" He exclaimed. "What the hell were you doing? I have never heard anything like that in my life! It was fucking great, man! Shit!"

I knew that while I was playing like that I was out of my mind. It felt right, but I don't know what it was. Every note was out of the blue! I went places I had never gone before with no fear. It made an impression on him, and me too. That was the beginning of something. I knew I was doing something that had just come out of me, not something I learned, but something that *was* me.

## Chapter Forty-One

Friends for Life

My manager, Elliot Roberts, plays such a large part in everything I am doing that it makes more sense to say what *we* are doing! I speak with Elliot five times a day at least. Everything we do, we talk about. He advises me on every move I make. I am involved in a lot of things and I am capable of screwing every one of them up without even trying. That is why I consult with my Wise Counselor on every little thing.

We fight. We argue. We laugh. We cry.

There is something to long-term relationships and loyalty that you learn over time. There are pitfalls to avoid, grooves that become ruts that you need to climb out of, and relationships that sour for one reason or another that still have to be managed gracefully. Because I tend to avoid the confrontations and delivering bad news, I am not good at doing any of that. Elliot is. He knows how to communicate where I don't. That is why I am where I am now.

With David Geffen (left) and Elliot Roberts, at Lookout Management offices in West Hollywood, 1971.

He has a cell phone as his instrument. He is tech savvy, but he is a people person, believing in face-to-face relationships and speaking relationships being at the core of any e-mail. He hardly ever writes an e-mail. He has to talk directly to people. Just as I wake up every day with a new idea, he wakes up every day with a new approach to solving the problems that arise with the projects I am already immersed in. There are a lot of them. This is our pattern.

As I've said, he is also one of the funniest people I have ever met. He is full of one-liners, and I love to hear him talk when he is on a roll. Oh my God, he blows people's minds with some of his insights and humorous comments. If there is a heavy meeting, he is the icebreaker. Let me tell you a typical Elliot story: We were having a meeting in an office in San Francisco. Our agents were there and we were talking about the future of our music system project, negotiating some fine points having to do with a lot of money and my control of the business. It was a little tense in the room. The negotiations continued. Elliot made some strong statements, and the other people there did, too. It was not an easy situation, but we all had a common goal. Elliot reminded everyone of that. Eventually we got what we needed. The room was still tense. Elliot looked his adversary squarely in the eye and said, "I just want you to know, we have no issues at all with your partner's drinking problem. It's really not a problem to us." There was a pause. Everyone started laughing uproariously! Elliot had brought the house down. His ability to move seamlessly from one mode to another is unbelievable.

Elliot navigates the rocky shoals of Respect. He is not perfect, and neither am I. If we shipwreck, we jump in the same lifeboat and row like hell. Thank you, Elliot.

Elliot and I have a long history with David Geffen. David started in the mailroom at William Morris, as did Elliot. David was a master of the deal, as was Elliot. David shaped a lot of things and was an artist himself. He played a deal like it was a Stradivarius. He was always on the phone in his office when we all started out together. He and Elliot were Geffen-Roberts, our managers. A superstar in his field, David was used to winning and expected to be successful at everything he did, and he was successful at *almost* everything he tried to do. His first foray into film was not a success, and I can't even remember what it was. That was a rarity, in that he did not succeed. Geffen Records was not the success I think he expected it to be. He had a lot of great artists on board and wanted to re-create Asylum Records, which was a total success, giving artists freedom. It was the ultimate label. The Eagles were one of the first acts. David's taste was great, having started with Laura Nyro, who we all loved as a great artist and unique presence, but Geffen Records never quite achieved the success he'd hoped to reach.

I think David's biggest failure was with me. I was happy to move to Geffen Records. Things had fallen off a bit at Reprise, and my last couple of records had not been that successful; that was not because of Reprise, it was because careers go up and down. Some records are hits and some are great but are not commercial. That's just how it is. Reprise did a fine job of presenting all of my records in a way that did them justice, even if they were not commercially successful. *Tonight's the Night* is a great example of that, as is *On the Beach*. They were not *Harvest*, but they were good representations of where I was at the time. I was really interested in communicating what I felt at the time, more interested in that than succeeding commercially, and it was in that spirit that I moved to Geffen Records.

I made a record called *Island in the Sun* about the planet Earth and invited David over to hear it at the house I had rented in Hawaii. He was not impressed with it and asked me to do something else. That was the first time that had ever happened to me. It was a good record, and I liked it. To accommodate David, I thought I would do a record that was a combination of that one and one that I was already hearing in my head to follow it up. The second one, *Trans*, was inspired by my son Ben and his communication challenges. Because of Ben's quadriplegia, he couldn't talk or communicate in a way that most people could understand, so I made a record where I sang through a machine and most people couldn't understand what I was saying, either.

I felt like it was art, an expression of something deeply personal. I called it *Trans*, meaning trying to get across from one world to another, being locked in a body without an intelligible voice, trying to communicate through the use of machines, computers, switches, and other devices. It was a very deep and inaccessible concept.

I had visions of a series of videos to support it. They were set in a hospital with a lot of scientists and doctors trying to unlock the secrets of a little being who had so much to say and no way to say it. *Trans* should have been just that group of songs, not a combination of those and some from *Island in the Sun*, which diluted it. There were a lot of robots and half humans in the video dreams. Even though I had ideas on how to do it inexpensively, Geffen Records would not fund those videos.

When *Trans*, my first record for Geffen, was not a commercial success, it was obviously because it was a weird record in the eyes of some of my listeners. I was singing through a vocoder about things they did not understand, and they could not see the characters I was doing because there were no videos to go with them. Geffen Records tried to present it like it was a hit record, using their publicity machine. But it was incomplete without the videos and should not have been overpresented. It should have been pushed subtly. I had different goals from my new record company. So the lesson from that is I should not have caved to Geffen in the first place. I should have put out *Island in the Sun* in its original form and then I should have done *Trans*, with more room for the *Trans* songs to establish themselves as a complete cohesive atmosphere. I had betrayed myself by not staying true to my art and following the muse.

After that, the Guy Who Was President of Geffen started telling me what to do. He told me to make a rock and roll record. So perhaps vindictively, I gave them a record called *Everybody's Rockin'* that was traditional old rock and roll, literally what he had asked me to do. I conveyed his misguided request into an expression by becoming an old-fashioned rocker. Of course, my literal interpretation was not what he had in mind. He wanted *Rust Never Sleeps*. I think the Guy Who Was President was under pressure to deliver big hits.

Then I made a record in Nashville called *Old Ways*. They didn't like it, either. I didn't put it out. Then I did another record in Nashville that I called *Old Ways* as well.

I liked it.

They hated it.

They released it, but buried it completely, just like my previous two records. They were not behind them, because they were not box-office hits.

I was not doing what I was told to do. And they sued me for making music "uncharacteristic of Neil Young." That was Geffen Records' biggest mistake, I think. The mistakes all started when I caved and didn't give them *Island in the Sun*. They wanted me to be commercially successful, and I wanted to be an artist expressing myself—those two goals are not always compatible. I was expecting to have the same artistic freedom that I had at Asylum Records, but Geffen Records wanted me to be a smash, selling millions of records. Most important, Geffen was not hands-on at Geffen Records. He had other people doing that. It showed.

The lawyers got in a pissing contest and made things much worse. It was egos and Hollywood nightmares. But it's over, and I still love David. He just let his record company make a big mistake with me and was disconnected from what was happening.

Some people think there must be bad blood between us. No. There isn't any. David is still one of my best friends, a very brilliant, generous, and caring man, doing so much for AIDS research and so much for the arts, as well as the Bridge School and countless other projects. We go back.

Chapter Forty-Two

The Aloha Garage is part of our property in Hawaii. There is a red 1971 Cadillac Eldorado convertible in the Aloha Garage. It must be the only one on the island, maybe even the whole Hawaiian Islands! Given my history with cars, particularly Eldorado convertibles, you would have to agree that it is significant that that car was in the garage of the house Pegi found for us and was not known to us at the time of the purchase.

I think we may have found out about it on the list of things the owner was "throwing in" to the purchase. Anyway, there she sits. Really nice faded original red paint and beautifully worn red leather interior. When we fly over to the island, Tom and Nell, our caretakers, always bring the Eldorado out to meet the plane, and then Pegi and I drive back to the Aloha Garage, which takes around a half hour. It is so cool to see that car waiting in the middle of a bunch of SUVs at the airport!

As I sit here today, writing this book, I cannot help but wonder about the significance of that car and our big green lawn with the palm trees blowing in the wind, two of my biggest dreams, coming to me at the same time in the same place. Right now I am listening to the wind blowing and rustling through the palms, the sound of the ocean just feet away, and the sun is beginning to sink into the waves. I see that big green lawn and remember the crazy nights when I would be amped out of my mind on coke, just praying that someday I could find relief and just be in a place like this, with the elements all working together to caress my senses.

For a while that happened a lot. I was into the drug so much that I would end up having the same dream very often, just being there amped out of my mind, wondering if and when I would be able to sleep, wishing I were on an island with the big green lawn and the palm fronds rustling, feeling that gentle wind. It was a recurring dream then, and now it is a reality.

Marc Benioff and Greg McManus are our neighbors in Hawaii. Marc, founder of Salesforce.com, and Greg, who owns and operates the Napa Valley Wine Train, scooped me up to go to Kona and trip around Costco and Sports Authority for an afternoon. These two guys are my good friends, and I very much enjoy hanging out with them. Costco and Sports Authority are like cultural centers here on the Big Island. You might get a similar feeling from walking around in them for a few hours, looking at the displays, as you would in a big museum in some forgotten future.

We started off at Costco by mistakenly going in the OUT door and being redirected by a helpful associate. First the flat-screen TVs greeted us with their shiny displays mirroring all of the neon lights in the ceiling. I learned that some screens are less reflective and noted that for a future upgrade to our existing TV. I also noted all of the online services that are now available on standard television sets. Things are evolving at a rapid rate.

My first big purchase was a set of replacement brushes for my Sonicare toothbrush, a product I am very impressed with. I really needed those and had been wondering how to find them. We wandered on through aisles of myriad products before we reached the book department, where Marc purchased several books for his little daughter, Leia. She is a beautiful and bright child who calls me Uncle Neil and asks me where my guitar is. We made a note to look for a guitar for her, but only found ukuleles at Costco. A plan was made to locate a music store. There were no records for sale at Costco except for local Hawaiian. I was happy for the locals.

The food department was awesome, with organic chicken breasts, much to my surprise. I am very big on organic food and did not expect to see it in Costco. Further exploration led to a staggering variety of fruits and vegetables, meats, fish, and local foods. Endless rows of packaged goods dazzled the eye. A guy went by with his cart completely full of chips, overflowing with a wide variety of brands.

For a moment I remembered the mom-and-pop record stores of my youth and the little towns I had lived in with families running the stores and restaurants, gas stations, clothing stores, and bakeries. I felt pretty old for a moment. Then I regrouped and realized I was alive and should be thankful.

You can find anything at Costco. After about two hours of walking the aisles, we had finally made it to the checkout with my new Fisker.

Next, Sports Authority beckoned, and the guys made some purchases. I came up empty. Greg got a nice wearable camera. Eventually we made our way to a music store. I was excited to get a guitar for Leia. Oddly, the store was called Kona Bay Books, and was located in the industrial area at the end of a funky parking lot. It featured CDs and DVDs, new and used. The doors opened and we entered an expansive store of used books, literally hundreds of thousands of them, categorized alphabetically by type and author.

The aisles were huge, very, very long, with the books stacked on homemade wooden shelves. Marc was way down one aisle along the wall looking in a box on the floor marked with a big letter Y. There was my life's work, all my CDs thrown in a box on the floor.

"Here you are!" said Marc.

As he sifted through the CDs, I saw the titles flying by and had flashes of memory of each one. There were about thirty or forty different albums in the box. I felt suddenly very sad. All of these people had given up their CDs! The original vinyl versions all sounded much better than the CDs, but they were still important to me. I had spent so long making each one, pouring myself into it, making it sound great. Now they were all in this little box, shadows of their former selves. If someone wanted to hear one of my old records, it was either on CD or online. This store was closing in on me. I found an old Clive Cussler book I must have missed back in the day, bought it for $2.50, and headed for the door. That place had become very depressing. I was overwhelmed with the reality of what had happened to my lifetime's work.

Stopping at the checkout, I inquired, "Do you carry vinyl?"

"Oh no, there's no demand for that," said the young lady at the cash register.

Next was a health food store located next door. I was not

really comfortable in there for some reason, so I waited outside at a little plastic table and chair, looking at the parking lot surrounded by a barbed-wire fence. Greg came out and offered me some coconut water. I was down. I was actually tanking.

"That's what's supposed to happen!" Mark said later. "We go on that trip to screw with our minds. That much sensory input is going to overwhelm the subconscious. It's the best way to shock your system out of the Hawaii nirvana!"

I am fascinated by the power of nature.

When the great Pacific earthquake hit in the spring of 2011 and the resulting tsunami devastated Japan, I was wondering how our beach house would make out when the waves reached the Hawaiian coast. Like everyone else, I watched on TV and the Internet. Our neighbor Greg had set up a webcam so we could watch it live. We couldn't see much, but could tell that the water level fell and then rose a few feet at least. Actually, the water rose and went right under our house! It went around the back of our house first and then went right under, leaving some debris there and doing about $10,000 of damage to the property. It knocked a hole in a gate we had that opened up so we could walk out to the shore. That had to be repaired. Some appliances that were located under the house had to be replaced.

I wish I had been there to watch. I would have liked to stay on the property and see that. Of course, that would have been too dangerous, because no one was really sure how big of an event it was going to be. We were so lucky compared to our Japanese friends.

Katy Lowry, a beautiful young lady of about ninety who grew up in our house a long time ago, has some stories about the old days. She told us that the house was built with wood that was brought into the bay on little boats, dropped into the water, and floated ashore. She also pointed out to us that there used to be sand in front of the seawall where there is only water and lava now. The water has risen a remarkable amount since the 1920s, more than you would think when you compare to the statistics of how much the sea level has risen in the last one hundred years— quite a bit more. Katy also told us that when other tidal waves have come in the past, fish and eels have been found on the lawn behind our house.

We should invite Katy down for dinner sometime. (Pegi says she brings her own food in a Tupperware container.) There are more stories I would love to hear. We could have a great dinner and screen all of the old movies of the area that we have collected that show the old ways and original buildings, how everyone used to dress, the old fishing traditions, dirt roads, and overgrown areas. Time passes, and these events are a way to keep track, to keep the history moving. The older I get, the more important things like that are to me. We are living right on the edge. They would never let us build here now with the regulations that are in place. I would love to stand on the upper deck of the house and watch a tsunami happen sometime, but I am sure the authorities would insist on our leaving and going to a safe area.

Time, the great healer, also brings the future. No one knows what is going to happen, so it is scary and exciting. That is why every day is so valuable and every minute so precious. On-the-spot decisions on what to do next are abundant. Life is unpredictable. My neighbor Greg called to see if I wanted to fly to Maui with him this morning, and I said that I think I will stay because I am writing. Poncho is coming by at eleven for a visit. It takes Poncho a lot of preparation to leave his garden. He is a bit of a recluse. I don't want to miss that visit. The flight to Maui is appealing, though. It's just a short one. I have made my decision, but it is lingering, and I've gone over it a few times. Basically I don't want to leave this spot. I am here and grounded. That would change big-time if I were to fly to Maui.

Ben Young is out on the deck with his team, having breakfast through his tube. I wonder how that feels. He seems to be content with it, although I am having some trouble reconciling the fact that Ben does not get all the big tastes anymore. He used to love Milanos and milk after every evening dinner. It was a tradition. Sometimes we still give him a tiny taste, just for old times' sake. He is so accepting. It's a marvel. He is the most accepting human being I have ever met, and he is very happy. Not all the time, mind you; he has a flair for impatience if he is going somewhere and there is a delay. He just yells! You know he is pissed. There is no stopping him. More power to you, Ben Young!

We had to stop feeding Ben Young by mouth because his lungs have become compromised by all of the aspirating he does.

It's a complex thing, eating. The body does a lot of work to protect itself and keep food out of the lungs. Ben's body is not working like a normal body does. Ben and Dustin and Uncle Tony are out on the deck listening to tunes on the computer and grooving. Ben's next support team is incoming for a shift. Uncle Marian and Ben Bourdon arrive in Hawaii today from the mainland, and the switch takes place around twelve-thirty. Time marches on. Because of this support, Ben has a very full life and keeps moving around, doing things, seeing people, and going to events. I reflect on this. Life is good.

Chapter Forty-Three

B ack in Omemee, there is a grade school called the Scott
Young Public School, named after my dad. The original
town school, the one I went to for grades one and two, was
down by the swamp or bog, as it was called back in the day. That
school is gone now. My first teacher, Miss Lamb, used to pick me
up by my chin whenever I was misbehaving or not heading in the
right direction. My partner in crime back then was Henry Mason.
He and I laughed a lot at the funny faces we all would make behind
Miss Lamb's back. He was hysterical, as I remember. This was way
before my dad became a famous Canadian writer.

I did take the family up to Ontario from California for the
opening ceremonies of the Scott Young School in 1993, and that
was quite an event. The ceremonies were held on the stage in
the gym, doubling as an auditorium, as was the tradition with most
schools in Canada. I think the choir sang "Helpless." There were
a lot of talks about the past and the history of the old school by

My brother, Bob, holding a rifle, and me with a bow, Omemee,
Ontario, 1955.

various speakers and local luminaries. Most notably to me, Miss Lamb was there.

My dad spoke. He was always comfortable in front of people and was relaxed and happy about the whole thing. He recognized a lot of people who were in the audience, and mentioned those who had passed away, and then made a joke about not talking too long and forgetting what he was saying. I am very proud of my dad. I remember having a good feeling that day. He was very eloquent, and everybody liked him.

The new school was right where the old baseball field and hockey rink used to be. That used to be right behind the Omemee train station, and ball games were regularly played there, which I attended. An old steam engine used to haul a passenger train through town twice a day when I was a kid, and we used to go back to the tracks about a half mile behind my house and put pennies on the rails to watch them get flattened by the train as it rumbled by. I would put my ear down on the rail so I could hear the train coming before I could see it. Once we heard the train, we would carefully place the coins on the rail and then wait for the big moment to arrive.

Recently my brother, Bob, and I took a walk along the track bed. It's a walking trail now, really beautiful. The rails are all gone. We crossed the old bridge where we used to play when we were kids, down by our boathouse where my dad kept his boat and outboard. The tracks, station, and train are all gone now. So are the boathouse and boat. But they live on in my mind, along with my mom and dad. Bob and I had a nice long walk that day and thoroughly enjoyed it, talking over memories of the old days when we were kids in Omemee and life was in front of us.

When I was about ten, my dad and I used to get up at six every Sunday morning and drive about five miles down Brock Road to the intersection with Highway 2, where the newspapers for my paper route were dropped. This was a weekly event that we shared. I really liked it. On the way back to the house, we would stop at about four houses on the way and I would deliver *The Globe and Mail*, which was the paper my dad wrote for, being careful not to wake the residents. Daddy had a daily column on the first page of the second section where he wrote human-interest stories. Every day he would write about a different subject, and I think he was very happy doing this job. He also was the host of *The Hot Stove League*, a TV program that ran between periods on *Hockey Night in Canada*, which was on every Saturday night across the country. Now that was a really big deal because, as you may have heard, hockey is the national game of Canada.

When we got back to our house, I would take the remaining papers and jump on my bike, riding through the rest of the route that took me about an hour and a half to complete. It was a rural area, and that meant not many customers over a large piece of ground. First I would ride away along the road and drop off papers at about ten houses. Every one had a long driveway, and a dog was usually present. I would carefully survey the situation and move in for the delivery, trying not to wake the dogs or the customers. I was pretty darn good at it.

At the end of the first part of the bike ride, I would arrive at the schoolhouse. This was an old rock building of two rooms with a creek running behind it. A potbellied stove heated each of the rooms. Grades one through four were in one room, with five through eight in the other room. Two teachers taught all the kids. Right in front of the school was the playground. We used to play baseball there, and home plate was right in front of the main door of the old schoolhouse. That schoolhouse was like something out of a history book, and it was about a hundred years old when I was there as a kid in the mid-1950s.

I went back there about thirty years ago and it was still there. When I checked again more recently, it was gone, removed to make room for the new wide road, I suppose. That was a depressing event, the day I saw it gone. The big trees that were on either side of home plate were gone, too. So was the little store and gas station that used to be on the corner next to the school.

The new modern school that I went to for grade five, four hundred yards up the 4th Concession Road, was gone. I went there when it was still brand-new, ran right into the glass door leaving class one day and got a concussion. Now it's all gone.

On that 4th Concession Road, past the new school, there were four more *Globe and Mail* customers, and the last one was the LaBrie family. That's where Marilyn LaBrie lived. There was a bridge crossing the creek at the bottom of the canyon near her house, and I crossed it on my bike every Sunday morning delivering the route. Sometimes I would walk Marilyn home after school, and one weekday afternoon, carrying her books home for her, I kissed Marilyn on the bridge. I think that was the first time I ever kissed a girl. What a thrill! Thank you, Miss Marilyn.

I didn't make much money on my route, but then again, I didn't need much money. Besides selling golf balls I had found to golfers on the course across the street, I had about fifty chickens in the henhouse that my neighbor Don Scott helped build. Like my son Ben Young's own organic egg business, my egg business was my largest source of income. Those were some lucky chickens, because Don had a glass business in Toronto, and my chicken house had a huge picture window looking out over the endless field behind it! Those lucky chickens had a great view.

Foxes were a big problem, though, and kept killing my chickens, so I slept on a cot out by the hen house in a pup tent, listening for the first sign of any problem (although I don't remember ever hearing anything or getting up to save the chickens. Probably just my presence out there was a great inhibitor). Anyway, every morning my dad would come to the back door of the house and whistle. He had a most shrill whistle! It was very loud, and it was quite impressive the way he could put two fingers in his mouth on his lips a certain way and make this amazingly cutting sound that carried for a very long way. Hearing that whistle, I would stick my skinny arm out of the tent, signaling that I was up and ready to feed the chickens. On the weekends, though, I would feed the chickens only after the paper route was delivered.

Anyway, when my route was delivered and I had ridden my bike up the driveway, parked it, and entered the house, I would go into the kitchen, where Daddy would be creating a batch of pancakes for breakfast. Every week he tried something new: banana, blueberry, strawberry, combinations, you name it. (Once he even tried orange, and we both agreed that didn't work.) Every week it was a surprise to get home and find out what he was creating. We would sit at the table and enjoy the pancakes together, just my dad and me—nobody else was up yet.

I hope I have given my kids something like that to remember. Those Sunday mornings with my dad were a real gift. I did that route for a few years, and then something happened. I think I was growing up and didn't notice it, but time passed. A lot of time.

## Chapter Forty-Four

In 2005, Pegi and I went to the Rock and Roll Hall of Fame ceremony in New York, where I was inducting Chrissie Hynde and the Pretenders, who we love. She is one rockin' woman. We had a great time there. I had been to the Hall of Fame ceremony a few times before. Once in 1995, when I was being inducted myself, Pegi and I had flown out with David Briggs and Bettina, his wife. On the flight out to NYC from San Francisco, we were smoking weed on the Warner Brothers plane, living it up and celebrating the occasion, when the captain came back and busted us. He was very upset. I guess they thought they might get high or something because they were breathing the same air.

Anyway, in 2005 when I got up at the hotel the morning after inducting Chrissie and the Pretenders, Pegi was down in the gym working out and I was talking with Amber, Topher White (her boyfriend at the time), and Ben Young in our suite, looking at the great view of Central Park. I noticed suddenly that I couldn't see very well. What appeared to be a shard of glass was in my vision, kind of like looking through a broken mirror. When I described it, everyone was alarmed. When I called the doctor, he told me to lie down and call him when it stopped. I went into the bedroom and lay down. Eventually it grew and blocked my eye before it went away. I had noticed that it was in both my eyes and did not go away when I closed one or the other. So it was in my brain. That was very disconcerting. I had a headache. I called Dr. Rock Positano, who was my New York doctor. He was referred by Marsha Vlasic, who had been my agent and a very close friend to Pegi and me for many years. Marsha booked all of my own shows and the Bridge School concerts, and her husband, Peter, often accompanied her to the performances.

After Dr. Rock arranged with experts in neurology, we went to the doctor's office, and he set me up with a neurosurgeon and scheduled some tests. They were magnetic imaging tests to look at the inside of my brain. Then I met the neurosurgeon, whose name was Dr. Dexter Sun; I liked him immediately because he was very focused and friendly.

A few days later, Pegi and I went to see him in his office to review the tests. We were waiting in a little room to view the images when the nurse came in and said the doctor would be right out. That was odd, because we were planning on going into the room to see him. He walked out to us with a handful of films. He put them up on a light board to look at. This was not normal, was my first thought. Pegi and I held hands. He explained the different parts of the brain and settled on an irregular-looking part of the image that resembled the state of Florida, hanging off the southeastern United States.

He said to us, "This is what I found. It is not an emergency right this instant, but we have to take this out of your brain as soon as we can. This is a very bad thing to have staying in there." He then showed me how it was like a balloon or tube that had expanded in one area but not burst, and that it had blown out again and again and again. Several times to be sure. He said the surgeon who could remove it for me was Dr. Yves Pierre Gobin, who would be back in New York in ten days.

Pegi and I left the office and went back to the hotel. We were scheduled to go to Canada, and I was supposed to do something at the Juno Awards in a couple of weeks. It was a huge thing in my home country, recognizing Canadian musical talent. I did not want to perform on TV or be under pressure and was feeling a little shocky. I was not told that I couldn't travel, just to take it easy.

I decided that waiting around a week in New York would be impossible for me. We booked studio time in Nashville when I decided that the best thing to do was make some music. I began writing an album of new music called *Prairie Wind*. I felt it would keep me occupied until I had to go into the hospital. I called Ben Keith, and he began rounding up all my friends to do a recording session; Ben always was the kingpin for my Tennessee recordings. Pegi and I flew to Nashville together.

In Nashville we set up at Masterlink recording studios, formerly Monument Records' recording studio, where Roy Orbison had recorded years before, and began recording with Chad Hailey and Rob Clarke. We stayed at the Hermitage, and I wrote whenever I wasn't in the studio recording. Pegi stayed with me the whole time. At one point, in the middle of the sessions, Pegi and I flew back to New York to meet the surgeon, Dr. Gobin, and he scheduled the operation for a week later. We returned to Nashville to complete the recording. I did a lot of eating and gained about ten pounds in the week we were there. We did the whole album except for one or two songs, and then Pegi and I flew back to New York for the operation.

News was getting out among my friends. Quincy Jones called at the hotel and comforted Pegi, having gone through the same thing himself. Bob Dylan sent me a thoughtful collection of gospel music I think I mentioned earlier; he really is quite a musicologist with a deep knowledge of the roots of popular song, and his gift, which was beautifully presented in a wooden box, struck me as very thoughtful—I really appreciated it. Willie Nelson called me the night before the operation and wished me well. It was reassuring to hear from these musical friends. I really appreciated that. Pegi was right by my side.

Anyway, the time was upon us. The day before the operation, the surgeon, Dr. Gobin, assured me that the procedure was something that had been done with no complications many times at this very hospital by himself and his team. Of course there always is risk. I signed the normal paperwork so Pegi would have all the authority she needed if it was called for, then we went to bed. When we woke up we went right to Admitting in the hospital at some very early hour of the morning. They came to get me and I said, "See you soon," to Pegi. We exchanged a deep look. I was then taken to a small room and sedated.

When I woke up it was all over. I was in recovery. My leg was secured so that I didn't move it and disturb the wound where they had gone in through my femoral artery and up to my brain, where several platinum coils (like tiny little Slinkies) were carefully placed in the aneurysm. They would attract scar tissue, which would fill the entire problem area and redirect the blood flow correctly from that moment on. I had to stay absolutely still for about forty-eight hours, but was then allowed to go back to the hotel and begin slowly resuming my normal life. I returned to the hotel, happy to be out of the hospital. Following doctor's orders, I took it easy. A lot had happened. I did not want to do much or be booked for anything where I had to be there. I was scared to think about going to Canada. We moved slowly. Pegi was with me all the time, and Marsha and Peter were in close contact with us. Marsha was a good friend to Pegi throughout this whole situation.

After a couple of days in the hotel, I was stable, and since Pegi had previously had brain surgery of her own, and since we knew we had the best team ever to look at her radiological results, we decided to get her checked out too. While she was doing that, I decided I needed to go for a little walk down to a restaurant we knew. I was going with Eric Johnson, Elliot, and his son Zack. It was my first time away from the hotel or Pegi. We left the hotel, moving slowly along near Madison Avenue, and were half a block down the sidewalk when I took one more step and felt a pop above my thigh. My leg got really hot. I noticed it was wet. My shoe was filling up with blood and my pants were soaked. I called to Eric and turned back toward the hotel. I was weak. He helped me walk. I tried to make it to the hotel, but started fading fast near the front door.

I eventually made it to the elevator with Eric's help. We were there waiting for the elevator. I'm so glad it didn't come! That would have been so wrong! I would have had to go up and come all the way back down to go to the hospital, wasting precious time. I collapsed right in the lobby, crumpling slowly downward until I was on my back, my blood running all over the floor.

Eric was right there. He had figured it out and was applying massive pressure to my leg where the wound was, holding back the flow of blood. The incision point in my artery had failed to hold. I do credit Eric, absolutely, with saving my life. No question about it. We stayed there for a while on the floor, waiting for the ambulance and paramedics. Eric was holding my leg in the air and pressing on the wound. The hotel was calling for help. Elliot called Pegi to say what had happened and that there was an ambulance coming to pick me up; Pegi, who was getting ready for a CT scan of her own brain, went straight to the hospital to meet me. After about ten minutes, certainly no more than that, the paramedics arrived. I was on a stretcher, moving into the ambulance, and one very bright and strong EMT guy was saying, "Neil, stay focused! Stay right here." I tried to say something funny, but nothing came out. "Dropping! Dropping!" someone's voice said.

Bright lights and a siren came on above my head. "Which one?" "Lenox Hill!" "Not close enough, which one?" We sped through New York City.

The one face kept saying, "Neil, talk to me. What's your name? Where are we?" I looked at him and tried to speak. Tried to tell a joke again. I was full of them. But nothing came out. "Okay, fluid is in, fluid is in!" "We got him." "How do you feel, Neil? What's up? What's your name?" "Stabilizing!" said a voice. Then one guy kept yelling, "Stay with me! Stay here. No sleeping. Stay here!"

Then I felt really cold and good. My body was vibrating wildly! I was freezing! They turned off the street and I was on the runway to Emergency. We stayed there for a few beats, then into Emergency. A nurse put warm blankets over me. One of the doctors on the original operating team was with me then. The team that did the operation! I was back there!

He said, "I got you, Neil. You will be fine, just don't move your leg." He was pressing right where Eric had been pressing. I was starting to get warm again, but I was still shaking uncontrollably. A nurse brought more warm blankets. I was moved to a bed in my own room overlooking the river and a huge bridge into Manhattan. I was sedated, and when I finally awoke, I was with a very nice and floaty old black lady nurse from South Carolina. She moved slowly around the room, seemingly on air. She was my angel guide.

"You are fine now," she said. "He doesn't want you yet, or He would have taken you."

It was dawn. Headlights were crossing the bridge in the fog like diamond water drops dripping from a hanging leaf, continually forming and falling; commuters heading to work. She continued floating around the room, telling me how fine this day was. I will never forget her. I may even see her again. Pegi had arranged for me to have extra night care so that I was never alone, both after the original procedure and this emergency. So it was Pegi who provided my guardian angel.

The original procedure was on the Monday after Easter Sunday, and we were scheduled to fly to Winnipeg at the end of the week for the Juno event. It was a big deal because I was from Winnipeg and the Junos had never been held there. We had been trying to be quiet about the medical situation, but after the disaster happened, realizing there was no way we could make the Juno ceremonies, we alerted the family to what was happening so they wouldn't read any sensationalized stuff and be scared. Then we put out a press release explaining why I wouldn't be there. The folks at the Canadian Consulate in New York City were kind enough to offer us an opportunity to watch the Junos on satellite at the residence, so we did.

## Chapter Forty-Five

With the Lincvolt project in its fourth year, I am becoming much more experienced and less idealistic about what is possible than I was at the outset, but I still have the feeling that Lincvolt can make a really strong point about what is possible. I am trying to make a luxury car that has the ability to be environmentally responsible. I am realistic about what people want in this country. Small cars will never be what *everyone* wants, so big cars and pickup trucks need to be environmentally friendly. That will make a big difference. The people who like luxury vehicles have the ability to pay for this innovation, and they will if it's available.

Granted, a 1959 Lincoln Continental convertible is not necessarily the answer, but it is a great way to draw attention to the possibilities for change in design of large luxury cars and trucks. This car draws a crowd wherever it goes. I write articles for the Lincvolt website we created to tell the ongoing story of the development (www.lincvolt.com). It has been a joy. The ups and downs have been many, and I have made my share of mistakes, but I love this idea. It is worth it to me. One article from the *Lincvolt Gazette* reads:

A Ghost from the Past

Lincvolt is a constantly evolving vehicle. We have just announced our new A123 Battery system, far superior in every respect to the previous battery pack. We have made many more changes in design and we will be announcing them as the weeks unfold. The work will be done in California, home of the greatest hot rods on earth, both in Northern California and Southern California. We will be telling you more about that, too.

Here at Lincvolt.com, you have seen Lincvolt at Brizio Street Rods in South San Francisco for the last couple of weeks. A bare metal body, painstakingly restored at Camilleri's in Sacramento, is now covered with primer and ready for the rebuild. What you can't see is that the suspension and parts of the power train have been put in place or prepared for placement under Lincvolt's massive and beautiful uni-body during the last weeks.

Lincvolt has been redesigned in and out. When all of the new components are installed and tested, as a final stage, an aerodynamic covering will shroud the underbody, reducing drag and allowing Lincvolt to cut through the air more efficiently than ever before at high speeds. We expect the undershrouding to have more of an effect the faster the car travels. These measurements will allow us to see how much energy is consumed for highway cruising. A typical 400–500 mile day at highway speeds of 70 mph or more on changing terrain is nothing for a Continental, so she has to be ready for that challenge. Many of the changes we are about to announce are designed to make long trips at highway speeds a reality. This is what the Ford Motor Company's Lincoln Continental was designed for, not just arriving in style like a '50s dream. That is why Lincvolt is destined to be a Continental Electro Cruiser like the world has never seen, like a ghost from the past, arriving smoothly and silently at every destination.

You can see the love I have for this project, this car. I am so into this that I sometimes wonder where all the energy to keep doing it is coming from. I am not exactly sure, but it feels so good! Basically I just love the car. The idea to do this just sprang to mind one day as I was looking at the car, knowing what a guzzler it was. Since I was a kid I have loved big cars. It's just in me. I wanted to do something. Try to make a difference somehow. I didn't care if I failed or not, I just wanted to try. Having no knowledge is sometimes exactly what is needed to find a solution, so I qualified. I have come to think that electric power generated from natural sources like wind and solar is the optimum solution, but we need something created domestically to keep the power flowing, a fuel from the United States that does not require wars.

The movie about Lincvolt's odyssey is a monster project. After four full years of work, we have time lapse of almost all of the projects in the various shops. There was some pretty flaky stuff happening in the beginning, and I was so enthusiastic about it all that I couldn't really see what was going on. Using water for fuel was one of those things. We spent a year plus on that. The guys I was working with believed it could happen. Light was finally shed. Then we moved out of Wichita back to California and eventually had our fire accident (or thermal runaway, as it is sometimes called) because one of our team made an error and left an untested system plugged in. It was a human error, not a fault of tested battery technology.

When the car burned to the ground, it gave us a good opportunity to start over with the insurance money. And when everyone saw I was not pausing, that I was continuing with the project and was doubling down to get it right, they all started helping me like never before. I am overwhelmed with the support we are getting from Ford Motors, AVL, A123 Systems, UQM, and Brizio Street Rods!

The movie, though, is a whole other thing.

Shakey Pictures has an epic on its hands! My favorite part by far is that first ride out to Wichita in the original car with Larry Johnson. We had such a great time! I am so glad to have that memory and a recording of it. It is a beautiful thing to have, and it makes me feel so happy! All of the footage surrounding the Wichita build may end up on the cutting-room floor, though. Looking back, it doesn't make me feel very good, because the task of building the car became so difficult. But I am going to go through it, pull out the gems, and tell the story. Johnathan Goodwin had great energy and enthusiasm for the car. He gave us a good "proof of concept" and proved an electric car with a generator was feasible, but we kept getting derailed by undisciplined process, lack of planning, and not enough attention to detail. He gave it everything he had.

Anyway, I became so emotionally involved, I was talking to the car. It got personal. The movie is going to be nuts. We did a lot of episodes in my junkyard at the ranch, recapping progress. The one we did after Larry passed is going to be hard to watch. There is a scene where Larry's son, Ben Johnson, and I are driving in the car and talking about how we are going to handle Larry's passing in the film. Ben is editing this with me and is the cinematographer as well, now that Larry is gone from our lives. Not really gone; just physically not here with us. There is a lot of reality in this project. It is a labor of love. We are in the editing process now, and Ben has made a portable editing room we can take anywhere. Just the sort of thing his father would have done. I am constantly amazed by Ben's uncanny ability to continue in his dad's footsteps while completely retaining his individuality. Writing this book and finishing this film with Ben Johnson are my two big goals right now.

Today I have zero interest in touring or playing music, but that is not a threat to me. It has happened before. The muse is out and about and no doubt visiting with someone else, making magic. A little more rest in Hawaii and I will be ready to dive back into the Lincvolt movie with Ben Johnson. What a journey of discovery that will be.

## Chapter Forty-Six

I became very interested in filmmaking around the time I was recording *Harvest*. I was looking for another outlet, and film had a lot to offer, especially when combined with music. I saw it as a logical extension of my work. My first movie, with Larry Johnson and David Myers, *Journey Through the Past*, was a wild and crazy experiment that showed no fear. Larry and I, along with David Myers and Frederic Underhill producing, fashioned this documentary/fantasy piece and completed it in 1972. It was a great experience and the birth of Shakey Pictures.

My favorite filmmaker was Jean-Luc Godard. I loved long uninterrupted shots that played out and told a story. I was not a big fan of fast cutting and preferred to not use dissolves. I learned so much from David Myers. He was a gifted cinematographer. I learned how one camera could cover a live event and provide everything the editor needed to cut a sequence, and I learned the virtues of a fixed lens in documentary filming. David's 5:9 lens is still my favorite tool to create a documentary. I was editing on a KEM Universal table, an electromechanical editing machine that was able to run three reels at the same time, and I was learning as I went along.

It was all new and very captivating. It was an incredible experience, an absorbing way to edit film, so creative and empowering to put the pictures and music together and create a whole new experience.

We started editing in my house, and when the ranch studio was finished being built, we moved over there and continued. It is impossible to explain what that movie, *Journey Through the Past*, is or what it means; you just need to see it to understand. It is not *Citizen Kane* or *Gone With the Wind*. (The reviewers made that pretty evident.) I am not a mainstream movie guy. But it was a *way* early music video long form, in some obscure ways. We were proud of it. I wish Larry Johnson was still around so we could continue our life's work together. I guess that's why they call it "life's work."

We began by going to the South and doing some filming in and around the Carolinas and then Nashville. I had released "Southern Man" and wanted some aerial footage to use with the guitar jamming instrumentals. There was a good CSNY version we had on film that I wanted to embellish. While we were in Nashville, we started traveling around doing documentary shoots. We did one in a junkyard and one at a barge launching. Anything was fair game. We went to a radio station and I did an interview with the DJ, and we shot that. It is interesting to see that episode today because it shows what radio used to be like when there were still real people involved. I mean when the DJs chose their own content to play as well as the top hits and weren't following a formula devised by a media marketing company that had been hired by the station. (There was a kid in the reception area, Gil Gilliam, who had a unique look because he had a liver problem and had grown up with it. He was very talented, energetic, and outgoing. I liked him immediately. He had a great look, attitude, and presence. We asked him to continue with us in the film and he did a great job.)

Back in California we shot an old car traveling through redwood country and followed it to an old gas station. We put together a cast of characters inside the station and did a scene there.

Though all of the scenes were interrelated, there was really no thread of continuity that was obvious. I came up with a story about a graduate from school who was dropped off in the desert by some characters: an Italian mafioso, a Catholic cardinal, and an army general. They had dropped off this beat-up and bloodied graduate kid they had in the trunk, still in his cap and gown, out in the desert, and when he got up and started walking, we followed him until he arrived at the Pacific Ocean via Las Vegas and a lot of other places. Gil, the kid we met in the radio station, showed up at the gas station's restaurant with a card shark and they were sharing a booth. There was also a preacher walking and dancing with a truck. He eventually showed up at the gas station, too. There was a guy walking on the beach with his truck and the truck was talking to him. By the time the graduate got to the beach, he was a junkie. He kept his kit in a Bible he carried around. He broke it out and started to shoot up. A bunch of riders in black robes and hoods came charging down the beach at him on their horses. There was a Bible-thumping revival.

No beginning. No real ending. This was Shakey Pictures in full bloom.

We loved it!

We had the most fun making it and had no fear. We had our first screening at the Fox Theatre in Redwood City, California.

Shakey Pictures has a very particular fan base. People yelled at me after we first screened it for an audience. A mother who brought her kid to the screening was very offended. I completely forgot about the rating thing; the film wasn't really appropriate for a small child. It didn't make the Oscars, either.

It can be safely said that *Journey Through the Past* was ahead of its time. Of course, I paid for it all myself. There was no one going to take a chance on a hippie with a list of ideas and some friends with cameras, even if they were classics like David Myers and Larry Johnson. It was a very cheap film to make.

## Chapter Forty-Seven

Today I got another FedEx package from Gary Burden. Over the years I have received hundreds of these. Today's is a songbook proof for *Rust Never Sleeps*. These books just keep coming out. It seems like we have done this one before. This is a new edition with a new publisher, and we are doing it again. Looking through the Pegi Young and Joel Bernstein pictures, I remember how wonderful that 1978 Rust Never Sleeps tour really was!

It all started on the *WN Ragland*. We were in the Virgin Islands—Pegi, pregnant with Ben, Captain Roger Katz and his girlfriend, Suzanne (Pusette), David Cline and his girlfriend, Leslie Tellier, David Briggs and Connie Moskos, and some crew members, notably Reynoud Bos, our sailing Aussie doctor, and Joe Trailor, a sailor and shipbuilder who was now helping out crewing with us. We were down in the Grenadines, near Grenada, and had gone ashore in Saint George's to buy supplies. I picked up a school notebook, the kind with lines drawn on the pages. It was rough

Backstage with Larry Johnson (Larry in blackface for a Rust Never Sleeps show) and stage manager and friend Tim Foster, 1978.

paper, like we used to have in the Canadian schools when I was a kid. It had a political leader on the cover, a prime minister probably. I suddenly came up with an idea for the next Crazy Horse tour!

It was going to be from the standpoint of a young boy dreaming. All the amps were huge and there was going to be a giant microphone. It was going to be like Tom Thumb in reverse. The roadies were all like Jawas from *Star Wars*! A cone-headed wizard was the lighting director, and some scientists in lab coats were the sound mixers. It was all like a hospital experiment, with the scientists appearing in lab coats during the performance taking notes on clipboards and the Jawa-cloaked roadies with their illuminated eyes raising and lowering amp cases over the top of the amps from the ceiling by pulling on ropes with pulleys.

A thunderstorm like Woodstock would have a "no rain" chant, and announcements about the bad acid that should not be taken would be played over the PA. The show started with "The Star-Spangled Banner" played by Jimi Hendrix as the roadies (Jawas) raised the big mic into position like the soldiers at Iwo Jima with the flag. It continued with things like that for about a hundred minutes.

I took the little Grenada notebook and drew charts with song titles, effects, action, lighting, sound cues, all in a sort of data-based sequence I had handwritten in this grade school book. When I showed this to Tim Foster, my stage manager, who loved doing things theatrically, he got really into it! He dove right in and explained to the crew that they would all be wearing these outfits and be onstage doing things throughout the show. I was not using actors; I was using my road crew: Larry Johnson as assistant director, his girlfriend, Miss Jeanne Field, as production, Briggs as onstage sound, Stephen Cohen as lighting director, Sal Trentino my amp tech, Joel Bernstein my tuner (and also a great photographer who took all the pictures)—everyone in the whole crew was involved! It was quite a shock when everyone showed up for a rehearsal at the Cow Palace in San Francisco and learned what we were doing and that we only had a couple of days to learn it.

The "roadeyes" (the Rust tour name for roadies) put on their black face and head racks holding the two battery-powered lights placed to shine as eyes under a giant hood. Crazy Horse had the music down and the crew knew the songs and instruments, but that was the easy part. The rest of it put everyone in a state of shock. Our first show was in a few days. We had all the costumes made and the props built. Tim Foster and Larry Johnson did a superb job making this concept happen. It was billed as "Rust Never Sleeps: A Concert Fantasy," and it was even stranger for the audience because my brand-new album, *Comes a Time*, had just been released.

Comes a Time had been a completely different type of music recorded in Nashville with a different band! At that time I was in the habit of performing all of my new songs live first, recording them that way, and then taking the audience out of the mixes. Then I released them as studio albums. Crazy Horse was great live, and that was the most fun way to do it.

Of course, that was before the Internet, and it's not realistic to work that way anymore. Any experiment I try onstage is thrown up on YouTube, where people who think they know what I should be doing start shooting holes in it before it's even finished. This is the single most daunting challenge the Internet has provided, along with all the good things. The stage used to be my lab, where I could experiment in front of a live audience and see how it reacted and—more important—how I felt while I was doing it. That is how I created and adjusted most of my best plays, tuning them by feel. I try to avoid reading about myself on the Web for that reason.

Now I try to work things out in private while I develop ideas. That way I have a chance to present the first time to a large audience, the way I envision it. Unfortunately that is not as adventuresome for me. The first couple of performances of *Rust Never Sleeps* were full of disasters, from things not working right to not working at all. If that was today, the rap on the show would have been so bad on the Net that the show would have been killed before it even was fully born. That's life!

Things change. *Rust Never Sleeps* was named Album of the Year that year by *Rolling Stone*. The production of the concert got some awards as well and was seen as bold at the least. That made Briggs and me feel pretty good. The movie we made of the concert is one of my favorites.

#	ACTION	EFX	LITES	ROAD EYES
1	~~SET UP~~		FADE IN STAGE	BRING OUT MIC
2	"	STAR SPANGLED BANNER	STAGE	IWOJIMA/MIC
3	SET UP PIANO	DAY IN THE LIFE	STAGE	LIFT ANVIL CASE STAIRWAY IN PLACE
4	NEIL WAKES UP		STAGE/FADER DELUXE	ROAD EYES SCATTER TO HIDDEN POSITIONS
5	SUGAR MTN 12 STR G AMP		STAGE/FADER DELUXE	RODIS STAY HID.
6	NEIL DOWN STAIRCASE		STAGE/FADER DELUXE	STAY HID
7	I AM A CHILD		STAGE	HID
8	COMES A TIME		STAGE	HID
9	ALREADY ONE		STAGE	HID
10	GOLD RUSH		STAGE/PIANO	HID
11	THRASHER		SPOT	HID
12	OUT OF THE BLUE		STAGE	HID

#	ACTION	EFX	LITES	ROAD EYES
13	NEIL IN SLEEPING BAG		STAGE	PEEKING 'ROUND AMPS
14		WOODSTOCK	FADE TO HALF	DRAG BAG OFF STAGE
15	SETUP AMPS STAGE PIANO DRUMS	WOODSTOCK	HOUSE TO HALF LITES	SETUP AMPS Y DRUMS ENTER DR DECIBEL Y CONE
16	SETUP	WOODSTOCK	STAGE	LIFT ROAD CASES DOWN DROM GRAPHIC
17	CHEK INSTRUMENTS	WOODSTOCK	STAGE	TUNE Y CHECK INSTRUMENTS MAC ON ENTER CLONE
18	CHEK SOUND	WOODSTOCK	STAGE	DISROBE RODIS BECOME BAND
19	WHEN YOU DANCE		STAGE	SCATTER TO POSITIONS LEAVING DR DECIBEL CONE Y CLONE
20	THE LONER		STAGE	
21	TUNE UP	TONE ON CUE	STAGE	BRING OUT TUNING FORK MAKE TONE LEAVE STAGE

Original performance notes and cues for
the Rust Never Sleeps tour, 1978.

#	ACTION	EFX	LITES	ROAD EYES
22	BRIGHT SUNNY DAY		STAGE	HID
23	WELFARE MOTHERS		STAGE	HID
24	COME ON BABY LETS GO DOWNTOWN		STAGE	HID
25	STORM	WOODSTOCK RAIN	BLACK WITH STROBE	BRING OUT 12 STRING
26	STORM ENDS	WOODSTOCK RAIN FADE	FADE IN SPOT CENTERSTAGE	BRING IN & SET PIANO
27	NEEDLE & DAMAGE DONE		SPOT	
28	LOTTA LOVE 12 OR 6...		STAGE	
29	PIANO STRIKE		STAGE	ROADEYES STRIKE PIANO

#	ACTION	EFX	LITES	ROAD EYES
30	SEDAN DELIVERY (BRING BACK)		STAGE	HID
31	POWDER FINGER		GROUP	HID
32	TUNING	TONE	STAGE	BRING OUT TUNING FORK MAKE TONE LEAVE STAGE
33	" "	SEAGULLS & WAVES	STAGE	HID
34	CORTEZ THE KILLER	FADE WAVE SEAGULLS	STAGE	STAY HID
35	CINNAMON GIRL		STAGE	KEEP HID
36	TUNE & SET UP HURRICANE	TONE	STAGE	BRING OUT FORK ETC FLY IN STRING MAN BRING IN & SET FANS
37	HURRICANE		STAGE	OPERATE FANS
38	COMPANY BOW		STAGE	ON STAGE
39	APPLAUSE	WOODSTOCK BEGIN & UP	STAGE	ON STAGE
40	BAND LEAVES		GROUP/STAGE	ON STAGE CHECK EQUIPMENT

#	ACTION	EFX	LITES	ROAD EYES
41	BAND RETURNS	~~~~ STObK	STAGE + ~~~~	
42	OUT OF THE BLUE			
43	STRIKE		HOUSE LITES	1 ROADEYE PLAYS ~~~~ PIANO OTHERS TEAR DOWN
44	. .		. .	DROP ANVIL CASES

Chapter Forty-Eight

It's better to burn out than to fade away.

John Lennon disagreed with that.

Kurt Cobain quoted it in his last letter.

People have asked me about that line since I first sang it in 1978. I wrote it referring to the rock and roll star, meaning that if you go while you are burning hottest, then that is how you are remembered, at the peak of your powers forever. That is rock and roll.

At sixty-five, it seems that I may not be at the peak of my rock and roll powers. But that is not for sure. The idea that I should have died earlier is not the point. There really is more to life than its charged peak, because other things continue to grow and develop long afterward, enriching and growing the spirit and soul.

I wrote that song right after the death of Elvis Presley, one of my childhood heroes, and sang it first for Bruce "BJ" (Baby John) Hines, part of the original Crazy Horse family. He was visiting the ranch for some reason, and I had just finished the song. It was written as an acoustic song. Rather reflective.

During the filming of *Human Highway* when I played it with Devo, Booji Boy sang it in his crib, pounding on a synthesizer. I played it on Old Black. I remember seeing the video of that, and the peace signs and doves on Old Black's strap played against the visual of Booji Boy, and the image created a feeling I can't describe. It was the feeling of the hippie generation and the new punk generation juxtaposed. Devo's influence and where they came from is something that I have never seen adequately described. They were true originals. It was just one of those moments.

That was the defining original rock version. Booji Boy added some new lyrics and sang, "It's better to burn out, 'cause rust never sleeps" or "than it is to rust." I'm not sure which. One of the Devo members later told me that there was a sign on a shop in Akron, Ohio, where Devo originated, that read RUST NEVER SLEEPS. It was a maintenance and rust-prevention service. As is the case with many of my songs, some of it came from real-life things other people said or did.

Another time that happened was on my bus with Poncho. We were cruising along in the mountains between Spokane and Seattle. Something about the Berlin Wall and the recent unrest was on TV. "Keep on rocking in the free world," said Poncho. I said, "What?" Then I wrote that whole song and we did it that night. Poncho thought he should have credit for that and told me years later he had always felt that way. Now he gets credited and paid whenever that song is involved.

It's part of the process. I just do what I do and keep my ears and eyes open. Things are happening all the time. You put it out there and shit happens. Yesterday we were on our way to the movies and I heard some guy pouring his heart out in some song on the radio. I said to Ben Bourdon, Ben Young's caregiver and friend, "That sounds like Jimmy Fallon doing me. What the heck does that mean?" It was funny. It really did sound like me. We laughed our asses off! Ben Young thought that was really hysterical. Fallon sounded like a twenty-year-old me. Maybe not as good. Maybe better.

How about that Jimmy Fallon? He is a classic. He does me so well, I don't have to bother anymore. He looks great, and I am an old guy who doesn't want to be on TV, so Jimmy has done all of my television performances for the last year or so. Thank you, Jimmy!

As an aside to you, the reader: Writing this has been a lot of fun so far, even the tough parts where I have lost some of my best friends. As we make our way through this experience and I grab some thoughts out of the bag while waiting patiently for ideas that come out of the blue, inevitably we are going to get to some of the longest run-on sentences in history, ending in places I may have been avoiding, but not if I can help it! Seriously, though, there are still quite a few boulders to climb out from under.

Chapter Forty-Nine

In August 1968, Briggs and I began making our first record to-gether, my first solo. This was a big thing to me. I was finally going to create my masterpiece. Buffalo Springfield was fine, but I was creatively frustrated, with a lot more to give. I think Stephen felt the same way about CSN. He had a lot of arranging and production concepts, just like I did, that he wanted to try; Greene and Stone's production of Buffalo Springfield had made us both interested in doing it ourselves. Just singing on some of the songs was not good enough for me anymore. I was writing every day. I picked up the guitar first thing in the morning and started right in. I was imagining arrangements and couldn't wait to get started recording. Looking back, I don't know why we didn't just do solo records and keep the Springfield together as well. That might have worked. Don't look back.

Elliot made a solo deal for me with Reprise, and David booked some time at Wally Heider Studios on Selma Avenue in Holly-

Formal portrait, sitting in the Big Chair at home in Topanga Canyon, with Danny Whitten behind me, while recording Everybody Knows This Is Nowhere, *1969.*

wood. A lot of great records had been made in that place. I really respected the Beach Boys, who had worked there quite a bit, and Wally Heider had an engineer named Frank Dimidio who had built some incredibly good-sounding recording equipment. The place was state-of-the–art, with 8-track tape machines and a Dimidio recording console, known in town as the Dimidio Board. George Grantham and Jim Messina were the rhythm section, and I was recording by overdubbing most of the other instruments. Soon Briggs discovered that I needed to drink some beer to do vocals. In those days I didn't sing live; I overdubbed. I was very unsure of my singing, especially after my previous experiences in the studio with Greene and Stone producing Buffalo Springfield.

They tried feeding me amphetamines to get me loosened up enough to sing "Burned" with the Springfield, a song I wrote about having a seizure. Now there is a hit song idea! I sang "Burned" for about four hours after it had been recorded, unable to stop. David Briggs suggested an Oly—Olympia Beer was my favorite. It loosened me up quite a bit, and I actually sang a song, "Last Trip to Tulsa," that was about ten minutes long, without overdubs. Once I got loose and in the groove I was fine, although it still sounded like me. Briggs always said my voice was good. It was unique, and that's what we needed to make it.

Briggs and I always had a good groove working together. For another recording session at Sunwest Recording Studios on Sunset Boulevard, Jack Nitzsche came in and did "The Old Laughing Lady" and "I've Loved Her So Long" from my first solo album with me. Later on, Briggs and I did some work there with Crazy Horse. Pat

Boone owned Sunwest. I bought some monitors from the studio that I still have today in my living room. They are totally antiques now.

There's a quote from Briggs that I want to share, which comes from an interview (that I asked him to do) with Jimmy McDonough for his book *Shakey*. Here it is:

I can teach you everything I know in an hour. Everything. That's how simple it is to make records. Nowadays, buddy, the technician is in control of the medium. They try to make out like it's black magic, or flyin' a spaceship. I can teach anybody on this planet how to fly the spaceship. If you look at the modern console, there'll be thirty knobs—high frequency, low frequency, mid-frequency, all notched in little tiny, tiny, teeny *tiny degrees— and it's all bullshit. All this stuff doesn't matter, and you can't be intimidated. You just ignore it—*all *of it.*

I walk into studios with the biggest console known to mankind, and I ask for the schematic and say, "Can you patch from here to here and eliminate *the ENTIRE board?" I just run it right into the tape machines. All the modern consoles, they're all made by hacks, they're not worth a shit, they sound terrible. None of it touches the old tube stuff—like the green board from Heider's.* It has *two tone controls—high end, low end and a pan knob—and that's* it. *I had great good fortune when I was a kid and started makin' records. I made 'em at Wally Heider's, Gold Star, so all the people that taught me were Frank Dimidio, Dave Gold, Stan Ross, Dean Jensen—these guys were the geniuses of the music business, still are.*

They taught me more about sound and how sound is made and the principles of doing it, and it's unshakably correct *what they said to me: You get a great sound at the source. Put the correct mike in front of the source, get it to the tape* the shortest possible route—*that's how you get a great sound. That's how you do it. All other ways are work. The biggest moment of my life—the one I haven't been able to get past ever, really—is 1961, when I first got to LA. I got invited to Radio Recorders to see Ray Charles, and I walk into the studio, and Ray's playin' all the piano parts with his left hand, reading a braille score with his right hand, singing the vocal* live *while a full orchestra played behind him. So I sat there and I watched. And I went, "*This *is how records are made. Put everybody in the fuckin' room and* off we go.*" In those days everybody knew they had to go in, get their dick hard at the same time and deliver. And three hours later they walked out the fuckin' door with a record in their pocket, man.*

Of course, in those days they didn't have eight-, sixteen-, twenty-four-, forty-eight-, sixty-four-track recording, ad nauseam, to fuck people up, and that is what fucked up the recording business and the musicians of today, by the way—fucked 'em all up to where they'll never be the same, in my opinion. People realized they could do their part . . . later. *Play their part and* fix *it* later. *And with rock and roll, the more you think, the more you* stink.

It's very easy for people to forget what rock and roll really is. Look man, *I'm* forty-seven years old, *and I grew up in* Wyoming, *and I* stole *cars and drove* five hundred miles *to watch Little Richard, and I wanna tell you somethin'—when I saw this nigger come out in a gold suit, fuckin' hair flyin', and leap up onstage and come down on his piano bangin' and goin' fuckin' nuts in* Salt Lake City, *I went, "Hey man, I wanna be like* him. *This is what I want." Even* today *he's a scary dude. He's the real thing. Rock and roll is not sedate, not safe, has truly nothin' to do with money or anything. It's like wind, rain, fire— it's elemental. Fourteen-year-old kids, they don't think, they feel. Rock and roll is fire, man, FIRE. It's the* attitude. *It's thumbing your nose at the world.*

It's a load. It's such a load that it burns people out after a few years. Even the best of 'em burn out. People get old—they forget what it's like to be a kid, they're responsible, they're this and they're that. . . . You can't have it both ways. You're a rock and roller. Or you're not.

I wanna tell you somethin': Neil's never been insecure about anything in his fuckin' life. First among equals is Neil Young, and it's always *been that way. When Neil's got his ax in hand, it's like the Hulk. His aura becomes solid—he becomes eight feet tall, six feet wide. The only guy other than John Lennon who can actually go from folk to country to full orchestra. The* only *guy. I think when it's all written down, he will unquestionably stand in the top five that ever made rock and roll.*

During these recording sessions at Sunwest, my love affair with cars continued. I bought a 1934 Bentley close-coupled Mulliner Coupe that Briggs and I cruised in between the Hollywood studios and Topanga Canyon while we were recording. It had a lever on the floor that bypassed the muffler for high-speed efficiency that was really a cool feature for saving fuel. It was loud as hell. Briggs and I cruised home in that car every night after the sessions, grooving on the cutout muffler bypass and the hairy sound it made as we flew along the interstate and into Topanga Canyon's backroads.

When we finished our first record, Reprise had some new technology they wanted to try with us. It was called the Haeco-CSG system, a new way to produce albums. According to the good folks at Wikipedia:

> *The Haeco-CSG or Holzer Audio Engineering–Compatible Stereo Generator system is an analog electronic device and method developed by Howard Holzer, Chief Engineer at A&M Records in Hollywood, California. His company, Holzer Audio Engineering, developed the system in the 1960s during the years of transition from monaural to stereophonic popular music recording . . . The idea behind Haeco-CSG was to create stereophonic vinyl LP records that when played on monaural equipment would allow the two-channel stereo mix to automatically "fold-down" properly to a single monaural channel . . . Generally speaking, Haeco-CSG has a degrading effect on the performance of both stereo and mono sounds processed through the system. The effect can vary substantially from one recording to another depending on the characteristics of the original unprocessed sound. The system "blurs" the focus of lead vocals and other sounds mixed to the center of a stereo recording. As bass frequencies are centered on most recordings, it also causes a*

partial loss of low frequency information, making the resulting
sound somewhat "tinny."

Holy shit!

This completely fucked up my first solo record, *Neil Young*, so
that it didn't sound anything like the mixes! What a beginning! My
first solo record release! My masterpiece! I was totally blown out,
being a technical freak of sorts even at that age. We went back in
the studio and, of course, overreacting, remixed a few tracks and
took the process off the other tracks. We should not have done any
more remixing.

Then the next version of the record (which was also called *Neil
Young*) was released with the changes. Unlike the first edition, it
had my name across the top of the album cover in big letters so
you could know it was a different edition. Some copies of the original made it into the marketplace, and they are collector's pieces
today.

Ultimately, the record was disappointing to myself and to my
fans. All the people who were really waiting for it went out and got
the bad version. That was a big learning experience.

I started thinking about how much fun it was to play with a band,
not be *in* a band, but play *with* a band, where I could direct the
music and interact with other musicians. I was tired of overdubbing. It's a lonely job. Since that first album, with few exceptions, I

have only done minor overdubs for color on some tracks, mostly just a chord here or there; the rest has been playing live with other musicians in the same room at the same time.

Singing live in the studio was the next big hurdle for me to overcome. I could visualize myself singing live in the studio like musicians used to do for the old records, where there was a real performance, not some contrived built-up creation, but a real piece of music. I began building confidence in my ability to sing and play with a band at the same time while recording. I was doing that live onstage, so I figured it shouldn't take too much to do it in the more analytical environment of the recording studio.

Soon after that first record, *Neil Young*, came out, I remember meeting Billy Talbot and Danny Whitten from the Rockets at the Topanga Center. As I have said before, I met the Rockets first in Hollywood at the Whisky and visited them a few times in their house on Laurel Canyon Boulevard while I was still in the Springfield. We visited with a friend of Billy's at a Topanga house. It was way across the canyon from mine, and it was visible from near my place. I always wondered what it was like inside because it was an incredible house on a beautiful piece of land, set aside from any other houses. It was pale yellow in color and was quite striking to me.

After we visited that cool house in Topanga, I asked if they would like to play with me and try some stuff out. I just wanted Danny, Billy, and Ralphie from the Rockets, though, because I was looking for a simple band sound. I invited them up to my house in Topanga, and we got together in the living room. We hit it off instantly, jamming just like we had many times in the Laurel Canyon late-night pot fests they had at their house.

That was all before music became a business, an industry, a commodity, or an asset for any of us. Music was more important than "making it." It seemed to be more down-to-earth to me, and I think that is why I was more relaxed hanging there with the Rockets at the Laurel Canyon house. It was so cool, with everyone sitting in a big circle talking and sharing songs together or playing solo. Music was our language. We passed the guitar like Native Americans passed the pipe. It really was our language of love, our shared interest, our common bond, our own. That is the feeling we shared with our audiences back then, too. We had a bond.

The Rockets had a lot of friends back then, including Robin Lane, a musician singer/songwriter. She was Danny's girlfriend, I remember. I was unaware of her history with Danny and the Memories, but I could tell this group of people had been friends for a good long time. I always felt so comfortable jamming over there with Danny, Billy, Ralphie, Robin, and their friends. There was a lot less pressure there than there was around the Buffalo Springfield scene. There were no big expectations. Just dreams.

A few weeks before the people who would found Crazy Horse (as yet unnamed), Danny, Billy, Ralphie, and me, got together in my Topanga living room, I had been sick with the flu, holed up in bed in the house. Susan was bringing me soup and good stuff, but I still felt like shit. I was delirious half the time and had an odd metallic taste in my mouth. It was peculiar. At the height of this sickness, I felt pretty high in a strange way.

I had a guitar in a case near the bed—probably too near the bed in the opinion of most of the women I had relationships with. I took it out and started playing; I had left it in a tuning I was fond of, D modal, with the E strings both tuned down to D. It provided a drone sound, sort of like a sitar, but not really. I played for a while and wrote "Cinnamon Girl." The lyrics were different from how the song eventually ended up, but all those changes happened right there, immediately, until the song was complete.

Then I took the guitar out of D modal and kept playing. At the time, there was a song in E minor on the radio that I liked, "Sunny" or something like that. I remembered hearing it in the drugstore at Fairfax and Sunset while I was shopping for something to ease the flu. The song kept looping in my head, endlessly, like some things do when I'm sick and maybe a little delirious. So I started playing it on the guitar, and then I changed the chords a bit—and it turned into "Down by the River." I was still feeling sick, but happy and high. It was a unique feeling. I had two brand-new songs! Totally different from the last album!

Then I started playing in A minor, one of my favorite keys. I had nothing to lose. I was on a roll. The music just flowed naturally that afternoon, and soon I had written "Cowgirl in the Sand." This was pretty unique, to write three songs in one sitting, and I am pretty sure that my semi-delirious state had a lot to do with that.

So there Billy, Ralphie, Danny, and I were in the Topanga house living room. It was all so easy, just like falling off a log. We played so well together. Simple, down-to-earth rock and roll. There is a cool picture of us all in that living room, grouped around a big

I wish to marry a cinnamon girl
I would be happy the rest of my life
With a cinnamon girl

Purple canaries that live in the air
~~That would be happy it could offer no pearl~~
We could be flying away from the world
With a cinnamon girl

I wish to marry a cinnamon girl
Purple canaries would fly through the air for
a cinnamon girl

Purple canaries that live in the air
Look at them flying

I want to marry a cinnamon girl, Purple canaries
that live in the air for a cinnamon girl.
I want to find a cinnamon girl, someone to
take me away from the world a cinnamon girl
~~some~~ your diamonds and rattle your pearls
Maybe I'll buy one and carry home for my cinnamon
girl

The original "Cinnamon Girl" lyrics, 1969.

chair Briggs and I had found at an antique shop in Echo Park and brought back to Topanga. The only thing wrong with that picture is the suit I had decided to wear. It was the suit I married Susan in. Should have left that one on the rack.

Anyway, I remember saying to the guys when we were playing "Cinnamon Girl," describing the modal instrumental theme that introduces the song, "It's like the Egyptians rolling giant stones up to a pyramid on logs. It's huge and it's moving. Unstoppable. Think Egyptians!" Soon we were in the studio recording those songs with Briggs at Heider's. It was massive. I was so freed by this music. I was happy as hell.

Somewhere along the line I had suggested the name Crazy Horse after the great Indian chief, and the guys liked it. Neil Young *with* Crazy Horse. Not *and*. There was a distinction there. I am not sure why I did that, but I liked it being different. I liked that I was *with* them. Like we were together, not separate.

The idea was that the Rockets would still continue on. We asked Bobby Notkoff to play violin on "Running Dry," and it was great. I think that was my first live vocal on an electric track; it is really different from all the other electric songs on that album. I know we all sang live on "Round and Round": Danny, Robin, and me. All gathered in a circle like at Laurel Canyon, singing and playing. The vocals are so great—Danny singing on the top, and Robin's rich voice on the bottom. Danny's soulful acoustic playing. Amazing. That whole album is so pure. I love that music. I love that old feeling of just the music. Nothing else mattered to us then. I can remember singing that song with them in the studio like it was this morning. There was no success, nothing to live up to, just love and music and life and youth. That was a happy time. That is Crazy Horse.

In Cleveland, there used to be a little club called La Cave; Crazy Horse and I played one of our first gigs there. The club held about two hundred people, and we stayed in a funky hotel just a few blocks away. I was playing Old Black through my little Deluxe amp, and we all had these other little Fender amps, too. We sounded perfect for that size of room.

I remember doing Danny's "Look at All the Things." It's too bad that Danny didn't get to sing more of his own tunes back then. It must have been frustrating for him to be so great and not be heard completely. Everything he contributed had that special edge. We were really great and we knew it. We were playing for ourselves. I would go out and play five or six songs acoustic, and then the Horse would come out and we would rock the place. We never did "Cowgirl" and "Down by the River" in the same set. We saved the long jam songs for the end, and focused on the shorter songs in the beginning. Every set had one of Danny's songs.

When we were finished at La Cave, we went on to the Bitter End in New York for a week in the Village. While we were in New York we stayed at the Gorham Hotel. It was a funky, soulful place on West 55th Street (now closed), and I stayed there every time I was in New York for years afterward. Once I played Carnegie Hall solo and the set list was written on Gorham stationery and taped on the top of my guitar.

My set list taped to my Martin D-45 guitar
for a show at Carnegie Hall, 1970.

Anyway, the tour continued, and when Crazy Horse finally arrived in Providence, Rhode Island, we were playing down in the shipyards. I noticed when we arrived that there were a lot of slot machines in this club. I'm talkin' a *lot* of slot machines. A funny feeling was in the place. It was not like the other gigs. The owner was friendly enough, but nervous.

We set up our equipment and went out for something to eat. BJ was our roadie at the time and stayed back with the equipment. It was always necessary to watch the equipment in these gigs. We never left it alone. It was irreplaceable. We returned to play, and eventually people started showing up. This was a club with almost no chairs, maybe some around the edges with a few tables, basically a dancing kind of place, so people were standing around looking at the stage, which was not a stage. We set up on a riser, possibly six inches higher than the floor. At least it was a one-nighter, not a weeklong gig.

Night was falling, and the shipyards took on a different look, with the bright lights outside shining down on the decks of a few ships being serviced and loaded with cargo. There was no acoustic set. We just started playing, and soon the crowd was into it. During the second set, we were doing an extended version of "Cowgirl in the Sand" when a fight broke out on the floor. All hell broke loose, and people were leaving! The fight got really big. A lot of people were just beating up our audience. We just kept on playing. One of the cardinal rules of club gigs is KEEP PLAYING in a fight situation. Stopping is taboo. It was very surreal, playing this long jam while people were getting beat up all around us. We still don't know quite what happened that night in Providence, but it was clear that our audience had the shit beaten out of them by unknown thugs from somewhere else.

We packed up and left without getting paid. There was no money.

In mid-1970, on the last Crazy Horse tour with Danny, our final show was at the Santa Monica Civic. All of our friends were there, and it was a big success. We played great. We had also played the Fillmore East on that tour, and a performance series CD was recently released that documents our shows there. I am really happy that I recorded all of that and have something to show for it, because there was nothing like it in any of the Crazy Horse records made at that time.

One of my instruments, a very rare and valuable D'Angelico New Yorker guitar, was missing after that tour. It was never found. I'm not sure there was a connection, but I had a suspicion that one of our roadies had sold the guitar for drug money. I don't blame them, but junkies will do almost anything to score, and there were a few junkies with me. Danny was using heroin, and I didn't know it. Jack Nitzsche was playing piano with us on that tour. Bruce Berry was a roadie on that tour, too. So was BJ.

One day after that we had a group meeting at the Lookout Management offices in the Clear Thoughts Building. I made a big speech about the group not being able to go on if Danny was still using. It didn't feel right even as I was saying it, the wrong approach. Danny was hurt, the other guys were with me but uncomfortable. I hadn't learned how to deal with a dependency or addiction. It was a stupid thing to do and didn't solve anything. I think that was the last time the group played together for a long time. I went off with CSNY to San Francisco and recorded *Déjà Vu*.

When I returned to Topanga, Dean Stockwell came by the house with a screenplay called *After the Gold Rush*. He had cowritten it with Herb Berman and wanted to know if I could do the music for it. I read the screenplay and kept it around for a while. I was writing a lot of songs at the time, and some of them seemed like they would fit right in with this story. The song "After the Gold Rush" was written to go along with the story's main character as he carried the tree of life through Topanga Canyon to the ocean.

One day Dean brought an executive from Universal Studios to my house to meet me. It looked like the project was going to happen, and I thought it would really be a good movie. It was a little off-the-wall and not a normal type of Hollywood story. I was really into it. Apparently the studio wasn't, because nothing more ever happened.

I went on to record most of the album in the studio I had built in my house. Ralphie and Greg Reeves were the rhythm section, with Nils Lofgren mainly on piano and also on acoustic guitar on one song. Nils had come to LA after I met him in Washington playing a solo gig at the Cellar Door a month earlier. Nils was very young and had a lot of energy for the music. He came to LA to get started, and Briggs was going to produce him.

Nils, probably because he had no money, had walked to

Topanga from the airport, about fifteen miles. Greg Reeves had just done *Déjà Vu* with CSNY, and I put him together with Ralphie and Nils to see how it would go.

We had finished a lot of the recording when word came through Billy that Danny had cleaned up. He came out and we played "When You Dance I Can Really Love" with him, Billy, and Jack. Crazy Horse was back together again. We rerecorded a lot of the chorus vocals with Danny singing, and they were a lot better than what we had before. It was great having Danny back! It really made the record better, and it felt so good to play with Danny again. Jack, too! Jack's piano on that track is unreal. We were really soaring! But that was it for the original Crazy Horse with Danny and Jack.

## Chapter Fifty

In 2010, I decided to make a record with Daniel Lanois, a great record producer. I have always, with few exceptions, had a direct hand in the production of my own records. This is how I do things. When I started this studio recording with Daniel, though, I said to myself, *At this time I don't like participating in the production as much as I like writing songs and performing them. I just want to do that and leave the production to someone else.*

Daniel had always seemed interesting and creative to me, so I called him up and asked him to produce a record with me. I wanted to do a solo record. I could see myself doing a collection of new songs in the folk tradition, acoustic and live, similar to Bob's earliest recordings. He was interested. I had written a few new songs in Hawaii, so I was already started. It's very simple to write songs and play them, and I wanted to return to those roots.

We got together at Lanois's house in Silver Lake in Los Angeles and started. When I arrived there, I was very impressed with what he had going on. He had prepared a group of rooms for me to play in and set up the sounds in advance, even prepared some instruments for me to try. It was a very interesting way to start. He had really done his homework. Dan's team consisted of Mark Howard (engineer), Adam CK Vollick (cinematographer), and Margaret Marissen, a lovely Canadian lady who supplied hospitality and food. Keisha, who lived in Dan's guesthouse, also helped Margaret at the sessions. I don't want to forget to give credit to them for what they contributed to the recording. I also met my new guitar tech, Ian Galloway.

I told Dan I wanted to cut the album on the full moon and the days leading up to it every month until we were done. That's the way I like to do it. I noticed early on that a lot of my best recordings were cut on a full moon, and I started to make it a habit to schedule sessions around the moon cycles. It seems very natural to me.

For the first sessions I drove to LA with Eric Johnson in my old Cadillac Eldorado, a white '57 Biarritz convertible that is all original. The ride down was magnificent. Taking Highway 101, we carved our way along the California coast and inland, through Gilroy, Salinas, San Luis Obispo, Santa Barbara, to Ventura and into LA. That trip really opens up my head. Ben Keith and I had done that same ride many times. I checked into the Beverly Hills Hotel, into a bungalow with a nice fireplace and a peaceful vibe. There was a grand piano in the room as well. I felt very good. We started recording the next day. It took me a while to loosen up, and the first couple of things I tried we didn't end up using, but eventually we hit a groove and recorded "Love and War" and "Peaceful Valley Boulevard," two songs written in Hawaii, and an older song called "Hitchhiker" that I hadn't cut yet. The previous night I had added a couple of new verses and changed some words to make it more relevant to me now, and it was "a good 'un," as Ben used to say. I did that song on Old Black through some amps Daniel had set up, and it sounded rockin'!

When the moon started to wane, I returned to the ranch with Eric in the Eldorado. It had been a good start. I loved the low sound that Dan was triggering from my bass strings. He certainly had some ideas I had never used before. We went along for a couple of moons, and I went out on the road, doing a solo tour, using the effects Dan and Mark had crafted on my guitars while I was playing both electric and acoustic. I took my old pump organ, my grand piano from *Tonight's the Night* that Amber had painted, and my old *Gold Rush* piano that I had rented when I made that record, then loved so much that I purchased it. I was happy with the way the tour was developing.

We decided to do three-week runs throughout the year with that show and intersperse trips to LA to record at Dan's house. The house was actually a mansion from the thirties. I loved the architecture of the place. It was so Old Hollywood! It reminded me of the film era, with its spiral staircases and Mediterranean look; the beautifully designed windows and arches everywhere were pleasing to the eye. Dan was recording analog masters and using a digital recorder from Canada called RADAR. Things sounded good, and I was happy with how things were going. Dan told me that the analog masters were not working for mixing because we were doing so many dubs that were dropped into the digital. I was cool with that. I loved the dubs he was doing with Mark. It was very creative, and we were getting a quite unique sound. I assumed that the digital was recorded at the highest resolution.

In the midst of recording, Dan and Keisha were involved in a motorcycle accident; word at first was that Dan might not survive. I was devastated. I called the hospital and found out that the reports I had gotten were greatly exaggerated, although Dan did have some broken bones and was confined to a wheelchair for a couple of months. I got him hooked up with the best doctors, and they took good care of him and Keisha, who had suffered some broken bones in her arm.

When I first heard the news of the accident, I was thinking about Larry and Ben, both of whom had passed in the last year, and I was wondering whether I was jinxing people close to me. Thankfully that thought passed.

Dan recovered, we resumed, and when the album was done I loved it. It was a mixture of electric and acoustic solo performances with dubs. I called it *Le Noise*, after Dan. It was a French Canadian joke, a very English way of saying *Lanois*. I was doing a show that introduced a lot of the songs, and things were going great. I was very happy.

Recently, I got my very first Grammy for a track on *Le Noise* in the category of Best Rock Song. We also won Juno Awards in Canada for the record. That was a great honor. The whole team, Daniel Lanois, Mark Howard, Adam Vollick, Margaret Marissen, and myself, were all Canadians! It was a massive amount of fun.

There were some dark spots, though. When I put the master to one of the songs from *Le Noise* on my PureTone demo player, I noticed it did not have the same openness and fidelity as the other tracks. Checking with the studio, I had them analyze *Le Noise*'s "Walk with Me," the strange-sounding track. It was a low-resolution digital master! It was recorded several steps down from high resolution. I couldn't believe it! We checked with Mark, and he verified it. It was a complete surprise to me, and it sounded decidedly inferior to all of my other high-resolution masters. There is no extra work involved with making something high resolution. It is just a matter of having the correct equipment and pressing the right buttons. If that can happen to me, imagine how many other contemporary artists record at suboptimal resolution. In the future, those recordings will be seen as unfortunate.

After a few months, I decided to do one more leg of the Le Noise tour and film the last show with Jonathan Demme in Toronto's Massey Hall. It turned out to be a great night. Everyone was very happy because we had captured it. During a review of the digital files, we realized that the resolution was not full; it was a stepped-down quality, not the best it could be. My own team's excuses were not adequate, because I was not informed of the decision to go to a lesser quality. Lesser quality is so accepted as normal now that even I had used it unknowingly! I went back to Massey Hall and set up a PA system like the one I used at the show, played back the mixes through the PA, and rerecorded the house sound at the highest resolution. I did the best I could with a bad situation. It does sound great now. Thankfully, the PA mix was only one step down from the highest resolution, so when it resonated in the hall and was rerecorded at the highest level, a high-resolution hall sound was captured.

## Chapter Fifty-One

On the Road

I n Feelgood's Garage there is a 1954 Corvette. I purchased this little car in a place called Old Time Cars on La Cienega Boulevard in LA. It's white with red interior, and when I purchased it in 1971, it was in very nice shape. John McKeig did a fine job at my old car barn bringing little details all the way back, fixing them as the years went by.

I was driving back to the ranch in it with Carrie in 1972 when she told me she was pregnant with Zeke. We were not getting married, because we had both decided not to. I think it was just something we weren't ready for, and of course, we knew nothing about the responsibilities of raising a kid. When we got to the ranch, she started to refer to the embryonic child as Goober. I was not particularly fond of that name. There were always a lot of her friends around the house during those days, and I was not particularly happy about that, either. It was like what my mother used to call a gab fest.

I just was overwhelmed and did not know how to deal. I was so young, even for my age. Confrontation was not big on the list of things I knew how to do—especially with women—so I didn't make a strong point about how uncomfortable I was with all these people around all the time. I really was happiest when things were quiet because I was not a very social kind of guy. Things never did fall into much of a groove with Carrie and me, so I have few memories to share. I guess I was not much of a partner. I was still adapting to lots of things, like this entourage of friends. That was not natural for me. I was happiest when I was with my musical cohorts, playing or touring. So that is the backdrop for our pregnancy period. It just seemed like another group encounter or something to me. Helluva guy I was. I was a fish out of water.

Traveling long distances in big cars is one of my favorite pastimes. There is really nothing that compares to the road. All of my days working with Lincvolt have been focused on the day when I would just get in the car and take off. Larry and I used to talk about that all the time. Of course I am sad that's not going to happen now, but I will do it with Ben Johnson. We will both do it for ourselves, but also because we wanted it so much for Larry. He will be with us every mile.

One afternoon, not long ago, I was making my way down to LA in the '78 Eldorado, listening to the PureTone system at loud volume on Interstate 5, making excellent time, when I noticed the fuel was low. I pulled into the next station, a Chevron with a convenience store, and fueled up, proudly remembering my zip code for the gas pump. I had Nina, Pegi's new dog, in the car. Nina is kind of like a poodle/pug/terrier mix, black and curly and soft. This was our first big trip together. Dad and Nina in the Eldorado for seven hours! She had water on the floor, and I had fed her at an In-N-Out Burger in Gilroy on the way. She was feelin' fine.

I left the AC on and had the engine running, but I locked the car as I went into the convenience store for water. It was 106 degrees. When I got back in the car she was ready for a walk, so we went over to the parking area and I let her out on some grass. She looked around and did nothing. After a while, we got back to the car and I noticed it was losing water from the radiator. I cruised around looking for a faucet and couldn't find one. In the whole complex I could not find water. I decided to keep going and find some water down the road at the next oasis.

Nina and I resumed our trip and headed south at about seventy-five miles per hour. I was looking for another exit for water, and we were about ten miles out when every alarm known to man started going off! The Eldo was talking to me. I turned off the AC right away and kept limping along at about forty-five miles per hour. No signs of an exit were forthcoming. The alarms kept flashing and buzzing. I decided to pull over and see what was up. There wasn't much room on the shoulder, and I was right on the side of the freeway with trucks roaring past at seventy miles an hour. The sun was high in the sky and it was really hot out there. Getting out, I left the windows down for a little ventilation. Nina got down on the floor. Raising the hood, I noticed it created a little shade, which I got into, although that was also where the engine heat was.

After a few minutes, I called Bruce Ferrario, my mechanic in South San Francisco, and told him what had happened. Bruce told me to wait for an hour before I tried to take the radiator cap off because it would be too hot and could scald me. Some folks I recognized from the last rest stop stopped and gave me some drinking water. That was kind of them. They said they knew Daniel Lanois and knew I had been recording at his home in the previous year. What a small world.

They also said they had seen fluid coming out from under my car at the area near where Nina had her little walk. I remembered a large puddle of dirty water about ten feet away from the car and I put it all together. I gave the fresh water to Nina and kept some for myself. She appeared uninterested in the water. About forty-five minutes remained until I could open the radiator and relieve the pressure, and it was really hot out there. I took off my shirt. Then I put it back on, fearing sunburn. I got out my wallet and called AAA. I finally got an operator and found out my card was expired. I told the operator that was not possible and to check further. I had all my cards out on the seat of the car, spread out everywhere. Cards from my whole life seemed to be appearing randomly from some source I was not aware of.

The heat was becoming quite intense, and the phone was losing its charge. For some reason it did not occur to me to charge the phone from the car. I waited for AAA to call back, but they didn't. I worried about the phone. Then I went through the procedure again to get someone on the phone. I finally did, and they discovered I was a "discontinued premier member." I told them to look further, and lo and behold! They discovered my card was *not* expired, though it would be in a month and a half. They informed me a truck was on the way. I stood in the shadow of the hood of the car. The heat would hit like a gust every time a semi went by, two feet away. A car pulled over in front of me and stopped about two hundred yards along the road. They sat there for a while. Then they took off farther down the road. I wondered who they were. Another truck flew by at about eighty! Credit cards and receipts went flying in all directions! One of the greatest collections of expired AAA cards ever known was lost. I was thinking to myself that this was the beginning of a seriously bad situation. I had a new awareness of heat stroke and the ramifications of that. I knew I was not thinking as clearly as I usually do. Nina had a credit card on top of her. She seemed unfazed.

Another half hour passed. Nina and I were beginning to get very uncomfortable. She was not moving, staying low, and panting a little. She would not drink water. A truck coming in the other direction crossed the median behind us, passed us, and pulled over in front of us. It was AAA. I had been sitting there a little over an hour. He backed up and got out of the truck, came back and told me I was a premier member so he could take me all the way to LA if I wanted. It was within the two-hundred-mile range.

Looking at my card further, he asked, "Are you Neil Young?"

I said, "Yes I am."

He asked, "Who is Cinnamon Girl?"

I told him he would meet her in LA—she was my wife and had the most beautiful eyes in the world.

He loaded the old Eldorado onto the back of the truck and chained it down. Nina and I climbed up into the cab. It was air-conditioned. We stopped somewhere near the Grapevine, a mammoth grade that climbs out of the valley. I got a sandwich at Subway and took Nina for a little walk. Along the way my mind drifted to dreaming about making that trip in Lincvolt someday, pulling into the hotel in LA silently, without a motor running, in a beautiful 1959 Lincoln Continental. I knew the dream was going to come true.

We got into LA at night, pulled up to Sunset Sound studios, where Pegi was recording, and just as I had promised, there was Cinnamon Girl, waiting by the curb.

Chapter Fifty-Two

"Good 'Uns"

Today is one year from the day Long Grain died in 2010 at the age of seventy-three.

Ben "Long Grain" Keith was a close friend for forty years. I was cruising along in the bus with some of the boys, including my brother, Bob, and Dave Toms. The phone rang. It was Pegi crying and crying. I knew something was really wrong, so I went to the back of the bus with the phone. "It's Ben!" she cried. "Oh, I'm so sorry, Neil. He's gone."

I let out what Dave described as a primal scream. I was consoling her, thinking that she was talking about our Ben Young, when she finally said something that told me it was Ben Keith, Long Grain. I felt a sigh of relief, but then a different sadness came over me.

Long Grain was always there. He was such a friend, such a cohort. I could do anything if he was with me, any kind of music at

With Ben Keith at the Fox Theatre in Redwood City, California,
October 2007.

all, and have a lot of fun at the same time. His death settled in on me. The giant bus rolled along over the Manitoba prairies.

It was time to call Heidi, Ben's beautiful daughter, the mother of a wonderful family that Long Grain loved. He was Grandpa. She answered. I told her and she cried. We talked and I comforted her as much as I could. I can never forget the feeling of that moment.

Ben was a wonderful man, gentle as the rain. The bus rolled on. He was a magical musician. It sank in and in. I realized right then that this was the end of an era. I could never play "Heart of Gold" or "Old Man" or any other songs from *Harvest* with anyone else on steel. That would not be right. I was so used to looking over and seeing him there, giving and giving. We spent so much time together.

Long Grain never understood why I would keep on mixing and mixing some of the records we made. "Let it go, Neil. It's a good 'un!" he would say as he walked out of the studio. "Call me if you are going to do any more." The bus kept rolling and the wheat fields floated by. Ben Keith was revered by all steel players as the original. His style was known around the world. He arranged horn sections, produced records, and played guitar, dobro, Autoharp, finger cymbals, piano, horns, and bass. He was a great singer. There will never be another like him. I still feel sad today that he is gone. He was taken too soon.

The silver bus rolled along, approaching the outskirts of the city of Winnipeg. He was not ready to go. I know he had accepted it in his heart, but he was not ready. Then we got to Winnipeg, which was the next show, and parked downtown near the theater. I went outside and sat in a little park on some grass behind the theater. I went inside. There it was, the stage I would walk out on, knowing I was more alone than I had ever been before. He was like a big brother to me, and he had been ill, but not *that* ill, I thought. I know his death could have been avoided with a doctor who was really on top of it. He had so much life in him. It was wrong. I played my way through that first show and did "Old Man" for Ben at the end. I looked over to my right and he was out there somewhere, but not next to me anymore.

In January of 1971, I was doing a solo tour of Canada and a few U.S. cities. It had started in Vancouver. Joni Mitchell sent me a hat she made for me. It was a beautiful knitted tuque with a seashell hanging on the front of it, made of wool in soft earth tones. I could feel the love in it. I wore it a lot on that tour. I was taking some Soma Compound to loosen up my back and drinking a little Michelob. My brace was with me everywhere I went, and I used to hurt a little at night and in the mornings from the slipped disc, but it wasn't too bad. The show in Vancouver went fine, and we flew to Edmonton or Regina after that. I remember the parking lot of the gig had all of the plugs for block heaters lined up on posts in front of the parking spaces so folks could plug in and not have their engines freeze up during the shows. Winnipeg was next, but my mother was down in Florida. She would have been there if she was in town, proud as could be and telling all of her friends. I met a girl named Nancy Eaton at the show there. She was one of the Eaton family, owners of a large chain of department stores across Canada.

(A relative of hers was the backer for the Mynah Birds when I played with them.) Nancy and I liked each other, had a good time, and planned to hook up again down the road.

Next came Toronto at Massey Hall. That was the biggest gig. It was a homecoming. When I walked out onstage, the place got really loud. It was a feeling like no other. It was where I had worked at Coles Bookstore, played at the Riverboat Hootenannies, lived on Isabella Street in my little flat writing songs, gone to school, experienced my mom and dad's breakup, bought records by Roy Orbison, delivered newspapers. It was a big moment in my life to be sure.

My dad was there for the first show, at six-thirty P.M., which was added because the originally scheduled show was sold out. I saw him and we chatted briefly. He said it was a lot different from the last time I had been in Toronto. Remembering the job at Coles and the little flat I had on Huron Street, eating macaroni for dinner every night, the uneasy feeling I had in his house when I first arrived in Toronto from the west, and the help he had given me finding a rehearsal space for my band, I agreed. It felt good to see him. It had been a long time. I played my heart out.

Briggs was living in Toronto at the time and had started a studio called Thunder Sound. He recorded the Massey Hall show. He thought this live show should have come out right away, and was disappointed and disagreed with my decision to instead put out *Harvest*—he thought it was not as good as the Massey Hall recording.

"It's great, Neil," Briggs said. "Put it out there." But that was not to be.

An announcement in the Toronto Star
of the added show at Massey Hall, 1971.

When I heard the show thirty-four years later while reviewing tapes for my archives performance series, I was a little shocked—I agreed with David. After listening, I felt his frustration. This was better than *Harvest*. It meant more. He was right. I had missed it. He understood it. David was usually right, and when I disagreed with him, I was usually wrong. Every time I go into the studio or onstage, he is missed.

After Toronto, I went on to the States, played in Stratford, Connecticut, at the Shakespeare Theatre, and ultimately to Nashville to play *The Johnny Cash Show* on TV. It was an opportunity to perform with my peers, but I felt I did not do as well there as I might have, for whatever reason. I played "Journey Through the Past" on piano. I'm really not that good on the piano. Maybe I should have done a different song, something where I played guitar. But something extraordinary came out of this trip.

While I was in Nashville, I wanted to do some recording. We met Elliot Mazer, a record producer who helped us get a session together. We went to a studio called Quadrafonic that he had recommended. He was going to record us. Elliot had a whole new group of musicians I had never met before waiting there.

We got Kenny Buttrey on drums; Kenny had played on many hits. Tim Drummond on bass had played with James Brown, JJ Cale, and Conway Twitty, among many others. Tim was responsible for finding the musicians, I found out later. There was a gui-

tarist named Teddy Irwin. He played the beautiful harmonics on
"Heart of Gold." John Harris was on piano. He was quite an original, obviously a genius live-wire player with an amazing touch.
Then, as we started, a tall guy walked in and set up his steel. Ben
Keith was his name. He was very quiet. As we started playing, I
mentioned to Ben to just play some simple pads under certain sections to separate them and to also play some long, wide tones very
spaciously, not like regular country-oriented licks. He made a few
sounds and we talked some more.

"Ben," I said, "can you play the same note on a couple of strings
and sort of phase them against each other instead of a chord?"

"Like this?" he replied, and played a long, deep, wide note that
rang forever.

"Yes," I said. "That is definitely what we are looking for."

Then we recorded "Old Man" with the signature Ben Keith
sound that went down in history. What a musician! Over the next
few hours we played "Heart of Gold" and many other tracks that
are on *Harvest*, and some that are not. "Journey Through the Past,"
in particular, is a great take that did not make it onto *Harvest*. (It is
included in the *Harvest* section of the archives.)

Ben and I played together for forty great years, and I wouldn't
trade that experience for anything on earth. I was so lucky to meet
Ben and Tim and Kenny and John on that memorable day. Thanks,
guys! What more can I say? I loved playing with you all.

This is a time for reflection. There is no time like the present.

As I sit here reflecting on my good fortune to have met these
guys and made music with them, I miss them. I wish we were still

together, and a lot of them are gone now. "There are very few of us left," as Waylon Jennings liked to say. "The mighty few," as Tim Drummond would say. What a great bass player and character Tim Drummond is! As deep as the sea! I just called him, and he told me I should have a mai tai for him. I didn't tell him I don't drink anymore. He still does. At least I can still talk to him.

## Chapter Fifty-Three

N ear the end of 2010, I did a leg of the Le Noise tour that
dipped down to the Gulf of Mexico to play for the people who had been hit hard by the oil spill and Katrina.
The economy down there had taken a tremendous hit. At the time,
I thought it was the last leg of that tour. We lowered the price of
the shows to an amount that let everyone come who there was
room for. Johnny Tyson, an old friend of mine from many years
back who is a music lover and a man who likes to do good things for
people, followed us around with a semi of Tyson poultry products
for the food banks.

The devastation from BP's Gulf oil spill disaster, plus Hurricane Katrina's aftermath, lingering for years, was an incredible
load on those folks. I just wanted to go down there and help. I took
Lincvolt, and after each show we would jump in the car and go. Ben
Young, Zeke Young, Ben Johnson, Dave Toms, and I piled into
Lincvolt with the top down and rode into the Gulf night. The
warm air and gentle breezes make the Gulf area one of the most
inviting places on earth. It was such a rush to cruise along the

coast of the Gulf of Mexico in a big electric convertible with the laughter of friends and the wind in our hair! We were in the zone.

The shows were very close together, and it was easy to make it to the next motel or rendezvous area with the buses. Lincvolt would then ride in the semitrailer that we brought along. It doubled as a gym in the front and a garage for Lincvolt in the back.

We met with folks along the way who told us of the planes going out at night under cover of darkness to drop chemicals on the Gulf and disperse the deadly oil slick to the bottom, where it was out of human sight and, therefore, out of mind. These people were very upset at the deception being perpetrated by the media that everything was being cleaned up. Some of the coverage that actually reported the cover-up and night flights of dispersants dropped on the Gulf was indeed good, but a lot of coverage reporting that the Gulf was cleaned up was total fiction, according to the locals.

In Mobile, Alabama, we met a young man who would only tell his story if we filmed him from the neck down and didn't show his face. He was scared of recrimination. He told us how they were working on a fleet of boats paid by BP that had been working on cleaning up the spill for weeks, and suddenly had been given three days off. When they came back to work the oil slick was gone. Everyone working knew it had to have been dispersants from airplanes. Locals told us the planes flew over all night for three nights in a row. The oil was dispersed to the bottom, killing untold sea life.

A lot of folks were greatly intimidated by the oil power that controls so much of the area. People were down, frightened, yet strong. They are not going anywhere. This is their way of life, their roots and family history. Fishing families with four and five generations of history working the Gulf are not going easily. These things don't change.

The shows along the Gulf went great. I was so happy to play the casinos and smaller halls. Old theaters full of happy folks who I would likely never have played for were enjoying the night and the music, the togetherness and the moments of laughter and tears. You could see it in their faces.

Around the back of the venues after the show, people came to look at the old electric Lincoln, defying preconceptions of what a car like that could do. It silently glided out of the backstage lot, full of our family and friends, Ben Young being gently and easily held in the front seat by a giant Dave Toms, whose long white hair was streaming in the breeze, Zeke Young and Ben Johnson holding down the backseat. At nineteen and a half feet, Lincvolt can hold a lot of happiness.

We played Panama City, Clearwater, Hollywood, Biloxi, Mobile, Pensacola, then we headed north to Farm Aid in Milwaukee. Farm Aid was a departure from our normal shows on that tour because of the forty thousand people and a stadium, but it was a good 'un! It's all about the music. If the music soars and you feel good, then the show is good. If for whatever reason the music does not soar, then it is not a good show. There is no way to tell what it will be like. It's like the weather.

That short tour will always be one of my best road memories. Maybe it's because I had Zeke out there again! I'm looking forward to getting back out there with Lincvolt and the boys for another trip someday soon. Maybe I can get Amber to come next time, too. It really felt good to wind down from the show behind the wheel of that old convertible. I guess I was harkening back to the days when entertainers would travel in Cadillacs pulling trailers full of band equipment.

Only the headliners of the biggest shows could afford that back in those days. I wanted to be like them and just keep going to the next town. When I saw Roy Orbison in Winnipeg Municipal Auditorium around 1960, he had a big motor home; very impressive. Gene Pitney had a Cadillac and trailer. So did the Crickets, with Waylon and Sonny Curtis, when I saw them at Winnipeg Beach, sixty miles north of Winnipeg. Dick Clark's Cavalcade of Stars all rode in one bus when they played the Municipal Auditorium— eight artists and the band all in one bus with the master of ceremonies, Fabian!

Those were my glory days.

## Chapter Fifty-Four

In 1974, on the night Carrie's mom died, I woke up in bed at the ranch and I saw her head in the air screaming at the foot of my bed. It was a nightmare I will never forget.

Although Carrie and I had just broken up, I went to Chicago to help support her in her grieving and be with her family. There were rumors of some strange circumstances around her mother's death that would lead one to believe that it was very traumatic. It was investigated and concluded to be a carbon monoxide suicide in a garage. I was very uncomfortable, but I felt I should still be there with Carrie because she needed me. Zeke was back in California with a friend.

While I was there in Chicago, I called Ben Keith, who was in Nashville, and Crazy Horse in LA so that they could come and play with me at Chess Recording Studios, the historic Chicago studio where so many great blues records had been made. I had already played with Poncho once at Billy Talbot's house in Echo Park. Billy and his new, young wife, Laurie, had been there with a few kids.

With Crazy Horse (Ralph Molina, me, Billy Talbot, Frank "Poncho" Sampedro), in a Copenhagen hotel room, March 1976.

We had played on the porch, and the music had echoed in the canyon outside. I guess that's why they named it Echo Park. Poncho had fit in real well, and we'd been able to jam on some cool stuff. I don't remember what we were playing, but it had a good sound. Poncho is Spanish, Billy is Italian, and Ralph is Portuguese; three Latins and a Canadian, I thought to myself. There was something sympathetic about the way we played together. It felt really fluid and hot, yet funky and solid.

When we all got to Chess Studios, we found it on the fifth floor of a big old brick building that really had a historic vibe. I felt I was in a hallowed place. It was funky and there was nothing high-class about it, like some of the studios we had played in Hollywood. It had everything it needed, though. We recorded one song, "Changing Highways," at that session. It was kind of an experiment with Poncho in the studio, and it went well. We rocked. Crazy Horse went back to LA.

After that session, I said good-bye to Carrie and her family, and Ben and I drove south to Nashville in the '59 Cadillac Eldorado I bought in Chicago—the as yet unnamed Nanu. That did not happen until Mr. Briggs first laid eyes on her and named her Nanu the Lovesick Moose. The car was really cool, and we had a good trip. It felt great to be on the road again; I was relieved to be free from all of the feelings around the death of Carrie's mom and the aftermath of my breakup with Carrie.

When we got to Nashville, we had a series of sessions with Levon Helm, then Karl Himmel, and, on one track, Kenny Buttrey on drums. Elliot Mazer was in the control room. Tim Drummond and Ben Keith were on all of the tracks. It felt really good. It was the beginning of an entire album I have held back, entitled *Homegrown*. I was making so much music then, it was hard to keep track of all of it and complete a record. The creative process was spinning slightly out of control because I had so much music to record. When *Homegrown* would normally have come out, I put out *Tonight's the Night* instead, because we all listened to both of them and *Tonight's the Night*, although almost two years old, just had to come out. I had delayed it originally, having felt it was not yet the right time for release, and also I had a sense that it needed something else added to it for perspective. I did find those tracks eventually, and then the record was complete. Now when I listen to it, I am not sure about that decision. Some things take a while to settle with me.

When I got to LA, I was soon in the Malibu groove. Briggs and I were up to our old tricks, having a lot of fun in the bars at night and lying around in the sun all day. I had rented a house on Broad Beach Road. Nanu became a regular on the Pacific Coast Highway (PCH). Ben had driven the car out from Nashville and brought it to LA. Nanu was the scene of many good times. There was a bar named the Crazy Horse Saloon in Malibu that we frequented. Poncho had a house on the PCH, and we hung out there, too. There were lots of girls and we were living the dream.

I kept writing, and when I wrote "Cortez the Killer" and "Hitchhiker," I called for the Horse to come and record. We decided on Briggs's Point Dume house with the Green Board as the ideal location. I lived a few miles north near Zuma Beach. Malibu, with the Crazy Horse Saloon, was a few miles south. It was a perfect situation for good times.

The album *Zuma* is the first album we made with Crazy Horse after Poncho joined the band. It's one of my favorites. The cover is by Mazzeo and came out of a conversation we had on a day trip from the ranch to Zuma. We set up a Green Board control room in Briggs's den. We played in the garage. One day Bob Dylan, who lived nearby, came along and sang a blues tune with us. On a break, Bob and I took a walk around the neighborhood, talking about the similarity in some of the paths we had each taken. It was the first time we had ever really talked. I liked him.

Back at Briggs's, we kept playing day after day and partying at night. We did the original "Powderfinger" and held it back. We did "Sedan Delivery" and held it back. My song "Born to Run" was recorded, left unfinished, and held back. "Ride My Llama" was completely finished and mixed and held back. We recorded a lot of tunes and held them back, but we released "Cortez," "Don't Cry No Tears," "Stupid Girl," and a bunch of other tracks on *Zuma*. It has a great feeling to it. Today I like listening to all of those tracks together in a compilation I call *Dume* that is in *The Archives Volume 2*. Those were some of the finest, most alive days of my life. I was getting past the lost relationship with Carrie, living the life with my best friends, making some good music, and starting to get a grip on something: an open future in my personal life and a new future with Crazy Horse after Danny.

Recently, I was in Point Dume visiting my producer friend Rick Rubin and told him about the sessions at David's old house; we went for a drive and could not locate it. It may have been torn down. It was a classic ranch-style house with wooden shutters around the windows. I saw a few others still around in the style of David's but couldn't find the one. Strangely, though, when Rick ordered some fish tacos to go for us at the local place located in the Dume Shopping Center, it turned out to be the same spot where Briggs and I used to eat breakfast every morning back in the day.

## Chapter Fifty-Five

Bruce Palmer and I had been in LA for only six weeks when Buffalo Springfield played at the Whisky a Go Go for the first time. Buffalo Springfield had already done a hootenanny at the Troubadour, a club down on Santa Monica Boulevard that showcased new talent all the time and had folk-oriented headliners playing weekly. That showcase had been set up by Dickie Davis, our original road manager who worked the lights at the Troubadour, and Barry Friedman, our manager who had put us up and guided us through the first weeks of our existence. That gig got the record companies interested in us and also got the attention of some other managers.

All kinds of people got their start there. Sometimes ten acts would be seen in one night, all of them looking for a break. It was LA, and a lot of these acts made it. Just *getting* to LA was a big thing, a launching spot to the big time. We had a one-night showcase along with a few other bands. It was an event because a lot of people thought we were going to be the next big thing. We were good that night, and though we were really nervous, it was obvious to everyone that we had something. Stephen and Richie sang incredibly well, and because of the diversity of musical roots, the band had a blend of music that was largely unknown at the time. It was kind of folk rock, but kind of country blues with a rock and roll edge. Richie's great voice and Bruce's unique Motown bass style brought depth. Dewey's smiling face behind the drums was both incongruous and appealing. It was Stephen's soulful vocals and phrasing that set us into another class.

Our guitar interplay was also something no one had ever heard. Stephen and I would play these intricate parts off of each other all the time that were largely improvised, and people could hear that it was spontaneous. It was exciting, and we were young and very alive. Everything started moving really fast.

Record companies, managers, everyone wanted to talk to us. Dickie Davis tried to handle the whole thing. He did the best he could and, as I mentioned earlier, we eventually ended up with Charlie Greene and Brian Stone, two guys from New York who had handled Sonny & Cher, as our managers. These guys were real hustlers. Before we met them, when they first came to LA from New York, they had actually set up an office on the Universal lot and were doing business there for six months before anyone at Universal realized they were there. Imagine that. They just walked in, set up an office, started using services, and lasted six months before they were caught. It was not long after that we first met them and we decided we liked them the best. They told us their story. They were also record producers, they said. They had a big Lincoln limousine and Joseph, their own driver. We were way too impressed by that limo.

They bought out Barry Friedman, who regrets it to this day,

and so do I. He was a musical guy with some knowledge of who we were. Losing him was a very big mistake. It was too late to back out of our agreement when we found out that Greene and Stone had never really produced a record. Still, with their connections, we were getting some major dates. We got a gig right away opening for the Byrds and played about a week of local California shows. We were playing with the Byrds! They were our heroes. It was so fast. I remember a show we played where the Byrds were pretty messed up. They were one of the biggest acts going, and that night we blew them away. It was obvious to us all that the Springfield was a force to be reckoned with.

Shortly after that, by chance Greene and Stone booked us into the Whisky to cover another band's night off—we ended up staying for six straight weeks without a break. We were building a following. We started opening for Hugh Masekela and then Johnny Rivers. Headliners came and went, but we stayed. We built our own fan base that kept returning every night. Mario Maglieri and Elmer Valentine ran the place and treated us like their own. Elmer was the boss. Mario was the doorman and floor manager. They were like fathers to all of us in the scene: the groupies, the bands, all of us. Mario still called me Skinny years later when I would drop in and say hello.

We were also recording our first album during that time. Greene and Stone had signed us to Atlantic, because they had connections there with Ahmet Ertegun through their success with Sonny & Cher. When we got the album down and mixed, we felt great. We had been there guiding the mixing process and everything. One day we were leaving to go on the road for a weekend, and we heard Greene and Stone had to go in and do a stereo mix. We had only done a mono. We were so unaware, so green! Stereo was the new big thing.

In one day they remixed the whole thing into stereo without us, and we only heard it when we got back to LA from our weekend tour.

We hated it.

The mixes sucked and didn't have the energy we felt in the studio or on the stage when we were playing live. That was what was missing. The sound was very thin, and the mix itself was terrible. Stephen and I were so disappointed. They released "Nowadays Clancy Can't Even Sing" as the first single, and that was a big mistake. It was way too weird to be a single. We had "Go and Say Goodbye" and "Do I Have to Come Right Out and Say It," either of which would have been a much better choice. But we went along with it. While I thought it was cool to have "Clancy" out there, I doubted whether it was commercial enough. But what did we know?

It bombed.

Riots were happening on the Strip. Hippies against the war, cops against the hippies. Stephen wrote "For What It's Worth" about the riots. It was a great message song of the times, with his signature vocal phrasing. We recorded it at Columbia with the help of Stan Ross, owner of Gold Star, because Gold Star was booked. Tom May was our Columbia engineer. Stan and Tom got us a decent sound. They got the drums right. Thankfully, Greene and Stone were not there producing. We had our first hit and rereleased the LP with that song on it. If you listen to that record now, you can hear the difference in tonal quality and production between "For What It's Worth" and the rest of the *Buffalo Springfield* album. We missed a good chance to remix the whole album right there and never even realized it.

Soon we were back at the Whisky, headlining on a Sunday night. We were recording artists now, and our fan base was exploding. We started to feel different and act different, but we were still just a bunch of green kids. That was our beginning, and we went on for a year and a half until we broke up. Bruce got busted a couple of times and was eventually deported. That was the beginning of the end for us.

Chemistry is the big thing in any group, and Bruce was the element that made us unique. His roots in R&B (that he got in Toronto playing in his first band, where he was the only white guy) were so important. Stephen and I loved Bruce. He was a complete original. He played like Motown, but he had an added flair that was totally Bruce. Everyone knew he was completely off the charts. A genius player. Musicians would just stand there slack-jawed, watching and listening to him play. After we lost him, we were never the same. It was the beginning of the end, right there. We had Jim Fielder on bass for a while, and he ended up with Blood, Sweat & Tears. Then we had Jim Messina, who we had met at Sunset Sound. But we could never find anyone like Bruce, and it was killing us slowly. Stephen became frustrated with the rhythm section problems and started cutting his songs with other guys, Buddy Miles on drums and Bobby West on bass among them.

When we used to play at the Whisky, Bruce and I would be back there with Dewey holding down a groove with our backs to the audience, lost in the music. That was magic. That is why Richie and Stephen sounded so great. They were singing on a rock-solid foundation that breathed and pulsed. We were so into the music back there that the girls in the audience could feel that pulse, and it drove them crazy. We didn't even realize what we were doing. The way Stephen and Richie sang their asses off, if we hadn't lost Bruce, the sky would have been the limit for Buffalo Springfield. But we did lose him. When he got busted for grass in a hotel in New York while we were playing a club there, he was instantly deported. Bruce was gone.

That was why the Springfield broke up. All the fighting was because we lost Bruce. If he had stayed in, we would probably still be together today (if we had all lived). Sure, I would have done some solo records, but with that sound there, I always would have come back to it. It is as simple as that. We broke up because we were broken. We were missing the essential ingredient, and all the momentum in the world could not replace it. People say we were great and ask why we ever broke up. That is why.

If you want to see the Springfield, the best representation of it is a Dick Clark production, *Where the Action Is*. On that show, you can see the real group. We were lip-synching, but that was what we looked like. Those were the finest times of Buffalo Springfield, and it never, ever got better. Without Bruce, that was all gone.

Our last gig was at the Long Beach Arena. We walked out and the place went nuts. Our fans knew this was the last time. We started playing and the crowd left their seats and rushed to the front of the stage. Some authority figure turned on the lights and walked out onstage, admonishing the crowd to sit down. He repeatedly said, "Buffalo Springfield will NOT play until you return to your seats."

Eventually we started to play again. It was a bittersweet moment. I was wearing my finest Buffalo Springfield fringe regalia, Stephen had on his great cowboy hat and suit. We all wore our finest. Without Bruce! It was like a funeral. We were just a little more than eighteen months old as a band. It was nobody's fault. We were just too young and we had made a lot of bad and inexperienced decisions, starting with losing Barry Friedman. But losing Bruce broke our heart.

Thank you, Buffalo Springfield. There will never be another. It's about chemistry. Love and chemistry.

## Chapter Fifty-Six

I n Feelgood's there is a 1957 Jensen. It is a 541, one of just thirty-five ever made. In 1975, while I was down in Florida working on restoring the *WN Ragland* with Roger Katz and a bunch of shipbuilders and sailors, I found the Jensen in Fort Lauderdale in a little used-car place on Sunrise Boulevard. It was $2,750. I had never seen one before, and it was very beautiful. I needed a car. It was in original condition, faded red, well-worn, but nice. This was and is still my favorite combination; beautiful, original, and worn.

Its worst flaw was that the back window had been cracked from a falling coconut somewhere. It was a right-hand drive and had a unique little lever in the dash; if you pushed up, the horn honked, and if you pushed down, the brights would come on. Toggling it back and forth resulted in a classic European blasting-horn-and-flashing-lights combination effect. It also had been equipped with glasspacks. That meant it was loud as hell! I loved it and bought it the next day.

I drove it everywhere in Florida. Once I took it to West Palm Beach. I was feeling lonely and went lookin' around, found a little bar, and met a girl there who was playing pool. She had a white dress on. Playing pool with a white dress on blew my mind! She took me to the West Palm Beach Country Club the next day for breakfast, and I couldn't get out of there fast enough. I felt like a trophy. The Jensen got me back in a couple of hours of peaceful motoring along A1A, the Florida coast route. It is a beautiful highway along the Atlantic with motels that reminded me of going down there with my parents every winter from Omemee when I was a kid in the fifties. We went down to New Smyrna Beach every year for a few years. Daddy was working on books, and while he would write, Bob and I would go in the ocean. I went to school there for a couple of months for a few years in a row when I was about ten, because that was where my family was. No wonder I like to move. No wonder I love the South, especially Florida.

When I got back to the boat in Fort Lauderdale, I was always happy to see the progress and check in with Roger and the crew. On a Friday, after the traditional payday tequila, we headed out to the bars. Later that night I was driving the Jensen and got pulled over by the police. We were completely shit-faced! The car was full to capacity with drunken shipworkers. I explained that we were all good citizens who had been working hard all week and we were simply going to go and get some coffee. He let us off. Everyone in the car was amazed. So was I.

Later, after the *Ragland* was launched, Roger shipped the car back to California, and it was damaged along the way. I had to get it fixed. Afterward, they repainted the hood area that had been repaired. It was the European type of hood that lifted completely up, revealing the whole front end, wheels and everything. Now it was suddenly shiny red in the front. I was disappointed and missed the old faded look. We had to repaint the whole thing—John McKeig was great at mixing paint and finishing, and gave the whole car a faded look.

Today, it sits in Feelgood's in need of a big tune-up (at the very least). The horn/lights controller was broken when I left the car at a dealership to get something done. Some turkey got in the car and broke it with his knee. It has never been quite the same. I want to get it fixed, and that's what's happening now. I love that car. So does Pegi, because it's very sexy. Just seeing it in Feelgood's fills my heart with all good thoughts of an innocent time with really good friends.

A few meditations about success.

Somewhere along the line it always comes up. Are you happy with what you have done? Have you been successful? I know I am thankful for the things I have been able to try. Success is hard to measure. If you have lots of cash, that doesn't make you successful—it makes you rich. (Even if you're like me and have lots of stuff and not much cash relatively, that doesn't make you a success; it only makes you materially rich.)

Success is a tough one for me to define. I have my failings to be sure, and I'm working on them all the time, except for when I forget or am so preoccupied that I'm not aware. These are my personal successes and failures, and they have nothing to do with money or possessions. My children are perhaps my biggest success, and I share that with Pegi, because without her, it would not be like that.

You may have noticed that a lot of my time is spent tying up loose ends, getting closure, and completing things. One early measure of success I set for myself was very material. Remember that red 1959 Cadillac convertible I sat in that was in my twin friends' garage in the early sixties while I was going to Kelvin High School? The one that was driven back and forth to a TV station in the States by their dad? Remember when I was in the YMCA in Fort William calculating how many months I would have to work at the Flamingo Club to earn enough money to buy that kind of car? Well, as fate turns out, I had it and I lost it and I still have it. The situation wears on me. It's not a big deal, but it isn't a success, nor is it a failure. You see, that car is the famous Nanu the Lovesick Moose! But there is much more to it than that.

One day in 1975, I was leaving my ranch. The long road out is very narrow; there is a very steep hill with twists and turns through redwood trees on either side of the road. As I was driving along, climbing slowly up the hill in Nanu, a Volkswagen came flying down the road between the trees and, seeing me, slammed on the brakes and slid directly into Nanu, scraping down the whole side of the car and destroying its side panels and the rare stainless molding that identified this Eldorado as a Biarritz. The driver of the Volkswagen, a teenage girl, was terrified. She was nearly hysterical, crying about the trouble she would be in with her parents for getting in another accident. She had been going way too fast and should not have slammed on her brakes. (That was the worst thing she could have done; she had plenty of room to stop or pass, but she panicked, hitting the brakes and locking them up, and slid downhill straight into poor old Nanu, the Innocent Convertible.)

I let the girl off the hook. I told her right there not to worry, I would take care of it and she should just go home, which she did. There was a place called Coachcraft in Scotts Valley, California, near Highway 17 between Santa Cruz and Walnut Creek. Nanu was taken there to be fixed around the third quarter of 1975. I asked the man in charge to do a perfect restoration of the car. "Make it museum quality," I said.

He took it down to bare metal in his shop and started to paint the chassis. At some point he decided he would like to work for me and complete the car while he was taking care of my whole collection. I liked John McKeig immediately; we were kindred spirits, so I hired him. He moved to the ranch and began taking care of my cars, maintaining and cleaning the building and the old autos, which had grown in number. He redid the entire building, which took a couple of years and was a beautiful work of art.

John's standards were very high, but so were his mechanics. (You don't have to read between the lines here.) Years went by. Anyway, to make a long story short, Nanu sat on the ranch for thirty odd years in the same condition, always next in line to be worked on, until one day John had to retire. It was just not feasible for me to have that many cars anymore, so I started selling them; I even sold the part of the ranch where the beautiful car barn John had built was. That was heartbreaking for John. We then constructed Feelgood's, where the cream of the crop of my old cars would stay. Today, there is also a warehouse in San Carlos, where

Nanu sits in pieces, patiently waiting to be reassembled. I have been told that Nanu is worth a fortune. I have also been told by Brizio Street Rods, the shop building Lincvolt, that to put Nanu back together again would probably cost around as much as she's worth. So when Lincvolt is finally done, I plan on starting one more job. If there is any money left in the Lincvolt fire insurance fund, I will use that cash to start reassembling Nanu the Lovesick Moose, completing my seventeen-year-old self's dream in one more giant step toward success.

Walking has always been good for me. I love to walk. Long walks on the ranch or over the lava in Hawaii are therapeutic and result in a clear head. Ben Keith and I used to walk the ranch together on a ridge every day for a couple of years. It is usually my preference to walk alone, but with Ben it was fine. One day Ben told me that he got winded starting where I start, so we began starting at the top of the first rise, rather than at the bottom. He was having a problem getting enough air. We adapted, and everything was fine. I miss him now on that walk.

For a year or more, I stopped the walking because my feet were hurting. At a doctor's advice, I tried wearing special inserts in my shoes, but they threw off my balance. Eventually I learned from various body workers on the Big Island, most notably a Feldenkrais practitioner there, that correct posture is very important and my bad posture was putting a lot of strain on the bottoms of my feet. It's amazing what you can learn when you step outside the realm of people who are selling you something and into the realm of people who treat the body, not the symptom.

Where the doctor had not helped me and the inserts were not working, the body workers' advice was the key to success. I took it to heart and solved the problem by working on my posture, which is a lot better now than it was. I was well on my way to being a stooped-over old guy. That did happen to my dad. That was my problem, and I solved it by changing my posture. After that, things were pretty good.

But I had another thing causing the problem, too. When I find something I like, I stick with it, sometimes for way too long. I had been wearing the same brand of hiking shoes for a long time. At first I loved them, but eventually I found that I had to get new ones more and more often. One day I went to a different store and got some real good leather boots instead of those hiking high-tops I had been getting for years. These new leather boots kick ass. No more problems. Now I have really good boots and can walk a long way again! Fantastic. Maybe I should call this book *The Shoe Chronicles*.

There *is* a reason why I am telling you so much about my shoes and my feet. Walking and all kinds of movement from one place to another are very important to me. It has always been my way to think about things while I walk. I am always going over ideas, songs, album running orders, all kinds of creative stuff, while I am walking. I love to walk. It soothes my soul. My mother always told me that my Grandpa Ragland would walk every day and he loved his walks. He lived a long time.

My favorite walk is still up on the ridge overlooking the ranch.

I walk about a mile and a half to two miles every time I go up there, and always feel better afterward, rain or shine. Nina goes with me now when I go. On the ridge, there is a place I walk to where two eucalyptus trees have grown together. One tree has a branch that reaches over to the other and grows right through its trunk. These two trees are permanently connected. I call them the Trees in Love. I walk to the Trees in Love and back home every time I get a chance.

Now, in Hawaii I like to paddleboard too. It does the same thing for me, I open up and start thinking about all kinds of ideas about music, life, my family, all matters personal. I take all of this to heart in my personal time of reflection.

## Chapter Fifty-Seven

O nce, when Buffalo Springfield did a show in Albuquerque, I went for a ride in a rented car with Bruce Palmer and cruised the back roads around town. There was a road called the Old Indian Trail that ran along the edge of town and had a wonderful view of the mountains and the old Indian country on one side and the city of Albuquerque on the other.

As we were driving along we found an old roadside antique shop and stopped to check it out. Quite a selection of stuff was inside. There were a lot of old glass bottles and some old statues. The place had a vibe I really liked, and I spent a long time just walking around looking. I finally saw something in a corner I wanted: a bow and two arrows. The arrows were handmade, with iron tips that were jagged-edged and very sharp. They looked like hunting arrows. The arrows were long, very straight, and the tips were different on each one. The bow was very plain and I think it was lemonwood. At least that's what the old man at the shop said.

Anyway, the arrows had real feathers on the ends, tied with

With David Briggs, backstage at the Roxy nightclub
in West Hollywood, 1973.

twine that was neatly wound around the quills. They looked like authentic Indian arrows to me, although the iron tips were different. Maybe they were obtained from a white man, a trader. So I took them up to the counter and paid for them, along with an old Indian blanket I found, and when I got back to Laurel Canyon and my little cabin there, I stuck the arrows in the wall by throwing them at it and letting them stick.

I always took them with me whenever I moved to a new place, and I would again throw them at the wall and let them stick wherever they were.

They went to Malibu when Stephen found a house on Malibu Road and the Springfield lived there. I had a little separate place below the garage where we put up some paneling and a sliding glass door. It had an ocean view. A decorative llama rug was on my floor. A kerosene lamp was on my Monterey Spanish dresser. The arrows were stuck in the wall. When Bruce was allowed a second chance and returned to the USA with the help of lawyers, he got busted for the last time near that Malibu house, driving down the Pacific Coast Highway on acid without a license. That was really the beginning of the end for the Buffalo.

Later I moved to Topanga and stuck the arrows in the wall there in that house the same way, by throwing them at a wooden wall and letting them stick. Eventually, I packed the bow and arrows away in the back of my '51 Willys Jeepster and drove north on the 101 to move to my new ranch. When we were done renovating half of the living room, I leaned the bow up in the corner, threw the arrows at the wall, and left them right where they stuck for the first time. Every once in a while now, when Pegi and I move pictures around, we take the arrows down and I throw them at the wall again in a new place. They are still there for us to enjoy after all these years, whenever we return from our travels to our wonderful ranch home.

Of course, our little cabin has grown, and if you listen really closely on a misty morning, you can still hear little Amber's bare footsteps running gingerly down the long hall to the living room. At night, when a fire is flickering in the lava rock fireplace, you can see those time-aged and untreated redwood planks glowing in the warm reflection—pierced by two arrows from Albuquerque. I like to take a little bit of the past with me when I go to a new place, and those arrows really ground me. It's odd, but the way Pegi likes those arrows makes me feel like she knows me.

David Briggs's house in Topanga was known as Old To-panga Ranch and was hidden in the trees just off Old Topanga Canyon Road. I would visit David there, and we would listen to records and talk about the songs and records we were working on. There were a lot of good times.

On the weekends or at least on sunny days, we would all be outside around a fire pit or pitching horseshoes. Kirby, David's old friend from Wyoming, was there with us a lot, as was Shannon, David's wife and the mother of Lincoln Wyatt Briggs, David's son. LW, as he was called, was a great kid. Hannibal and Attila were David's two dogs, brown shorthaired hounds, who were always around in the living room somewhere. David produced a few records during this time with Spirit, Nils Lofgren, and Murray Roman, among others. Briggs is known to have driven several bands crazy with his temper and his rants about the inadequacies of certain musicians and bands. Subtlety was never David's thing, although he did work his magic in some pretty curious ways. His reputation grew and became legendary, and some musicians were actually scared of David.

David once said, "If you want to fight someone big, hit them first and run like hell!" He was fearless. But of all the records I made with David, what I most remember is his dedication to getting a great performance on tape at any cost. "Be great or be gone."

One time we traveled across the country from Key West to San Francisco together in Pocahontas. I was driving and David was navigating. When we got to the Rocky Mountains, we decided to give Independence Pass in Colorado a shot. It was about twelve thousand feet or so at the summit, and then it landed in Aspen on the other side. We were imagining all the starlets we would meet there, so we tried to take that two-lane road over the Rockies in a forty-foot-long bus. It was the wildest ride I have ever been on. When we got to the peak, there was a curve on the side of the mountain with a sheer drop down several thousand feet on the left side and a rock wall straight up on the right. The road was about fifteen feet wide at that point, less than two lanes, and slightly narrower than on a straightaway. I couldn't see around the curve because the rock wall was cutting down my angle. I swung the front end out over the line a bit to make it around the curve, when suddenly a car appeared coming the other way!

Quickly I turned away from it and simultaneously heard a

sickening scraping sound on the right-hand side of the bus where it had kissed the mountainside. We couldn't stop up there or anywhere, so we just kept going around the curve and down that road. We had peaked the summit and were on our way down into Aspen, and after about twenty minutes of driving we got to a place where we could pull the bus over and take a look. Holy shit! There was a gaping slash in the bus. The generator and the air-conditioning unit were both heavily damaged. We continued into Aspen and went for a series of beers. David was drinking Mexican coffees, a favorite of his, made of coffee and tequila.

When we exited the bar, we checked into a hotel to regroup. The next day we continued on toward California with no generator and no air-conditioning. A couple of days later we finally arrived at Alex's Bar on the mountain on Skyline Boulevard above the ranch, one of our old haunts. We went in, had dinner and a lot of alcohol. That was a trip to remember, but it was only one of the many experiences I shared with my good friend Mr. Briggs. I think I have time to tell you a few more, although I could never tell you all of them.

About twenty years later, in the mid-nineties, Briggs and I were making an album. I still call it an album because that is what I make. I don't make CDs or iTunes tracks. I make albums. That is just what I do. Call it what you like. I remember how I hated the shuffle feature on iTunes because it fucked up the running order I spent hours laboring over. Having tracks available independently and having the shuffle feature available sucks as far as I am concerned. Call me old-fashioned. I make albums and I want the songs to go together to create a feeling. I do those things on purpose. I don't want people cherry-picking the albums. I like to choose the singles. After all, it's my shit.

We were making an album at the Complex in LA that Briggs was producing with John Hanlon engineering. It was Crazy Horse, and it was cool. We were right into it. Briggs said at one point that this record was going to be Crazy Horse's Grammy. He was really into it then, and that surprised me. He never gave a shit about that in the past. Kurt Cobain had just committed suicide and left a note with my song quoted in it. "It's better to burn out than to fade away." He had been taking a lot of heat for canceling some shows. I, coincidentally, had been trying to reach him through our offices to tell him that I thought he was great and he should do exactly what he thought he should do and fuck everybody else. He was not just an entertainer; he was an artist and songwriter. There is a big difference. I knew him and recognized him for who he was. I wanted to talk to him. Tell him only to play when he felt like it. And that would be good enough. Be true.

So when he died and left that note, it struck a deep chord inside of me. It fucked with me. I wrote some music for that feeling: "Sleeps with Angels." David was right there with me because he knew. He knew the truth. At the end of that session, David did something highly unusual: He made a sort of declaration about the record and what we were doing. He did it on camera with Larry Johnson, who was there filming the sessions. I went back and revisited all that footage to see what the hell we were doing. I couldn't find that. I found a lot of other stuff. That is just one more loose end to finish up.

That was David's last album. He got sick after that. There was more recorded there than what we used. We missed something. I know it. He sleeps with angels.

There was a Crazy Horse tour, Ragged Glory, that Briggs and I did, with John Hanlon engineering, around 1990. I wrote a lot of songs in my car barn that were on that album. The car barn was a huge metal building with a gravel floor, and I set up my amps in there with a bunch of old cars. All my best shit. My Fender Deluxe with a Fender Reverb, my whizzer attached to it, my Magnatone feeding from that, and my Baldwin Exterminator feeding off of it, too. The fifties tweed Fender Deluxe I refer to is my original amp purchased from Sol Betnun Music on Larchmont Boulevard in LA in the sixties. That place was always full of old Fenders galore. I think it's gone now. I had that amp in my little Laurel Canyon cabin when I was in the Springfield. It had a fine sound. It sucked in a really good way when you turned it up to twelve! Yes! It goes to twelve! (Eat shit, Spiñal Tap!) At ten it is distorted and chunky but doesn't suck, at six it is nasty and edgy. At three it is just plain awful in a good way. The whizzer is something we built that turns the knobs manually so the signal doesn't get compromised. Any volume pot (controller) that's in the line fucks with the signal. The whizzer doesn't go in the line. It manually controls by rotating the master volume pot with a motor instead.

My Fender Reverb unit is from the fifties, too, maybe the early sixties. It has tubes and a spring reverb. It's very analog. If you rattle it, it makes a loud sound all by itself. It is a real effect. Not digital. Digital effects are trying to sound like this stuff. My Magnatone amp has a stereo vibrato. It takes a feed from inside the Deluxe at a point where the signal is least compromised and there is a boost to keep the level up. The Magnatone has a lot more balls than the Deluxe, but they are both run from my pedal board built by Johnny Foster, Tim's brother, attached with platinum switches built by Sal Trentino, the original tube amp guru. Thanks to Sal, I can bypass all that shit with one button if I don't want it, because it splits the signal, too. Thanks, Sal—rest in peace, my friend. (Of course, there's still that one platinum contact that the signal has to go through. If that was too techy for you, then you can just forget I said it, but it's staying right here in this book where it belongs.)

Anyway, back in 1990, I would go into my car barn with all this stuff and Old Black. I'd just started reviewing my archives, and I had recently heard some of my best shit, so I knew who I was and who I could be. I would come in every morning, smoke some weed, and start playing. Then the songs just came. *Ragged Glory*. The songs got written. We started recording and playing all the songs in a row two or three times a day for a week or two. No repeating. We'd just do a few sets a day. That was a cool way to make a record. No analyzing. Then at the end, we read our notes and went back and found the masters.

One day we were listening to tracks and we heard "Mansion on the Hill." It was a funky track, but it had the vibe. I asked David to play it one more time. David said to Hanlon, "All right then, let's hear it in all its ragged glory." That became the title. David had a way with words, an amazing vocabulary that he used poetically and to great effect always. So I finished the record, and we went out on tour with Sonic Youth and Social Distortion. Briggs went along, recording in an analog truck. We were a great bill; people got a real show. It rocked. I met Thurston Moore, and he told me about Nirvana, this great band, and how I should be taking them out, too, or at least hear them. Every night I would warm up backstage with Mike, my trainer, when Sonic Youth would come on, and they were fucking great. How original are they? Very. They would echo through the arena and sound like God. First, Social Distortion would come out cold and level the place. Then Sonic Youth! Then Crazy Horse! Because it was the Gulf War, we did an electric version of Bob's "Blowin' in the Wind." "How many times must the cannonballs fly?" It was just another great tour for the Horse . . .

One night in March of 1977, Linda Ronstadt and Nicolette Larson were in Malibu at Linda's house. I went over to see them and show them some songs I wanted to do with them for a new album. We made a cassette of the songs, and the two of them sang like birds. It was a thrill to be there with them. Everything was so easy. Unlike me, they always sang on pitch. It was like falling off a log for them. Linda has always been friendly to me and has helped me on quite a few records. *Harvest* was the first one of those. A few years later, I was very lucky to have Linda opening for me on the Time Fades Away tour. That was in 1973. She was dynamite. She got in trouble in Albuquerque for swearing onstage or something. I can't remember exactly what she did, but she caused an uproar.

I first saw Linda at the Troubadour in the sixties when she was with the Stone Poneys. She was great then, too. So young and beautiful! She blew everyone's mind with her big voice. Can you imagine sitting in the audience, seeing this girl walk up onstage, looking so amazing in her short shorts, and then hearing that huge voice? It was earth-shattering. She is always at the top of her game, but now Linda has become somewhat reclusive. She just dropped out to raise a family and live a "normal" life in the "real world." She used "real world" to describe me once. She told Nicolette not to get involved with me because I was "not living in the real world"! It didn't matter, though, because Nicolette and I did have a close relationship for a while. It didn't last for us, though. Life is like that.

Anyway, when I was getting to know Nicolette, she was at the ranch with Linda recording the songs I had shown the two of them in Malibu. (By the way, Linda was addicted to peanut butter at the time! Isn't that exactly the kind of interesting information you expect from a book like this?) That album, *American Stars 'n Bars*, we recorded in the White House with the Green Board, exactly like I want to do with Crazy Horse now. After we made that album, Nicolette came to Nashville and sang with me on the *Comes a Time* album. That is one of my best albums ever.

The tapes from *Comes a Time* were damaged en route to the mastering in New York, and I ended up purchasing all of the records that were pressed from those tapes, a couple hundred thousand of them, and remastered from a safety tape copy. All of the high frequency was missing from my master! I couldn't believe it when I got those dull test pressings and checked the master tape. It was severely damaged somehow. I don't know what happened

*With Linda Ronstadt riding
at the Broken Arrow Ranch, 1977.*

With Nicolette Larson, Linda Ronstadt, and Crazy Horse,
during sessions for the American Stars 'n Bars *album*
at the Broken Arrow Ranch studio, 1977.

to it. That was the last time I ever shipped a master anywhere. Now my guys hand carry.

The song "Comes a Time" is one of my all-time favorite recordings because it just has a great feeling. The song and the performance are a total mesh. Nicolette's singing is beautiful. I can see all the pictures. That is as close to a perfect recording as I ever have gotten. Karl Himmel laid down a unique groove on drums, and the band was locked in. Karl has the ability to play two grooves at once, which I have never heard anyone else do as well as he does. He is a completely unique musician. Chuck Cochran did the string arrangement. Rufus Thibodeaux played fiddle. JJ Cale played a guitar on it. Ben Keith played steel. Spooner Oldham played piano. There was a rhythm guitar section with six great guitarists all playing rhythm on old Martin acoustics. Everyone played and it was the country wall of sound, the Gone With the Wind Orchestra. What a sound!

Soon after I was so high on that orchestra that I did a free concert in Miami and took the whole group down there and played. But we didn't record it—I can't believe it. It must be the only thing I've ever done that I didn't record. I did "Sweet Home Alabama" at that show, and the folks loved it. (My own song "Alabama" richly deserved the shot Lynyrd Skynyrd gave me with their great record. I don't like my words when I listen to it today. They are accusatory and condescending, not fully thought out, and too easy to misconstrue.) We *did* record a rehearsal at the Musicians Union Hall in Nashville, and I have a tape of that from a room microphone for the archives. It was a golden moment.

In 1992, Linda's singing on the *Harvest Moon* album was beautiful, particularly on the title song. She really made that record what it is. She is a master. "Hangin' on a Limb" on the *Freedom* album is beautiful because Linda played such a part in it. She played such a part on all of those songs, and "Unknown Legend" was taken to new heights by her gifted arrangement and singing. When she came to Broken Arrow and sang on my records, she elevated everything she touched. I could never thank her enough. She never asks for anything, so I can't do any return favors for her. I am ready to anytime, though. She is like a sister to me, and I love her like that. So giving and selfless, just loving the music.

(Incidentally, I was playing really quiet on the *Harvest Moon* album because my ears were blown out from the *Weld* mixing. We mixed *Weld* twice because Billy Talbot and I were not happy with Briggs's mixes. We were wrong, and it was a waste of time. We should have used Briggs's work. Loud music hurt for a year after that. I still have and always will have tinnitus, ringing in the ears, from mixing too loud with low-quality digital sound. The resolution on those machines was nowhere near what we have available today. Tinnitus never goes away, but the pain does.)

Linda is now outside the pop music world, doing her thing. I don't know if there will ever be another singer who impacts me like she does. She is truly at the top of the class, along with Emmylou Harris and Nicolette. Some artists just have it. Like a painter who is great, you can't say why. I have been so fortunate to have these friends.

I find it unbelievable that Linda Ronstadt is not in the Rock and Roll Hall of Fame. There is something wrong with that. She should have been inducted a long time ago. I would be honored to induct her. Linda, Emmylou, Nicolette—these were beautiful ladies who gave to the music so selflessly. I have been truly blessed to make music with them all. The background chants by Linda and Nicolette on "Bite the Bullet" from *American Stars 'n Bars* will never fade from my mind. "Hold Back the Tears"—so rockin'! Linda has so much to give. In "Star of Bethlehem," the harmony of Emmylou and Ben Keith is so beautiful. So I have been lucky and life has gifted me. I know who I am and what I've been part of, but the music speaks when words can't. I will never forget those times.

These days, Pegi is singing her heart out about things that really matter to her, just like she dreamed of doing when she was so young. She is opening up her voice and her soul on her third recording, *Bracing for Impact*. It is really a true record; her songwriting is so focused and real. Her singing, so honest. More power to you, baby! I know we will have a lot more to look forward to!

Chapter Fifty-Eight

T
he Squires were ready to move. From August 8 through 14, 1965, we had a gig up in Churchill, Manitoba, on Hudson Bay. That was very far north, and it was a day-and-a-half-long train ride through Indian Territory. It was the farthest we had ever gone from Winnipeg, and we were excited. As the train rolled north, I remember seeing Indian villages by the tracks, teepees and little wooden and tin shacks side by side. The First Nation's people were in disarray, very poor, and their lives were brutal. Seeing and feeling that through the coach window was an experience I will never forget.

As the miles rolled by, characters of all kinds traveled on that train with us. When we finally got to Churchill, we found it a pretty desolate place, with a lot of trailers and some white buildings made of wood and concrete. They all looked the same to me. There were no trees there at all. The tallest bushes were so wind-blown that the branches all extended in only one direction, so the plants always looked like the wind was howling, even if it wasn't. And the people looked that way, too.

With Mort and the Squires before moving from Winnipeg to Fort William, 1965. Left to right: Ken Koblun, me, and Bob Clark.

We stayed outside the hotel in one of the buildings during the day and ate at the hotel. There was a restaurant/supper club there, and we set up our gear. The crowd was pretty subdued until the weekend, and that was when people got rowdy. Nothing happened to us, but we could tell that it could have. We were too young to be playing in there, but they didn't know that.

One night the place was very rowdy, and suddenly the floor started moving! A polar bear was under the hotel! Some guys went out and shooed it away. Some shots were fired, and everything returned to normal. Another night during the week, an Indian guy was drunk and had left to walk home. He stopped and leaned on a telephone pole to rest, fell asleep, and died right there. Frozen to death. They found him in the morning, leaning on the pole, frozen solid. That place was not on the Squires' list of places to return to.

After the long trip back to Winnipeg, we got into Mort the hearse and took off to Fort William. I had written a few songs about Churchill on the train ride and updated the song "The Birds and the Bees" with lyrics about Churchill. It was a funny song. One of the updated lyrics was "A penguin I know, and a thing called snow." I don't remember the rest.

Whenever we went to a new place, I always thought that since we were from out of town, we would have a mystique about us and be more interesting than the other bands. That turned out to be true, and the Fort William days, when we were on the road, were among the best in the history of the Squires. We were headed for the big time at last.

The sky was the limit.

Chapter Fifty-Nine

Life in LA

There was an apartment building called the Commodore Gardens on Orchid Avenue in Hollywood. It was there that I got my very first place to live in LA. The Springfield was playing the Whisky a Go Go, and I had some cash. Some girls who were real good friends of mine from the Whisky were living there. Their names were Donna Port and Vicki Cavaleri. I enjoyed their company. They had a girlfriend who was really nice who they were always trying to get me together with, but I wasn't ready for her at the time. We really hung out a lot.

They introduced me to the Commodore Gardens landlord, and I got my own apartment there. In an attempt to make it my own, I immediately broke all the rules and tacked up some matting on the walls that I had bought at Pier 1 Imports. I put a blue light-bulb in the fridge. It was an old fridge. I don't know what I ever put in it. Must have been Cokes and Twinkies. I wasn't into health food yet, that's for sure.

I wrote a lot of songs there for the Springfield, and it was an exciting time for me. "Flying on the Ground," "Do I Have to Come Right Out and Say It," and "Burned" were among the songs I wrote there. I was also dealing with my newly discovered seizure disorder, and come to think of it, I'm sure the food I was eating was not helping! We would come home from the International House of Pancakes on Sunset at about three A.M. after eating a bunch of German pancakes with sugar and lemon all over them. Those things were great because they reminded me of the pancakes I used to have back home in Canada, "rollers," we called them. Butter, sugar, and lemon juice, all rolled up and eaten like a hot dog. I did that almost every night after the Whisky, and we played that place for a long time and returned and did it over again night after night. We were the opening act for lots of stars.

We had lots of girls and lots of fun. I got a few sexually transmitted diseases and started to become aware that there was a responsibility connected to the decisions I was making. Breaking new ground, you might say. I visited the Hollywood Free Clinic a few times. That was a place by La Brea that had been set up that helped all the transient kids on Sunset to stay more or less clean and healthy. Those were simple days. Some of the support systems set up by the government actually worked for the people.

It was after that period at the Commodore Gardens that I got my next place up in Laurel Canyon. We were getting more successful. I had my own car, but no license because I was still an illegal alien and had no Social Security card. Driving my car was nerve-racking for that reason. I was always worried about getting stopped by the cops. The first car I got was a '54 Packard ambulance. The next one was a '57 Corvette that I got with my share of the advance money from Atlantic Records, approximately twenty grand for the whole band, split many ways, when we signed with Ahmet Ertegun. Charlie Greene and Brian Stone retained most of that themselves.

Once during the height of tensions on Sunset, just before Stephen wrote his classic "For What It's Worth," I got stopped and put in jail for not having a license. My friend Freddy Brechtel, a singer without a band, was with me, and he took the car back to my place. I went to jail at the Hollywood substation, just down the hill from the Whisky. While I was in the cell, one of the officers called me a stinking hippie. He was wearing horn-rimmed glasses. Shooting back, I told him he looked like a grasshopper. He came in the cell and beat the shit out of me. Slamming my face and kicking me around on the floor. That was traumatizing.

The instances of that sort of thing were many in those days. Hippies were targets. Eventually Charlie and Brian got an attorney and I was out on bail, but I was even more scared of the cops after that. There was never any thought of pressing charges, because I didn't have a leg to stand on. No license. We felt lucky that I wasn't deported. They didn't realize I was an illegal alien. They weren't thorough, just brutal. I still cringe when I see a Hollywood sheriff's cruiser, even though I have been legal for a long time.

Once Stephen and I and the rest of the Springfield went to a beach near Point Dume to do a radio promotional event. You got airplay that way. KHJ was doing a promotion where the Big Kahuna was arriving from Hawaii in a canoe and giving out cash to KHJ listeners. KHJ Boss 93 was giving away big bucks, and Buffalo Springfield was going to be on the shore to greet the Big Kahuna when he arrived. It was live on the air, and we were all doing interviews. Soon a grass canoe with outriggers rounded the point and the Big Kahuna appeared! There were a lot of babes there, and Stephen and I were having a great time.

Later we met the Big Kahuna and found out his name was Chris. He sold us some of the best weed in Hollywood after that. It was called Kahuna grass. (Another name is sinsemilla, for "no seeds.") This was some really potent weed that all the bands were smoking. The Big Kahuna had delivered the mother lode. This went on for quite some time, and Kahuna grass is still legendary today in old LA musicians' circles. It used to make me so paranoid thinking that I was going to have a seizure that I had to stop smoking it. If you smoked a little, you wrote a song. If you smoked too much, then you were toast. That was the reputation it had with me.

## Chapter Sixty

Farm Aid 26 is coming up next week. I haven't played much lately. I don't have a musical direction at the moment, other than my wish to play with Crazy Horse and explore the territory, see the view. At times like these, I am at a loss. Gigs that come up on a time clock don't really work for the creative process and are a disturbance for the muse. That has nothing to do with my support for the farmers, a lifelong commitment. It has to do only with the muse. How can I play if I have no direction? It's not just a job you do.

Usually I do benefits in October. That way I can prepare myself, figure out what I will be doing, and play three or four benefits during that month. This Farm Aid is happening at an odd time of year, August. If I'm not on the road, I'm resting in August, and that rest is very important. After a long time off, playing one gig takes at least a month of mental preparation to get an idea of what I'm going to do, where I will be drawing from. I have less than a week left now to prepare. I need to start playing every day so my hands are ready with calluses on my fingers and I know the words and songs.

I'm going to do my best Bob Dylan imitation! I will go out there with an acoustic guitar and harmonica. No electric. This will be a folk approach, based on story songs with lots of words and verses. I will be like a ghost from the past, totally a throwback to another time. (It's funny; I call it a Bob Dylan imitation, but Bob never does it. It's what everyone would like to see him do, and he never does it. I suspect it would be too lonely and singular for him, no band to hang with or friends to see every day when he gets off the bus.)

So that is my plan. I will play a few new tunes that I did on the last tour—"Love and War," "Peaceful Valley Boulevard"—and do them differently, with a pushier groove and more harp playing with a straight acoustic rhythm instead of the more sensitive finger-picking and bass-reinforced *Le Noise* sound. I may revert to history with some story songs like "Powderfinger" and a few others, punctuated here and there with some more personal lyrics like "Sugar Mountain" and "Comes a Time." I will probably not play any other instruments, keeping it way simple and focused on the old-time folk music approach. Maybe I'll play "Vampire Blues," maybe not.

Basically I will come and go, just being myself in a really simple way. No bells and whistles at all. This is something I think I can do and make it work. I have been thinking about this for about three weeks and actually worrying about it. That is how a forty-minute set can take a month of preparation. It would take the same amount of preparation for me to do a whole tour.

B ecause someone had the rights to the name PureTone, we changed our name to Pono. It is Hawaiian for "righteous and good." We love our new name. Negotiations for the Pono project between Pono and WMG have been ongoing for about six weeks now, trying to settle on the details of the founding partners group. This process is distinctly different from most every other thing I have done in the past. My friend Marc Benioff told me that I need to remember what I'm in it for, saving the sound of music and rescuing an art form, and just focus on that. "Business is not like a song, Neil; there is no last note. It just keeps going on and on, and there is conflict almost constantly," he told me one night when I called asking for his advice.

The exercise is very frustrating.

He pointed out that I need to focus on what I *can* do, not what I *can't* do. I need to figure that one out for my own sake, because it's too wearing on me. I need to let it happen the way it will and not try to control every little part of it. Control is my way of ensuring that things go right, and if I don't have control, I worry that things are going to get away and not be done correctly. You know, the videos I have been making that showcase me playing Pono for musicians and music lovers are coming along so well, and I see the happiness on the faces of people who are hearing great sound and enjoying it, discovering that music can be much deeper an emotional experience than what they've grown used to recently. I feel this is so important, and it is so gratifying to watch all of these car interviews, some twenty-five now, as the editing continues on the ranch. The musicians and music lovers are of all ages, and they are all unified in their strong, supportive, and positive reactions. This is most positive and reaffirms what I believed in the beginning. I *should* be so happy to focus on that.

The goal is so great, and the success of this will be so gratifying. Yet everyone cautions me about the strength of Apple and iTunes. I think that no matter what, this project will force iTunes to be better and to improve quality at a faster pace. I just hope what Apple does is great enough, not some measured response that is hyped so much that the consumers feel they are getting the best when they are not.

The record companies are sort of held hostage in a weird way by the Internet's dominance in their industry. But because the record companies still hold the gold, their high-quality music masters, it's time for them to step up and take control of their own destiny. I realize the amount of cash Apple has far exceeds the amount of cash the United States of America has, and everyone is scared of that. But I think public opinion and social networking could win over money, just as it has upset the status quo in the Arab Spring and all of the other revolutions around the world organized through social networking. This is just another revolution. Quality sound can make a return and be reestablished for those who want the best. The best is just not available right now in a consumer-friendly way. The Sound Revolution could bring it back, if the cards the record companies hold are played. That is the big If. Will they have the balls to stand up and take care of the music?

These days it's all about closure of this and that for me. I have too many things to finish. How can I move on until I clean that slate? My film *Human Highway* is one of those things. It should be available to the public. Dean Stockwell and Russell Tamblyn, my old friends from Topanga Canyon, and Dennis Hopper, a good old friend, were in this movie with me, and we wrote the dialogue as we went along. It is the dorkiest damn movie ever and it walks a very fine line right on the edge of being too dorky. Some may say it falls over that line. The film was never put to rest to my satisfaction, and for the last ten years or so, Larry Johnson had been struggling, trying to find some pieces of that film that may be lost now. He was very occupied with getting the quality preserved for David Myers's legacy. Not that we don't have copies. We do. We have everything we need to edit together the film in a way I can rest well behind content-wise. When I finish something, I want it to be right, or as right as it can be.

As I mentioned, *Human Highway* is just one of those things. I am not Cecil B. DeMille. It is not a great commercial movie. But it has never reached its potential, so I have never been able to let it go. I have carried it with me all these years. It was released, bombed, and was buried before I even felt it was done. With Larry Johnson gone and David Myers gone and Dennis Hopper, too, I am left with this drive to finish. I went into the editing room on the ranch, which is actually in the train barn as fate would have it. (I love that I can leave the editing screens and walk around looking at the trains and work on some small detail of the layout or clean and polish some wheels while I work out some editing challenge in my head. That is so liberating. It is the combining of two different worlds in a good way for me.)

I asked Will Mitchell, Larry's and my right-hand man, for all of the existing Shakey Pictures' *Human Highway* footage to be brought to the editing room, and when it all arrived, I sat down with Toshi Onuki and we reviewed what we had. There were three separate versions of the film. One version, which was based on the original cut, the director's cut if you will, had last been worked on by Larry and Toshi. It was exactly what I was looking for. I asked to see it, and then I viewed it while taking notes. When it was all over, we took a little break and then went through the film, making corrections. It really got good when we made the changes. Humor is all about timing, and I have learned a lot about that in the thirty years since I first cut this picture. We had a hodgepodge of prints and qualities, but were able to cut together the story.

I now feel the picture is in its final shape, and I love it. It's not the greatest picture in the world, but it is my picture, and I love what it does. It moves me now like I always wanted it to. I think it might still get panned, but I don't care. I like it. That is what matters to me. Once the technical aspects are all pulled together and the final sound mix is done, I can rest knowing I have done my best. I hope it is what Larry would have wanted. That is a good feeling. Thank you, Larry. Thank you, David. Thanks, Dean and Russell. Thanks, Dennis. I love you guys. I'll show it to you when I see you.

When my studio album *Prairie Wind* was finished, I talked to Jonathan Demme about making a picture. We had discussed the idea a few times before but had no direction to go in. Now we did. We talked about the songs and the feeling on *Prairie Wind* for a long time, the musicians of Nashville, and the great history of country music. We talked about my home in Canada, my dad, my mom, my upbringing, my dad's hometown on the prairies, my dad's passing, my cousins singing under the direction of my uncle Bob, who was a great musician and my dad's brother; we talked a lot about those things. What it all boiled down to was an appearance at the Ryman Auditorium, home of the Grand Ole Opry in its heyday. We decided to do a performance that was a tribute to those times, to that heritage, while also showcasing *Prairie Wind* for the very first time. We were going to assemble a cast of the great musicians and singers who played on *Prairie Wind* and perform it live at the Ryman in front of an audience of Nashville folks on the night of the August full moon! It was a great plan, and we were very excited to get started.

One night in Nashville we were eating in the restaurant at the Hermitage Hotel. It's a wonderful place. We were enjoying some fine wine and talking about the picture. I'll never forget the look on Jonathan's face when I said I had invited the costume director down to meet him at the restaurant.

WHAT? You've *chosen the costume director?* (Jonathan's thought bubble!)

Jonathan Demme always chose his own costume directors! Of course I have the greatest respect for Director Demme's taste and knew he would love Manuel, who originated in Nudie's shop in Hollywood. Manuel was the man who made every country artist's clothing. He made Elvis's gold lamé suit. He made Dolly Parton's and Porter Wagoner's clothes. He was *the* man. And there he was, walking into the restaurant. He joined us. He was wearing a very cool shirt and looked like he was already in a movie. Accompanied by a young lady and a young man assistant, he sat down at the table and took a little sip of wine. Then he started talking. It was fascinating. He blew everyone's mind with his stories. Then Jonathan told him the whole concept for the show, describing the backdrop art, the Ole Opry atmosphere, the *Prairie Wind* songs and feelings, the ambience around the songs being written, my life-threatening situation at the time, the newness of the music, the audience itself, and the camera angles, and asked him what he wanted to do.

"Don't worry," Manuel said. "It will be perfect, like a dream you are having."

Manuel did not offer one detail. It was a moment to remember. Manuel was totally in control. Jonathan was seeing a living legend. This was a great moment.

We went on to make the movie, and it is something that will last a lifetime. We are all very proud of this film. We paid tribute to those who had come before and left an enduring document to the greatness of country music and the tradition of Nashville. My favorite shot is one taken from the back of the stage. You can see Emmylou Harris and me singing "This Old Guitar." It looks like it's from the forties, a perfect time capsule. And through beautiful camera work, lighting, and a great instrumental performance, we left a living picture of one of the greatest country music artists of all time, Ben Keith.

## Chapter Sixty-One

You may remember Nina. She is Pegi's new dog. All curly and soft, little Nina weighs about twenty-five pounds. She went through that broken-down Cadillac Eldorado episode with me out on Interstate 5 in the 106-degree heat. We bonded. Well, now Pegi is on the road with the Survivors, and I am at home with Nina. Nina sleeps at the foot of the bed whenever I am sleeping. It feels good to not be alone. Pegi calls quite regularly to tell me what to do with Nina in this case or that case, and that is always helpful.

Last night Nina was barking incessantly at something outside. I let her out and she just kept on barking. This is something that has just developed recently, and whenever I told Nina to stop barking, she would just ignore me completely. The barking just went on and on. I was beginning to get irritated with this development. Was this dog going to take over the whole house? She was really cute, but she was really LOUD, too. Once she started barking, she would never stop.

I tried yelling at her, "STOP BARKING, NINA!" in my biggest "man voice." It had no effect. I was getting pissed. Eventually, she got tired and stopped, but it had gone on for a long time. My always active imagination was now getting the best of me in a barrage of images and thoughts. I was starting to visualize a dog barking for the rest of time.

The next morning at about six, Nina and I got up and went out to the kitchen. I put on some water to boil and opened the door and we went outside. I stood there with her as she peed on the lawn. She went about her business, sniffing and carrying on in doglike fashion. Eventually, we returned inside and I made some tea. Sitting down at the computer to check my morning mail, I heard her growling softly, then more loudly, until it developed into a full-on bark. Nina was standing in the kitchen, barking! I sat there, digesting the situation. She continued her barking.

In an epiphany, I softly called her name and gave her my special little whistle that was just for her. She came over to me and I held her little head and in a very soft voice told her, "Nina, there is nothing out there. Just lie down here with me and chill out. Everything is fine. It's morning now, and it's all good. Just you and me right here, you on the floor and me with my morning mail." I patted her little head. She lay down on the floor at my feet and fell asleep. The dog is my new guru.

Drummers are very important to my music and the success of any band playing my music. Ralph Molina is the drummer in Crazy Horse, and his feel is a big part of that Crazy Horse sound. He is very sympathetic to improvisation and can quickly go with any flow change. That is really a key thing if you are playing a long jam or instrumental à la "Cowgirl in the Sand," "Down by the River," "Big Time," "Change Your Mind," "No Hidden Path," or "Rockin' in the Free World," to name just a few. Those songs require the drummer to listen to the subtle changes in guitar leads and rhythms, and follow with changes in the groove. Ralph is the best at that for me. Combining that with Billy Talbot's simplicity, soul, and aggression, Crazy Horse's rhythm section is solid as a rock.

Yet at the same time, Ralphie is extremely subtle and can express emotions beautifully in both a ballad and a laid-back song. He is completely unique, emotional, and driving at the same time. His flourishes with my feedback at the end of a long song are always right with me, as if he knows right where I am going. Fact is, we are going there together, feeling our way, and that really applies to all of Crazy Horse. That is what makes the Horse as great as it is, and as cosmic as it is. That is the Force of the Horse. Making the new albums, *Americana* and *Psychedelic Pill*, I have found that this cosmic force has increased, not diminished, with time.

Kenny Buttrey, on the other hand, is a finesse player with a master's touch on any song he plays. His grooves on *Harvest* are in the pocket, and yet so original at the same time. On drums, he just doesn't sound like anyone else. Kenny was a complete original who I was lucky to know and play with. His bass player was usually Tim Drummond, a master in his own right. The two of them together were just what my music needed. Tim Drummond also played with Karl T. Himmel on many of my recordings. They also played with JJ Cale on a lot of his early stuff, which just had that amazing groove. The International Harvesters' *A Treasure* is one of the best illustrations of the massive talent of Karl T. Himmel. Karl played on "Comes a Time" and "Four Strong Winds," as well as a lot of tracks on *Prairie Wind*. Karl's feel is so fluid and sensitive, and I still love playing with him today.

Chad Cromwell is a unique drummer, different from all the rest. He is very strong and steady, the most reliable. You can count on Chad to always be on the money. A band could hang on his groove because it never falters. His playing on *Prairie Wind* and with the Bluenotes is totally awesome. Equally at home in any genre from country to blues to rock, Chad is a very authoritative, consistent, and powerful drummer who just kicks ass. His drumming on "A Day in the Life" was amazing when I played it with him on my marathon tour with the Electric Band throughout the world in 2007 and 2009. He just rolled with the changes in that song, one of the most difficult and challenging songs for any band, including the Beatles, to play live. When Paul did it with us in Hyde Park at the end of our tour in London, I know he was impressed with how we took that song and delivered it live to the masses.

Chad also played "Words" from the *Harvest* album with its alternating time signatures on that tour. No one other than Buttrey could even play that song, but Chad took it by the horns and slapped it around. The groove with him and Rick Rosas on bass was so huge that we left the ground every night we played it. Save the original version, "Words" was played the best by Chad and that band. The first time I ever saw Rick and Chad playing was at Farm Aid one year with Joe Walsh. I loved the way they supported Joe. I asked them to play a little with me, and we did *Freedom*, the Bluenotes' *This Note's for You*; then we did *Living with War*, and most recently, the Electric Band's *Fork in the Road*. These were all wonderful groups, tours, and records. Rick is a pretty quiet guy until he starts telling jokes and getting funny; then he is hilarious. We've had some great bus rides. He's a slinky bass player with a lot of soul. I always enjoy playing with him and Chad, and we have a lot of fun together.

Dewey Martin of the Buffalo Springfield is possibly the fastest and lightest drummer I have ever heard or played with. His kick drum on "For What It's Worth" is what holds the whole thing together. Drummers are the heartbeat of a song, and it has to be good or you die. So yes, I have been lucky to play with all of these guys.

The Rock and Roll Hall of Fame is hallowed ground in my mind. Originally founded by Ahmet Ertegun, Bob Krasnow, Jann Wenner, and Jon Landau, the Hall was a great idea and an amazing place to imagine. Originally, it didn't really exist as a place, and that was fine. I supposed it was big, kind of like the silver lining around a cloud. Not something you could actually see or touch. It was the honor of a lifetime for me to be inducted. A dream come true.

All or most of my heroes were already in the Hall of Fame when I was inducted: Elvis, Little Richard, Jerry Lee Lewis, Chuck Berry—the pioneers and architects were all there. It is the biggest honor in rock and roll, and rock and roll is what it is.

When people got up to accept their inductions in the first few years, you could feel the energy. It was electric. It was their chance to say what they thought, their moment to be heard and be real. People spoke from the heart and said some outrageous things. You never knew what to expect. A few video cameras captured the moment. People spoke off the top of their heads or from a little sheet of paper. People cried and laughed and settled scores. A lot of them settled scores. There was a lot to say for some of them, and this was their best chance.

Some of these artists had not been active in years or had not had more than a moment in the light and certainly did not make a fortune in the music business. But they all had soul. Some did make a lot of money, of course, but the Hall was about the music, about rock and roll as a way of life. Phil Spector, Mike Love of the Beach Boys, and several others have made long speeches that covered things they needed to say and they had every right to say, and they exercised that right. It was amazing to hear their takes on life, how they had been done right or wrong, who they blamed for their problems and thanked for their victories on the road to the Hall. It was an honor to hear them talking to their peers, to the others who aspired to be like them, and to those who they felt had attained even higher ground than they themselves had.

My favorites spoke with no notes. Some cried. Some laughed. Some thanked. Some just lashed out at those who had screwed them out of royalties and security later in life. Rock and roll is no cakewalk. It was and is a shrewd and unforgiving business if you made some bad decisions about your representation when you were young. A lot of bad moves were made, particularly in the early days, as great as they were, and this was a chance to set it straight, and the inductees did, exercising their new power and rights as members of the hallowed Rock Hall.

Then the worst thing happened.

The founders decided to make the Rock and Roll Hall of Fame induction ceremony a TV show! VH1! What could be LESS rock and roll than VH1? Now a place that was beyond classification had been relegated to a VH1 show. Gone were the long speeches. Three minutes on TV was the new speech. Good-bye, long rambling diatribes. Teleprompters were now available. I made a lot of obscene comments in my speech and swore a lot about everyone involved, but in the end, I don't care to mention them here. They may know who they are, and they may not. People make mistakes. They probably don't know the difference.

It reminded me of the Lifetime Achievement Award the Grammys gave Frank Sinatra in New York one year. A recently successful artist came out and introduced Sinatra in a very long-winded oratory, and then Frank came out. He had just started talking when he was out of time. The band began to play and the introducing artist came back out and walked him off. Sinatra was definitely not finished speaking. I would have loved to hear him, but there was no time left. Frank looked confused and disappointed when he was escorted off. He was just getting started and couldn't believe he was cut short. That's TV. A rambling intro that was much longer than Frank's cut-short speech meant that time was up for one of the greatest legends ever in the history of music. That's life. It pissed me off. But sometimes it's better not to blow up at someone.

I can save that anger and emotion for my guitar playing. A Crazy Horse tour is just around the corner. I'll use it for fuel. I don't want to write some damning thing here about somebody and have to live with that for the rest of time. I don't think that would be a very good idea.

A lot of times things happen and you can't believe it. You walk around cursing under your breath and it really doesn't help. Life is too short. Things shake out. They really do. Take the dickhead record executive who came out to hear me once and went back to his Hollywood record company telling them the material wasn't ready to record. He really pissed me off. Who asked him? I never worked like that before, and I never will in the future. It's my music. But now I'm letting go of that. I might buy him a beer and tell him to drink it sometime, but that's about the extent of it now.

I don't drink anymore myself, I'm moving on. And that's not to say I won't drink again. I'm not making any promises, but I don't think I was a great drinker. Some folks are great drinkers; they drink and tell jokes and laugh their asses off, and they are funny as hell. We buried one of those last week. Life is just a big test, and if you try hard, you fail. If you don't try too hard and fail a little but have a good time, maybe that is success.

I've seen some really happy and content people in this life, and I am not one of them all the time, just some of the time, but I am thankful as hell for them and lonely for the old times and old friends. Not all the time, though. I'm really happy doing what I do, and what I'm doing now is trying like hell to rescue recorded sound so people can feel music again. That makes me happy because it's real, and if I succeed, I will have helped a lot of artists and music lovers achieve nirvana. Who knows where the feeling of sound went? It went so slowly and gradually that no one noticed but me and a few other narky old buzzards, as my daughter Amber lovingly calls me occasionally. But she was the one who heard Pono in my car after listening to MP3s her whole life and looked at me and asked, "What happened? How did that happen?" She knows why I am doing what I am doing. She is *them*, all of those young people who haven't felt the real sound of recorded music.

I am doing this for them, and me. Let's not forget me. I want to feel the sounds again like I did in the beginning, or even better now, because technology is supposed to improve life. Of course, you can't go back, but when I see a young person react to hearing Pono for the first time, well, that is good enough for me. Yes it is.

All I have to do now is navigate the waters of venture capitalism, those treacherous shorelines of commerce, in the HMS *Pono*, a fine ship of significant age and worthiness, with a crew I barely know, but who seem to be committed to the great cause of delivering the cargo to safe harbor in the Heart of Music. I can't tell you how scary this is. I have never been here before, on this vessel, in these waters, with the cargo on board. I seek counsel continuously from a wealth of friends who are experienced in carrying the cargo home to port. They have done this before me. But this is my cargo. I chose it myself, and it has gone undelivered for what seems like decades. How often I wake up at midnight full of questions. Am I alive? Yes.

I may have been asleep for forty years. It's hard to tell. Some people have pointed out to me how great I used to be when I wrote a bunch of songs, but I'm not sure they know what they are speaking about, or the subject, even. Why so pensive about the past? What can it say or do for you now? Nothing much, I fear. I used to wonder if people recognized me, and I was even worried if I thought they did because I didn't really need to be reminded what I was like or when something happened or if I met you once.

Perhaps I overstated that. Forty years is not an amount of time to ignore, though. I think I will have to use my time wisely and keep my thoughts straight if I am to succeed and deliver the cargo I so carefully have carried thus far to the outer reaches. Not that it's my only job or task. I have others, too. Sacred things that I need to protect from pain and hardship, like careless remarks on an open mind. I need to guard against that and honor the source of my feelings, not hide them in a blanket of doubt. My songs are hidden now, orphaned from their melodies and structure that once contained them. How am I, some forty years down the road, to deal with that past accomplishment? Cast it off? Relinquish it to the others who value it more? Was it me? Or who am I now that I cannot see or meet myself the way I was? That is not for me to know, because I am busy with new things now and have no time at all. I am very busy with all of this, and every day is shorter and I wake up earlier and go to sleep at a different time than before. I dream all the time at night, not like before, when I induced dreams in the waking hours to snatch them in their innocence and commit them to song and melody and words captured. Not now. It is not now for that. It is far over for that, I think. I am hoping for a revelation of dreams I can remember, but that is never the case with dreams, is it?

So now I am in the song machine gone awry. I wander the halls of straightness, not knowing how to hallucinate. Finally the course is clear and the sound of waves on rocks is fading. The fog is clearing and there is so much sea. An endless chorus of waves, melodies, refrains, and codas, cropping up and fading away, are a reminder of the duty at hand and the wasted moments. It is the time to gather this and make something of it, or it is not that time. There is no clue. Just the clear sound of the waves on the wood as the ship moves dutifully toward delivery of the cargo. I am on the deck now, at the wheel even, the wind in my hair, such as it is. And my hat is gone, blown away by the same wind that powers me on. The Heart of Music to be saved, delivered, moored, and off-loaded. This is my life, my dream, my moment in the wind. Escape me if you will, songs. Let yourselves go now. We approach safe harbor.

## Chapter Sixty-Two

It is 9:43 A.M. on the West Coast. I will hit the "Buy it now" button at exactly ten A.M.

My latest love affair is a 1961 Lincoln Continental with about fifty thousand miles on it. Very nice original condition with a few hot rod appointments, and not what I usually go for, but this car really caught my eye. I was looking for a Ford product to replace the Eldorado in the video series. One reason for this is the damage I did to the Eldorado that day on I-5 with little Nina.

The other reason is the real reason: For the same amount of money it would take to rebuild the engine in the Eldorado, I can purchase another Ford product. (Of course, I will rebuild the Eldorado anyway, so the money is not really a valid reason.) "Why is that so important?" you might ask. It is important to me because I will be taking Bill Ford, executive chairman of the Ford Motor Company, for a ride and letting him feel Pono. I really like Bill because he is a futurist, and not many people would actually believe how much of a visionary he is, since he is at the head of one of the oldest car-manufacturing companies in the world. He is taking a hard look at the future while he is here on earth. He is trying to understand where traffic will be in twenty years, what cars will be like, what people will need for transportation. He and Jim Farley, head of global marketing for Ford, have changed a lot of things.

Today's Ford cars are very different from yesterday's. They have evolved the interior and its features into many levels while using the same exterior with few changes from the top of the line to the entry level. That is really revolutionary. The quality is added inside. It's in the user experience inside the car. That is where the big difference is now. This enables a lot of money to be saved and put into the inside of the cars, where people are. So I want him to hear Pono in one of Ford's own cars. No car in the world has ever sounded that good, and I think he will hear that. Being me, I have chosen a 1961 Continental over a new Ford Focus, but I want to take the prototype system out of the Continental and put it in the Focus to show how easy that is as part of the demo I plan for Mr. Ford.

So I located this Continental and plan on buying it at ten A.M. PST, when the owner will put it up on eBay for a prearranged price, which is actually still a little too high. I go by feelings, and my feeling is that this is the right car, even though it is not standard stock, because it has nineteen-inch wheels and a new exhaust system resonating the original 430-cubic-inch V8, and I am paying for extras I don't really want. That said, it is rock and roll and worthy of the Pono feature. It is quite possibly the Hot Rod Lincoln you have heard so much about! The rest of the car is a really nice, near cherry original, beautiful in every respect, a true work of automotive history. I have looked at this car for almost two weeks in pictures, checking out each one and reading the description over and over. I trust the seller.

The car is in Canada, and I may go up there and get it next week and drive it home, stopping in Seattle on the way back to celebrate Pearl Jam's twentieth anniversary with them. Sounds like fun. 9:59 A.M.! Gotta go!

## Chapter Sixty-Three

In Kansas City for Farm Aid 26, I found myself strangely lightened, with all of the harsh business negotiations I am so unfamiliar with over for the moment and gone from my thoughts. I thought of myself as a breeze blowing through Kansas, not worried, not pensive at all. I saw my old friends in the Farm Aid family: Willie, John, Dave, Carolyn, Glenda, Corky, David, and a couple of new friends, Willie's talented son Lukas Nelson, and Jamey Johnson, a great singer/songwriter from Alabama who has landed in Nashville, I imagine temporarily. Jamey and Lukas are the new guard. Real country. Real good. No bullshit. They are not the only ones, but if they were, they could handle it.

Musicians like to check the stage and make sure everything is working before a show. Some groups let their crews do it. Some don't. If a band is running late, then the crew has to do it. If you sing, it's good to know that the monitor speakers onstage are right for your ears. Some singers today use in-ear monitors and listen to their voices pretty loud directly in their ears. I don't do this. I love to hear the sound of the hall, the echo off the walls, and the sound of the instruments onstage blending together. That is key for me if I'm going to improvise or get lost in the sound. I want to walk around the stage with my guitar, finding the sweet spot where I can hear everything in balance. That is key for me playing extended jams. In-ear phones are way too sterile and clinical for me. I have to hear the speakers and the amps and the hall sound.

The night before the Farm Aid show, I had a sound check and it was different. I sang the set I was planning on doing in the empty soccer stadium. I started with "Comes a Time." There was so much echo that I really couldn't hear too well, and the monitors sounded really harsh to my ears. I sang "Powderfinger," and it was too high for me to reach the notes that night. I hadn't really warmed up and it was hard to sing those high notes. I tried a few things and nothing really sounded too good, so I asked Mark Humphreys to just turn off the monitors completely, which not many musicians feel comfortable doing. All I could hear was echo now, just the sound of the stadium. I sang "Sugar Mountain." Actually it sounded good to my ears; notes just lasted forever. Nothing was abrasive. I tried my harmonica. It was like floating on air. The echo was amazing. I did "Peaceful Valley Boulevard" and then "Love and War." I tried out the harp in "Love and War." It worked, and the sound just floated out into the Missouri night.

So the next day at the show, when I was watching everyone play, adjusting their monitors all the time, trying to find a good sound and struggling, I used no monitors at all. I just didn't bother using any. I knew it was going to be cool. Just like a breeze blowing through Kansas. Everything sounded beautiful. I did an acoustic set and really enjoyed it. One guitar, one harmonica, and six songs were all I needed.

There was something about that set that still haunts me. I was ready for the echo. The sound was like I was in another world. Every note just hung there in space. I drew them out and felt them all lingering and fading. Somehow, just by myself, I had become so free that it was almost transcendent. The place was not that great of a venue, really. It had everything going against it until I stopped fighting it and dropped the onstage monitors. When I did that, it was like the gates of heaven swung open. I swear that sound was like being in a hallowed place. I was so free and unencumbered, really a very rare thing, very rare. Especially solo. "Golden," as Briggs used to say. I love it when it works. That echo was a gift from the gods.

Earlier in the day I had gone out for a walk around the grounds with Carolyn Mugar, Farm Aid's wonderfully dedicated executive director and a good friend, accompanied by some security people. They (security) were pretty subtle, and it all was good. I kept moving. I have learned how long I can stay in one place in that kind of situation: Not very long. I listened to the music playing from the stage as I walked around the concession area through the crowd, wondering how I would sound with just my guitar and harmonica. Pretty good, I thought to myself. Then I saw a guy with a really old and cool Neil Young and Crazy Horse T-shirt. He was lost in thought. I walked up to him, tapped him on the shoulder, and said, "Really nice shirt." He looked up and I caught his eye. Then I kept moving. People were beginning to notice me, and a little crowd was following me. We disappeared into an elevator and went back to the bus.

The Zen art of paddleboarding has been creeping up on me now for months. Recently my friend Rick Rubin, a great record producer, has taken up the pastime. Rick is quite Buddha-like, and to think of him on his paddleboard is a very harmonic vision. I went out this morning and only fell off five times, which I am feeling very good about. My knees were shaking as I stood for the first time and surveyed the great open expanse before me on the bay by our Hawaii home. I paddled for a long time until some disturbance in the force overtook my groove and I plummeted face-first into the welcoming sea. Doggedly, as in "like a dog," I climbed back on board with my beautiful Koa paddle resting on top of the deck. Then, on my knees, I resumed paddling until the nerve to stand assembled itself in my balance-challenged form. Suddenly I was up again and under way, gleefully rejoicing in my newly found existence as a man of the water. I approached a rock outcropping and had deftly avoided getting too close to it when a subtle swell rolled beneath me, completely throwing me off balance and into the welcoming sea again. The water was relatively calm, and the swell was a little like jelly when it came through. I vowed to be more aware and reasserted myself, standing once more with paddle in hand, looking out on the distant shoreline and feeling at one with the board.

The time had come to make a turn, an adjustment in course, and I was experimenting with this, first paddling on one side, then reversing the flow on the other side, making the craft unwieldy, and once again I found myself in the welcoming sea. On my knees,

I continued toward the launch point, thoroughly worn out and totally invigorated by my new experience.

This, I felt, was the beginning of a new chapter for me, the basis of a more broad understanding of my place in the universe. Perhaps I was taking it a little too seriously, but the bottom line is I had a great time out there. On this journey, my maiden voyage, I was accompanied throughout by my neighbor and friend Greg McManus on his paddleboard.

I told you before that Greg and his wife, Vicki, own and operate the Napa Valley Wine Train, which he repairs himself, among other feats of engineering. Previously Greg's engineering prowess had been demonstrated many times, notably in the design and implementation of a system he developed for getting Ben Young into the ocean via a system of wires and pulleys that was tied off on the shore to a tree and in the water to a big lava rock under the surface. The system was devised because carrying Ben into the water over lava rock was obviously a source of danger and concern. So, with this new idea, we would get Ben Young in a giant sling with pulleys on it connected to an overhead wire and let him glide down along the wire until he splashed into the water and the waiting arms of his dedicated support team, Dustin Cline and Marian Zemla. Of course, Ben Young was laughing his ass off all the time and having a wonderful water experience! (Since Ben had his feeding tube implanted, we have not been doing this sort of thing, but I am not so sure we need to stop it. We are getting familiar with the tube, and it's really quite stable. It just takes some serious getting used to. Ben should still have those ocean activities, and I see no reason to stop if it's safe.)

Although Ben will not be able to paddleboard with me, I know he will enjoy watching. He always likes sharing himself with us by watching, which is one of those gifts he has. He just enjoys what we're doing through our joy. He has become a master of that. Life is short and should be lived to the fullest. We will be trying to do everything we can to get back in the ocean again with Ben Young.

Chapter Sixty-Four

So now I find myself rolling down a California two-lane high-way listening to the Pistol Annies' *Hell on Heels*, which I first heard on Rhapsody. The old fields and new factory farms fly by, the road full of cars I don't recognize, with young people be-hind the wheels talking excitedly about things of which I have only some understanding. A long grade approaches. My generator is cycled off and I'm running silent at about forty-five miles an hour. Visions of the future and past jostle for position in my coffee-soaked mind while the sun starts having its first warming mo-ments. My windows are not as clean as they were when I started my journey, so I'll have to try to do something about that soon. I like looking and listening. The music is really good! I crank it up and lament the streaming quality, wanting to download the album from Pono as soon as I can so I can hear what they heard, but I love the songs. Finally I am hearing something that makes me feel good! I love the vibe these girls have! The way they talk about real things.

"Trailer for Rent" comes on and I strain to hear all the words, making a note in my mind to Google the lyrics as soon as I can.

The ones I can make out are really good, and the harmonies are just great. It's all about struggling with life at a young age, trying it out, discarding it, and grabbing for more. I love hearing this energy. I recognize it from my own youth, and it gives me faith in life and makes me feel. Feelings, once awakened, can take me anywhere, and they do. Now happy, now sad, reliving the past again.

I'm noticing the approaching grade as the generator cycles on and my speed holds at forty-five miles an hour. I am in my element, traveling past the small towns now on a side road that reminds me of the highways my family used to take when Daddy drove us down through Georgia to Florida every fall. Actually it is the same vintage of road, but it is seldom used now. That is all on the interstate a couple of miles away, running more or less parallel. This two-lane with the faded yellow line is soothing somehow, although the roughness of the surface harkens back to smoother times. Rolling down the side window, I feel the air rush in and smell the grass in the fields as they fly by. Life is good!

Now I notice a bad smell and it gets worse immediately. Up goes the window. Cresting a small hill I see the factory hog farm that is the source of the foulness. In a few minutes it is past and I am upwind. I try lowering the window again. Now the sweet smell of the fields returns as I see a few small family farms roll by. I love this road. I wonder how long that factory farm has been there and how the locals feel about it, what it would be like to live downwind. Damn, that music is good, something about her husband being a hunter and never being home, always out with his coonhounds. I realize that I am loving this music because it's talking about a life that I can't see, kind of a mirage from the back country of the South.

"Boys from the South" comes on and again I am taken by this music. It appears from nowhere as a new release on Rhapsody. No radio play. No hype announcement. Just real good country. I suddenly realize that things have changed so much that I might be getting lost. The old ways I know are losing ground. My way is fading. But I still feel. No one can take that away from me. It is a gift I still have and I want my own music to feel as alive and vibrant as what I am hearing now. Will that happen? Will I just be reliving my glory days when I record again? Will anybody hear it? Doubt enters the picture as I slow to thirty and cruise by a horseshoe-shaped complex on the side of the road. RETIREMENT MOTEL, reads a neon sign. The vacancy light is there, but I can't make out whether the sign is lit or not because the sun is hitting it.

I keep rolling along, and the grade has gradually started. I try to call home but the cell reception is gone for the moment. Checking the GPS, I decide to cross over a few miles and join the interstate to make the long climb. When I get to the big road, the pace is much faster, and I am cruising at seventy or seventy-five with the generator cycled on at maximum. Fuel is a bit low, and I start wondering if I'll be able to get E85 (85 percent ethanol, 15 percent gasoline) or if I will have to refuel with pure gasoline. This is a big grade, really long. The interstate seems to stretch for miles in a straight line as the fields and farms give way to a more barren landscape. "Loneliness has been good to me" is playing on my personal radio, where I hear songs before I write them, and I wonder if this is just another mirage I will forget or if this will become a real song. It has been a long time since I've written a song, and the visits from the muse seem to be lessened by something. I still keep my faith that the muse knows best and when I am ready the inspiration will be there. I am trying not to look too ready. I know that just invites false promise.

I pass a hitchhiker going the other way, on the other side of the big road. You don't often see those anymore, especially on the interstate. Glancing in my rearview mirror, I can't see him anymore, or maybe it was a her. I am sure I saw someone, but I know looking backward is not a good idea, so I abandon the thought and continue on my way up the grade. The big Lincoln holds steady at seventy-four miles per hour, displaying the legendary power that makes it a true Continental, even though it is totally electric at the prime mover. A soft whine comes through the rear set as the two hundred kilowatts does its work.

A lot of insects have met their demise and the windshield is even harder to see through than it was earlier, so I try to clean the glass with the wiper wash system. Initially it leaves some big streaks, so I keep pushing the button until I can see clearly again. The only clean area is where the wipers are. The rest is really pretty useless for anything other than windshield protection. Halfway up the grade, the road begins to turn and I see a fuel station. Taking the exit, I cruise into a modern fuel stop where there is no E85, so I fill up with gasoline. Using the towels and cleaning tool available there, I clean all the Lincoln's windows and even the headlights, as well as the front of the car, which is packed with dead insects, the victims of my passage. A few minutes later I return to the big road and the long climb. The summit is somewhere ahead.

Looking for another dose of that great music, I try to restart the Pistol Annies' *Hell on Heels* on Rhapsody, but there is not a clear enough signal to stream it. Cruising along, I see the pollution from LA lingering at the summit ahead and remember the first time I smelled LA air in 1966. It was new to me then, a smell I was unfamiliar with.

It wasn't bad, but it sure wasn't good. I was twenty years old at the time.

Walking in the forest for me is like going to church. It is my cathedral, and I haven't been doing that enough lately. With the cougars getting so close to our house recently (we found some cougar shit fifteen feet from the back door), I suppose I have become a little fearful of the forest. I'm going to have to let that go. I need to connect again. Walking the forest floor is one of the most spiritual things I can imagine. Just thinking about it now makes me wonder why I haven't been there in a couple of years. I used to take Ben Young into the forest all the time. We would fasten his chair into the old blue jeep and off we would go together. We both enjoyed it a lot.

Next time we're on the ranch we'll load up and go for a trip together. Just like old times. Rolling slowly down the old jeep road, giant redwoods surrounding us, Ben and I will see the God-rays streaming down through the trees and landing on the forest floor. The old jeep crawling along the pathway silently in low gear, effortless in its motion, creates just enough noise to warn the residents of our arrival, and that is the way. Every now and then we stop just to listen and smell the forest. The birds become silent, then slowly start their chirping, warbling, and finally, as if triggered by some unknown event, a jay cries a warning into the forest. All becomes quiet, and then the cycle begins again with a few warbles and chirps.

I have learned through walking with my dogs here that there is an unspoken law. Always send a warning. Never surprise the animal life in the forest. So walking along without the noise of the jeep, it is wise to whistle a little tune and give the creatures some kind of an idea that you are approaching their area. This gives them a chance to adjust and find a place to hide, so they can watch you from their position out of your view. It is wise to follow the rule of the forest.

Once I was walking with my dog Carl, a golden doodle, in the forest cathedral when I realized that he was not with me. I looked around and called softly. I heard a little yelp. Then I retraced my steps about a hundred feet back on the path around an outcropping on the canyon side and found Carl, just sitting there in the path. I called him softly again. He came forward and sat down about ten feet from me, indicating that he would not come closer. When I turned to continue up the path, beckoning him to follow, he let out a soft bark. Carl was a very quiet dog, and to hear him talk was unusual, yet there he was, sitting on the path, unmoving in his resolve. It was then I realized what Carl was telling me. We were trespassing. There was something ahead on the trail and we were not supposed to go there. He was warning me of the danger. When I felt that and grasped it, I immediately reversed course and headed back along the way I had come. Carl ran on ahead, happily wagging his tail.

Carl is gone now, and Nina is with us today, but I think that the same will hold true for her should she choose to go for a walk in the woods with me. So Nina, that is the plan. When Pegi and I return to the ranch, I will take you into the forest for a new experience and a little religion. You can be my guide. You will instinctively know the language. I am reticent to enter the forest without guidance. I will take you to my beautiful church, the place where I find myself.

I really need to do that now. I feel it. Something is missing.

I read on the blogs that legacy artists (i.e., artists with long histories and large catalogs) are just trying to hold on to what they have and keep their money. There is some blogging jerk out there who feels he can generalize his way to validity. I don't like being put into any group. This guy thinks he knows the motivations of artists like me. I am a legacy artist, like it or not; I have my history, for what it's worth. I love streaming. What a great replacement for radio! But radio used to pay mechanical royalties every time a song got played. It was a minuscule amount and artists were happy. Just because I would like to know the formula for artists getting paid by streaming services does not make me a greedy person. I have been trying to find out what the formula is for these services paying the artists/record companies, and you'd think I was trying to infiltrate the U.S. Mint. I get a letter asking me if I want to be "in or out" of streaming, with absolutely zero information with which to make my decision. Like I said, I am not trying to get rich here; I am trying to make an informed decision. It is my art, my creation, that is being served here, and I deserve to know.

Yet I have been told that the deals are so new that they are changing all the time, and my music is being streamed on multiple services in the meantime. That does not seem like good business to me. I'm wondering what the heck I should be thinking about when I make these decisions. There certainly is a lot more to music than technology, and the creative flow of songwriting does not revolve around a computer. I would like some answers.

My friend and manager, Elliot, is going to Warner Brothers today to find out what the deal is and get me a copy of it so I know what I and other artists are doing. Every artist everywhere deserves to know these things. It is the right of the artist. That does not make legacy artists and record companies greedy. Listen, I love the new technology. It fascinates me. Steve Jobs was a genius, and I was deeply saddened by his death. What a pioneer. His death marked the end of an era. I was so close to getting to talk with him in person about the future of music, after one or two telephone talks and a few e-mails, but now he is gone. I hope he knew what a wonderful thing he had accomplished, and I only wanted to help him make it better by bringing quality sound along with it. Thank you, Steve.

(As an aside here, I want to say that I have now learned the basis of the formulas for payment of streamed-music royalties, and they seem to be pretty fair. Remember, there are different formulas for different streaming services. Someone needs to explain these models to artists so they can feel good about the knowledge. Artists need a representative and a clear message. It's a brand-new way of dealing with the payment of royalties, and it has been carefully worked out so far, although there may be adjustments to the formulas as time goes by and everyone concerned begins to understand the impacts of these new models on their lives and businesses. Time will tell. This is the beginning. Some things will work, and some won't.)

Personally, from what I can see, I would hate to be in the position of dealing directly with the technology companies without a buffer if I was an artist, which I am. I would say neither legacy artists nor record companies are the buffoons some self-righteous music newbies have made them out to be. This is an evolving picture. It needs to be watched.

I have been clean now for seven months. That is a good long time. I still feel cravings. Maybe I'd like a beer, maybe a joint. I heard the Pistol Annies sing about reasons why they're broke and so who would invest in their future? One's drinkin', one's smokin', one's taking pills. Well, they are writing their asses off. I know that. I haven't written a song in more than half a year, and that is different for me. Of course I've written over ninety thousand words in this book, and that is different for me, too.

I always wrote when I was high before. Getting high is something I used to do to forget one world's realities and slip into the other world, the music world, where all the melodies and words come together in a thoughtless and random way like a gift. I always have said that thinking is the worst thing for music, and now I would like to know how to get back to music without getting high. Some people are probably saying I should get high and write more songs 'cause that works. My doctor does not think that is good for my brain.

My brain has a lot of something else in it that you can only see on an MRI. I don't know what it is or what it isn't, but I do know my dad's history. He was a writer and lost his mind to dementia. What the hell is that cloudy stuff in my brain? I wish I'd never seen that shit. Anyway, I have been advised to stop smoking grass, and I have. As a matter of fact, I've written this whole damn book straight. It certainly is a quandary.

Of course there are many reasons to be straight and many reasons to be stoned, but that doesn't solve anything. There are many reasons to live and die, too. Where is this headed? I'll be damned if I know, Hoss; some highway at the bottom of some hill? Tell me about it. I've been there. I can still see myself out on that road, ripping it up in some honky-tonk or tearing down some arena with the Horse, but when I occasionally see myself in the mirror, it just doesn't add up. Where are we headed with this? Beats the hell out of lookin' back, that's for sure. I'm not sure of what's real anymore, I can tell you that. The straighter I am, the more alert I am, the less I know myself and the harder it is to recognize myself. I need a little grounding in something and I am looking for it everywhere.

Cravings. Yes, I have 'em. And they are not insignificant, but then I imagine where that takes me and it scares the shit out of me. I have been with some of you for a real long time, and others of you don't have the foggiest notion what I am or what I stand for. I am possibly joining those legions myself. I am okay when I focus on something and stay with it; I may get abrasive and overbearing about it, but at least I'm busy. It's those other times that get me.

"It's Those Other Times": is that a song or what?

When will I put it together? How fucking loose do I have to get to put a song together again? Why not? Have you ever heard of transference? Am I taking on someone else's battles? Is that it? How the heck did I get to this place?

Now, in a few moments, I know this will pass and I will focus in on something a little easier. Maybe back on that highway, climbing that grade, burning that damn gas, heading for that pollution. Listening to "Bad Example" by the Pistol Annies. (Check that one out. Those girls can sing.)

When I was onstage at Farm Aid in Kansas City a couple of weeks ago, that was the realest I have been in a while. I was really happy to hear that echo. That's the closest to being high I've been in a long time. It *was* being high. I was so into that moment, and everything was so easy. I have to remember how the heck I got to that place. Why did that happen? What was the key? At least I know it happened and I was there. If I can bring that to the Horse when we get together in the White House, then I will be really happy. Farm Aid was a solitary experience, though; just me and my old guitar were playing. No other people. Except for the thousands of fans in the soccer stadium—I forgot about that.

When I started out I did a lot of acoustic solo playing and

found it to be quite liberating, if confining in that it meant jamming was more or less out of the question, while improvising was definitely easy and totally unencumbered. Dropping beats and bars is no problem when you're alone and is part of the folk process and storytelling freedom. All the while in my life I have been on these two separate paths, acoustic and electric music. Some people like one and some like the other. I like them both. Especially with the Horse, I have fans who could totally miss my acoustic solo stuff and not care at all, while fans of the acoustic solo appearances have little use for the Horse. I have often wondered why Bob, who was so great with just his guitar and harmonica, has never returned to that form since his first foray into band music with Barry Goldberg, Mike Bloomfield, later Al Kooper and the guys. That was great sound, but so was his solo acoustic stuff that defined a whole era. He has just never gone back, and that is notable. I don't know why. He plays a unique guitar and his harp playing is definitive. His storytelling is beyond my description, so why doesn't he do it? I guess I'll have to ask him someday.

I would really like to make a solo acoustic record at some point. You really have to have songs to pull that off. Usually when I do try to do that I end up with a band, because you can always hear a band playing songs when you write them, at least I can. In the studio with the Horse, though, you have to be real careful. Analysis is no good for the Horse. The Horse defines music without thought. The physical feeling of playing with the Horse is like nothing else. It leaves your brain wide open, like you can feel the wind blowing right through it. I am looking forward to that relief, that feeling.

Another thing about the Horse is that knowing the song structure before starting is important. There are no run-throughs. Generally the best feelings are the early takes. First or second takes, mostly. Whatever you think of the music I have made with Crazy Horse, those songs are the most transcendent experiences I have ever had with music. That has an immeasurable value to me, and I think it will still be there when we get together to record.

Of course, I have seldom played straight with the Horse.

## Chapter Sixty-Five

S omeday I would like to write a book, *The Life and Times of David Briggs*. I could research everyone he touched and really get to the bottom of some things about my mercurial, mysterious brother.

He was born Manning Philander Briggs on February 29, 1944, and grew up in Wyoming with family members who took care of him. His best friend was Kirby, and one day in the mid-sixties they up and went to LA to find their fortunes. Kirby became a grip, working in the movies, and Briggs became a record producer, eventually marrying a Wyoming girl, Shannon, and having a son, Lincoln Wyatt Briggs, in Topanga Canyon, which is where I met him. Shannon was a great girl, and he loved her. He was a wild man, and she loved him. Lincoln was a good boy, and I'm not sure how he is doing now, although I worry about him sometimes.

Briggs and I made my best records, the transcendent ones, the ones where I am closest to the Great Spirit. I say that because She visited me more often with Briggs than when I was with any other

With David Briggs, the night I was inducted into the
Rock and Roll Hall of Fame, New York, 1995.

human being. Briggs and I had a way of getting to the place. We somehow knew the *way*. He was the most influential person on my music of anyone I've met. His guidance and friendship through the creation of countless pieces of music are one of the greatest gifts of my life, right up there with my wife's love and all of my children. I feel the loss. I feel the memories. I feel the weight of every mistake I made in our long relationship, the times he was right and I was wrong, the times I didn't use him to produce for the wrong reason, every battle we had. I feel the absence of his unbelievable energy for music, combined with mine. There is no replacement for that. It is one of life's little voids.

So there he was in his apartment in San Francisco with Bettina, his sweetheart. Barely standing and all crooked and bent over. Short in stature, this giant of a man, now resembling a tree with no leaves waiting for winter, was looking right at me. It was obvious he was dying from something and the process was well advanced. I was surprised at how far it had come in a short time, having only heard he was sick. It had been a few years since we had worked together, and this was not the Briggs I remembered. Be that as it may, there he was, barely able to stand, which he did, for some reason I can't remember. He was in pain from an ailment, a mysterious ailment that may have visited him once earlier in life, in the seventies. At that time, he had disappeared for a few months and come back as if nothing had happened. There was a rumor of cancer and a hospital stay in Sacramento, but nothing was for sure. David was mysterious, and that is the end of that. Nobody knew what was really happening with David, ever. That is why a book on the subject might be worth a shot.

So now here we were with David's second big bout against whatever it was, and it had pretty well gotten him. He was taking a lot of morphine for the pain and looked terrible, although the spirit was still in his eyes, weak as it was.

"Do you have any advice for me on my music going forward?" I asked David.

"Just make sure to have as much of you in the recording as you can," he said. "Stay simple. No one gives a shit about anything else."

He told me to keep it simple and focused, have as much of my playing and singing as possible, and not to hide it with other things. Don't embellish it with other people I don't need or hide it in any way. Simple and focused. That is what I took away. He didn't exactly say that, but I got that message. I have failed to do that in some instances. "Be great or be gone," his famous phrase, echoes in my head. I have to remember that for sure. Damn.

So I left the apartment after a hug. It was devastating. He died a week later. He wanted to go. His body was all fucked up, and it was not easy. His tenacious spirit would not let him go.

The last time I saw Danny Whitten, it was late 1972 and he had come to play in the Stray Gators with Jack Nitzsche, Kenny Buttrey, Tim Drummond, Ben Keith, and me at the ranch. We were rehearsing for the first tour since my *Harvest* album had been released. The tour was my longest and biggest ever. I wanted the band to be able to play well live, and just as CSN wanted me for that, I wanted Danny in this band.

I had heard he was doing well, and had called him and invited him up. I went to pick him up at the airport and take him to the ranch. He wanted to stop at a liquor store and so we pulled over in Millbrae, a little town near the San Francisco airport. There was something weird about that. I really can't put my finger on what it was, but something happened at that stop. I wish I could describe it, but now I just have a feeling. I think it was because he didn't want me to go into the liquor store with him. Anyway, he reappeared and got back in the car and we headed up to the ranch, where I set him up in a little cabin on the ranch called the Red House.

Rehearsals started the next day, and I was excited. It was great to hear Danny singing and playing with these guys, but it didn't last long before he had to take a break and go back to the house. Eventually I started to see that he was still strung out. I'm pretty sure Jack knew right away, and maybe Tim knew, too. But no one was talking. After a few days of this, it was becoming obvious that Danny wouldn't be able to cut it. He wanted to. You could really see that. I had to let him go, and that was difficult. So I got him a ticket home and a ride to the airport. It was sad, but we had work to do to prepare for this huge tour that was already booked. It would have been great if Danny was with us, but that was not to be. We rehearsed without him and got started rebuilding the band.

That night Carrie and I were asleep in our little bedroom at the ranch house when the phone rang. It was the middle of the night, and Carrie got up to answer it. I fell back asleep. She woke me up.

"Danny has OD'd," she said. "That was the LA county coroner. He had the ranch phone number on a piece of paper in his wallet."

I lit a fire and sat there in my rocking chair. We lit a candle for him. It was as simple as that. I knew that what I had done may have been a catalyst in Danny's death, but I also knew that there was really nothing else I could have done. I can never really lose that feeling. I wasn't guilty, but I felt responsible in a way. It's part of what I do. Managing the band and taking care of the music is very painful at times. It's a sad story. A moment I will never forget, years I can never replace, music the world will never hear, all gone in the turning of a second.

One of the true greats, Tim Drummond is a musician at the highest level, and a very funny character, full of expressions like "You crack the whip and I'll make the trip," "We are the mighty few," "Been around like shit on a wagon wheel," and "Front row, white socks," to name just a few. He called me Rainy. As I have said before, he played with a lot of greats: Conway Twitty, James Brown, JJ Cale, Bob Dylan, and Jimmy Buffett come to mind. He had the big groove. He was sometimes known as The Moth by the crew because he was always in the edge of the spotlight when it was on me. I never minded that at all, because he was always watching my foot to see what I was doing with the beat. His playing on *Harvest* was wonderful, and he is responsible for putting that band together. Tim played with me in many bands over the years and was one of the very best.

Something happened to him when he broke up with his wife, Inez. He gave up music. He has been drinking a lot and is in a wheelchair now. The last time I saw Tim was in Nashville when I flew him there to be with me for a party celebrating the release of *A Treasure*, which is one of my favorite records of all time, featuring the International Harvesters with fiddler Rufus Thibodeaux, Spooner Oldham, Joe Allen, Karl T. Himmel, Hargus "Pig" Robbins, and Anthony "Sweet Pea" Crawford. Although Rufus had passed away, the rest of the band except for Pig was all there at the party, and it was fun to see everyone together again. *A Treasure*, titled by Ben Keith, was a record that had never come out before, a compilation of beautiful performances from the eighties by a seminal road band. Tim is one of the best I have ever known, right up there with Ben Keith. I wish he hadn't given up his music. Something in him just broke. And I miss playing with him and having him active. Thanks, Tim.

Jack Nitzsche was the composer-arranger who did the charts for Phil Spector's Wall of Sound. These masterpieces always had Jack's brilliant orchestrations as the major component or influence. In the back room at Gold Star Recording Studios in Hollywood, a few doors south from Hollywood Boulevard on Santa Monica Boulevard, there was a legendary echo chamber. The magical tones of this chamber adorned many, if not all, of the Wall of Sound records by the Righteous Brothers, the Ronettes, and the Crystals, to name just a few. These records are part of the history of rock and roll.

The Wall of Sound featured multiple players in the studio, many people all playing the same parts together, multiple tambourines, basses, and pianos, with string sections always in the same room at the same time. These sessions exemplified the spirit of music as I know and love it. It was a capture of the essence of many musical forces, musicians all playing their hearts out at the same time, following a chart, or a loosely preordained order, arranged by Jack. Of course, this was an analog recording, and the overtones were all universal and real. The Gold Star echo brought it all together into the Wall of Sound.

Imagine all of these people getting together in the room, setting up, and then Spector in the control room with Jack in the corner with his charts. Legendary. This was real music, mixed with that magical echo. Goose bumps were felt every night, at every session.

The echo chamber itself was somewhat of a secret. Stan Ross, the owner of Gold Star, would never let anyone see it. No one could go in there. Unlike today's little echo machines, this was a real echo chamber: A sound was fed into a speaker in the chamber from the control room, and a microphone placed in the chamber picked up that sound, with the added echo in the chamber, and sent it back to the control room, where it was remixed into the music according to how much of the effect was desired. The echo effect amount was varied by how loudly you sent the sound into the chamber and how much of it you remixed into the music. You could turn it up or down, change the treble and bass by EQing it, but you never, ever went in there and moved that speaker or messed with that microphone! That would be taboo! No way. It was already great, and the sound was magic. If someone were to change the placement of the microphones it would be disaster and the sound could be gone!

It was spooky, that sound. It was as real as it gets, not some adjustment on a digital device. The sound was different every time something resonated it. You could lose yourself just listening to the depth. It was true magic.

Outside the studio there was a little lounge for musicians where multicolored phones hung on the wall for several answering services to call in and book musicians for sessions at other studios. These phones were each dedicated lines to the different services. Musicians were always moving around town, going from studio to studio, with their cartage services delivering drum kits, stand-up basses, amplifiers, you name it. The services would set up drums or electric instruments so the musicians could just arrive and start playing. Many drummers had multiple sets, and guitar players had multiple amps. Vibraphones and harps were all rented from instrument rental services and delivered around town to multiple sessions, day in and day out.

Then, one day in the eighties, Stan Ross sold Gold Star. Those Wall of Sound days were gone, and it was real estate. Stan called me and asked me if I would like to buy the chamber. I said no. I regret that. I felt it would never be the same if it was moved. I think I was right, but now I'm haunted by that decision. The legendary chamber was an abandoned meat locker.

There was another great Hollywood chamber at Sunset Sound. It was there for a long time, until digital music arrived. Prince recorded exclusively at Sunset for a long time, and I heard he had the chamber made into a lounge. That may or may not be true. I hope it isn't. Anyway, Sunset Sound is where Jack and I recorded and mixed "Expecting to Fly" with Bruce Botnick, one of the most influential and accomplished recording engineers in the history of recorded sound. Jack and I spent weeks working on the chart for "Expecting to Fly" in his house in Coldwater Canyon.

I remember one night going down to the sheriff's office to help get Jack out of jail for drunk driving. I also remember one day when Jack was broke, Phil Spector gave him five grand. That was a shitload of cash in those days. Jack loved Phil because Phil was a genius with a big heart, even though he was crazy and very eccentric. Jack was not a businessman. He was a renaissance composer. His music, if ever collected in one place, would stand with the classics. "Expecting to Fly" was just one of his masterpieces, played by real people and captured on analog for the ages, at a time when no one anticipated what was going to happen to sound. We couldn't know that our beloved tones and recording techniques would be just part of the past, a forgotten art. When I made music that Jack didn't think was up to my potential, he hated me for it. Then he would forgive me and we would move on. Thankfully, that only happened a few times over the years. Jack was a genius. He taught me so much more than I can ever say.

A number of years later, the midnight call came again with a different name. Jack Nitzsche had OD'd in his little home studio in Hollywood. I sent twelve dozen red roses to the service and quite a few floral displays. It was completely over-the-top, but I heard it looked great at the ceremony and made the family feel good. I couldn't go. I was on the road. I didn't know what else to do, so I just sent flowers.

So yes, there has been a lot of loss. It is important to remember the times when life is in full bloom. Those are the moments that give us the faith to move through the darkness when it falls.

## Chapter Sixty-Six

A lot has happened over the years. I am now a very successful musician with a lot of stuff and things of value. Music is a business. I have traveled a long way along life's pathway and have become somewhat of a hard person to work for, or with, because I set high standards and have lost some patience. The years have left a mark. Success has made it possible for me to form some bad habits, to lose respect for those I work with, to skirt certain responsibilities, and to make my own way in the world.

That said, now I am trying to find myself again and reconnect with the values I had in the beginning, find the love in the music with others again, return to the camaraderie that we all enjoyed back in the day, respect others, have empathy for them, be considerate, love myself again, and through that, be more true to myself and others, and above all, be deserving of Pegi. So yes, a lot has happened. I have a full plate, but I am up to the task, I think.

Changing the person one has evolved into is not a simple process, to be sure, but I know that with Pegi's love and support and

Videotaping Ben and Amber on a trip to New Zealand, 1987.

my family close, I will be able to learn to reach out and live life in a more caring and conscious way. Maybe I have never been good at that, and that's why it's so hard to find it in myself. It may never have really been there. I may be starting from scratch. I've always been told that what I am doing is right. Maybe it isn't. Maybe just some of it is. I need to dig deep and discover some things along the way.

How do I avoid being short with those I love and respect? How do I try to make people feel good about what they are doing for and with me? How can I respect others' tastes while retaining my own? This is the knowledge I am searching for. I can remember so many times in my life when I have hurt others and hurt myself. I really need to find a way to change those patterns for good.

The Times They Are a-Changin' in the book world. I got an offer from my potential publisher today. Borders closed their local store yesterday and announced plans to close them all in the next couple of months. The bookstore culture is evaporating, though the online sales of books was not as great as anticipated.

A group of writers in our living room smoking their pipes and talking into the night was not uncommon to me growing up. Books have always been close to my life, with my father being an author and our family knowing so many writers as family friends. Now huge bookstore chains have closed their doors and liquidated their stock.

These changes would have blown my daddy's mind.

Just as the online social media revolution has brought on mammoth upheaval in the Arab world, it is bringing big change to the publishing world as well. In the new world order there will be an altered landscape, and it is exciting to be around to see it, even as it causes a sea change for the things I do for a living. I believe music and writing will always be around. They are not going anywhere. Actually, I think the full effects of this revolution are just beginning to be seen, and many more areas of world culture will be changed in unknown ways. I am glad I am a musician, and I am looking forward to making my next record with Crazy Horse. I'm not sure how many more albums I will make in the future, since they're not even called albums anymore, but I'm looking forward to finding out.

A long time ago, I started having little birthday parties at the ranch. These parties have become famous in our small community. Pegi and I love traditions, so I thought every year I would invite the children of our friends to a marshmallow roast on the shore of our pond. The pond is a beautiful place, with reeds all around it and an opening near our house that expands onto a huge lawn. It is the perfect place to watch the sunset and listen to the birds. I love the sounds of the red-winged blackbirds! Once while paddleboarding around the pond I was chased and led by a flock of these singing birds flitting about from the reeds behind me to the reeds ahead of me. It was a circular dance, me on my board and about fifty of these beautiful little red-winged blackbirds that I love so much going in a big arc around the edge of the pond.

Anyway, every year I would invite the kids and tell them they could bring their parents. Presents were always requested in a certain category. One year, presents were all requested to be "something from the ground." I got rocks and dirt and little pieces of wood, many of which still reside on my train layout, representing something in a different scale. Each year the presents were a little different, but always something the kids could find around for no money. Also, as part of the tradition, I would set a fire with fallen wood from around the ranch, and when I had it all ready, Pegi would come down and light it. That was always a great moment for us, as we watched the fire catch and begin another year together.

The years went by, and the little kids grew up. Soon they were in college and could not make it for one reason or another, so a new crop of kids came along, then the older kids started coming back. This went on for quite a long time and was a really beautiful feeling and memory. I would go out and gather sticks for the marshmallows and prepare them to be used around the fire by the kids, big and small, and we all would roast them together with the sun going down until we were there in the dark with the bonfire roaring away. It was really great. So one year I went out into the bush to get some sticks for the roast and found a great source. Every stick in the bush was the perfect size. Amazing! What a find! I was so lucky to locate these babies, and I gathered them all up, cut them carefully to length, and stored them by the unlit fire in preparation for the evening's activities. That night we had a wonderful time, planning and remembering the future and past. All was well in the world.

The next day, one of the guests came down with a rash. The day after that, everyone had it.

I went down to the doctor's office and all my friends were there! Some of them were so disfigured as to be unrecognizable. All of them had poison oak! Oh my God! What a feeling that was! I felt like a Canadian terrorist who had infiltrated this little community and poisoned all of the unsuspecting residents in a crime that was years in the making. No wonder those sticks were so different! I had to share that here because it is the single most embarrassing thing I have ever done. All those innocent kids got poison oak because of me! Every year it comes back to haunt me as everyone jokes about it mercilessly. I am not allowed to gather the sticks anymore. What a tradition.

## Chapter Sixty-Seven

There is a song that I wrote in the middle of the night in front of my fireplace at the ranch that I think stands alone in its form and consciousness. It is a fairly long song that is pretty ambitious in a few ways. It was 1976. I recorded this song on a little Sony cassette player that had "Life is a shit sandwich. Eat it or starve" on a plastic strip label, applied by Briggs during the *Zuma* sessions right below the Sony brand marking. The door for the cassette opened right below the label so you saw it every time the cassette was inserted or removed.

Sitting on the floor late at night, I recorded in front of the fireplace with the cassette on the hearth, three feet from the fire, and you can hear the crackling and hissing of the fire as I played my old Martin guitar and sang "Will to Love," the story of a salmon swimming upstream. Laden with my own feelings of love and survival, the recording stands alone in my work for its audio vérité style, a

With friends at the Broken Arrow Ranch, 1981. Left to right, standing:
David Briggs, Ralph Molina, Larry Cragg, Steve Antoine, me, Jerry
Napier; sitting: Tim Mulligan, Billy Talbot, Frank "Poncho" Sampedro,
Sal Trentino. Crazy Horse and I were in the process of recording our
album re·ac·tor *around this time.*

live sketch of a massive production number with only the high-lights presented, fragments of parts, the sound of the fire, the underwater sound created by vibrato.

It has often been my dream
To live with one who wasn't there
Like an ocean fish who swam upstream
Through nets, by hooks, and hungry bears

When the water grew less deep
My fins were aching from the strain
I'm swimming in my sleep
I know I can't go back again.

I was scheduled to fly to Miami to continue recording the Stills-Young album with Stephen in the morning; the flight was leaving very early and I had decided to just stay up all night and drive to the airport in time for the flight. I had some drugs, had written this song on a piece of paper, and had decided to sing it all the way through for the first time so I would have something to show Stephen and the band in Florida. I didn't listen back to it that night, I don't think. It was complex in that there were pieces that would have to be added later that I could not sing myself. It was layered, so I had to just sing little pieces of choruses and then go back to the verses and releases.

The cassette of that song was never played for those sessions. It was too sensitive and complex and wouldn't fit with the rest of the tracks on the album, so I saved it for later. Later came in a few weeks, when I was back in Malibu at my beach house, a beautiful little house I had purchased on Sea Level Drive, at the end of the road, right on the beach. The house was wonderful, a Cape Cod cottage that was totally overgrown with bougainvillea. The roof and outside walls were covered in vines, with flowers everywhere. It was a magnificent place that I loved dearly, situated right in a bunch of evergreen trees on the ocean. A big rock was in the water right in front of this house, and the beach went on for miles to the right with no other houses on the sand. They were all on the top of the cliff that started right past my little house. That was paradise. One of the most beautiful houses and locations I have ever seen. The actress Katharine Ross was living there when I bought the place, and I'm sure she was sad to have to leave.

Placed in the evergreens around the patio was an Indian chief with full headdress. That wooden Indian was a work of art. A few years later Pegi and I were married there, and Briggs was my best man. The house and patio, on two lots, were my pride and joy, and I wrote a lot of songs there.

So one evening, Briggs and I went up to Indigo Ranch to record. Indigo Ranch Studios was way up in one of the canyons above Malibu, at the end of its own road, with a beautiful canyon right outside the studio. The place was magnificent and had a great sound, with wonderful equipment that Briggs loved. The owner, Richard Kaplan, was really into his studio; he was an engineer himself, and kept it up really well. It was a perfect place, and David recorded me there a lot. We loved it and always enjoyed being there.

I had asked David to get me a lot of instruments, including drums, an electric bass, a vibraphone, some of my old amps including my Magnatone with the stereo vibrato, and a few other things. They were all there when we arrived. We always smoked some weed on the way up there and were feeling fine as we drove by The Band's Garth Hudson's place on the little dirt road, the last house before the studio, which was about a half mile farther. I realized there was no way I could sing the song again or perform it, and I never have since. I told David that I simply wanted to play back the cassette through the Magnatone with vibrato so it would sound like I was underwater at times during the song, when I was taking the point of view of the salmon. That was the first thing we did. Then I started layering on instruments, one at a time. The drugs began to flow and soon it was the middle of the night and we were still hard at it. I was sketching, not painting, the track. Instruments came and went, indicating their presence without the cumbersomeness of staying. I played some drums during one section, just following the muse. Then I sang all of the choruses, filling them in so that I was singing on top of myself, and added the releases as well.

Somewhere in the middle of that night, we did a mix. That was the perfect way to work. Get it all at once. Put it on tape and mix it immediately while the image is fresh. As the last chords died away, I felt Mr. Briggs's strong hands massaging my back as I sat in front of the console with my own head in my hands, my eyes closed and covered, just listening. The sound was cascading over me and all around me, and I was swimming in it. Our work was done. That memory is one of my favorite moments and is the perfect example of a great life with my friend David, who guided me and assisted me in every trip I decided to take through the world of music.

It was time to jump in Nanu for the slow ride home to dawn on Sea Level Drive, carefully avoiding any actions that would catch the sheriff's eye as he patrolled the Pacific Coast Highway in his cruiser.

## Chapter Sixty-Eight

The Continental climbs along up the grade with seemingly little effort, and the grade never seems to end. Traffic is thicker now, with more and more vehicles joining the procession. Six lanes wide, the big road winds and dips through the mountainous terrain, and I am a little lonely. For some reason the GPS is not functioning and Rhapsody is not getting enough signal to deliver another round of *Hell on Heels*, but everything else is going to plan as I glance in the rearview mirror and see myself looking back. I look really good somehow; maybe it's the light, but my face doesn't seem all lined with age. I actually feel great and eager to get to the city and see what's going on, but also strangely hungry. Thinking back over the last many hours, I remember the Retirement Motel, the small farms with their green grass, the stench of that factory farm I passed, and as I trace back through the day, which seems to have started a long time ago, I can't remember eating a thing or having a drink of water. Looking around the front seat, I don't see any bottled water or snacks. From where I am, I can't see the sun in the sky, although I can feel the heat on the convertible top. It must be noon or thereabouts. My mind is wandering to women I have met and loved, and when I come to Pegi, I feel really good, kind of complete in a way, like I really lucked out in the end, getting the best of the best.

I remember some of the dreams I've had where Ben Young is walking and talking, dreams that seem so real and vivid. The things he says are so natural, like he has always talked, and he exchanges a knowing glance with me as his mother makes an observation concerning the feelings she has had her whole life.

Family business is on the agenda, and reckoning with things is at hand. The meeting is set for tomorrow. Business people are flying in, and the pressure is mounting, or at least the anticipation. Perhaps we may not be able to keep everything we have and we may have to make some decisions and lighten our load. All of these houses, five on the ranch and three on the Hawaii property, may be too much for us to handle, and the moment has come to make choices. We have never looked forward to this, thinking that ultimately something might happen to help us avoid the inevitable, but here we are.

Brake lights line up in front of me and I slow to a crawl. Traffic is lined up for miles in the sweltering heat. I try rolling the window down to get a feel for the surroundings, and it's excruciatingly hot outside, with a lot of fumes. The Continental's generator cycles off and we are running on pure electric power, able to crawl at less than one mile an hour with total control, completely eliminating the stop-and-go actions of the older cars with their prime mover internal combustion engines. Thank God for the air-conditioning, which is still working.

The sound system comes on again with a glitch, somehow set to the Crystals' "Da Doo Ron Ron":

I met him on a Monday,
And my heart stood still . . .

What a great song, so simple and innocent. Somehow I am connected to a vintage radio show on Rhapsody, with a real DJ talking
and old commercials. What a trip. Technology is amazing! It even
sounds old. I remember that there is a café up here and decide to
get off the interstate in a mile or two and take that two-lane road I
remember to a little town Briggs and I used to visit, and get some
food. That may give this traffic time to clear. After about twenty
minutes of crawling along under five miles an hour, I finally arrive
at the exit and discover it is closed. Looking about carefully, I spy
an opening around the roadblock and decide to take a chance.
There's nothing better to do, and the most that can happen is I will
have to back up and lose some time. The Continental just fits!

Making it around the roadblock, I turn on the two-lane and
find myself cruising along with no problem; the other direction
was completely blocked, but this way is fine. How lucky can you
get? This is the old road we used to take every time we made this
trip back in the day. It's in pretty good shape really, and there is
no traffic to speak of. A sixties car passes going the opposite direction, and I think to myself, *Wow, will they be bummed when they get
to the interstate.*

It's very quiet out here, and I pull over at a place near a creek
where I can just get a drink from the flowing water. Parking roadside, I get out and stretch my legs. I feel great! It's a beautiful day,
and this road is just the kind I like. Now, watching my step on the
rocks, I edge my way down to the creek, cupping my hands and

scooping up some of the crystal-clear water. I love to drink this way; it's so refreshing. A couple of fish are visible in the pool in front of me, so I sit down on the shore to watch them for a while, remembering how I used to hang for hours near creeks in my boyhood, catching crawfish and chub and taking them back to my house in a little pail. Then I would store them in a little makeshift water scene I had created in one of my mother's old roasting pans with some water, sand, and rocks placed carefully to give a natural look. I used to stick little green grass plants in the sand and make believe they were trees. I feel so good here, I decide to just take a little nap.

I get back in the Continental and continue down the road to the café. Then I pull in and there's Larry Johnson's '57 Ford pickup in the parking lot. As I enter the little café, I see Larry and Briggs in the corner, drinking some coffee and having a late breakfast. I go right over and sit down with them. We don't say much. David says something about Kirby getting a job at one of the studios. Kirby is very good with his hands and can fix anything, plus he has a very friendly personality. We are happy for him. Larry has to make a call and gets up, heading for the pay phone in the corner. He asks us to get him another coffee when the waitress comes back. Briggs looks at me and asks what I've been doing.

Acknowledgments

I would like to thank all the people in
this book and my next book. There can
never be enough pages for you.